How   Reading

Is   *Astrid*
                            Lorange

Written

                            A BRIEF

INDEX TO   GERTRUDE

        STEIN   *Wesleyan*
                        University
                        Press

                        Middletown,
                        Connecticut

WESLEYAN UNIVERSITY PRESS

MIDDLETOWN, CT 06459

WWW.WESLEYAN.EDU/WESPRESS

© 2014 ASTRID LORANGE

ALL RIGHTS RESERVED

MANUFACTURED IN THE UNITED STATES OF AMERICA

DESIGNED BY QUEMADURA

TYPESET IN SCALA AND TRADE GOTHIC

WESLEYAN UNIVERSITY PRESS IS A MEMBER OF THE
GREEN PRESS INITIATIVE. THE PAPER USED IN THIS BOOK
MEETS THEIR MINIMUM REQUIREMENT FOR RECYCLED PAPER.

LIBRARY OF CONGRESS CATALOGING-IN-PUBLICATION DATA

LORANGE, ASTRID.

HOW READING IS WRITTEN : A BRIEF INDEX

TO GERTRUDE STEIN / ASTRID LORANGE.

PAGES CM

INCLUDES BIBLIOGRAPHICAL REFERENCES.

ISBN 978-0-8195-7511-1 (CLOTH : ALK. PAPER) —

ISBN 978-0-8195-7512-8 (PBK. : ALK. PAPER) —

ISBN 978-0-8195-7513-5 (EBOOK)

I. STEIN, GERTRUDE, 1874–1946—CRITICISM

AND INTERPRETATION. I. TITLE.

PS3537.T323Z698 2014

818'.5209—DC23

2014013666

5 4 3 2 1

FRONTISPIECE: LUKE BEESLEY, *WORD*. PENCIL AND
PASTEL ON PAPER, COURTESY OF THE ARTIST.

How Reading Is Written

WORD

This book has emerged over a number of years and with the support of many people. An earlier version of the manuscript was submitted and examined for the degree of Doctor of Philosophy at the University of Technology Sydney in Australia. Thank you to Stephen Muecke, whose supervision in the first year of my project has left an indelible trace in these words and in my thought. Thank you to Martin Harrison, my supervisor throughout and a most extraordinary and generous friend and mentor. I have finished this project at the College of Fine Arts, University of New South Wales. Thank you to my new colleagues, students, and friends, for welcoming me so warmly. Thank you especially to Ross Harley, Jill Bennett, Anna Munster, and Caleb Kelly.

Thanks to everyone at Wesleyan University Press. Working with a press that I admire so much is a true thrill. Thank you to Suzanna Tamminen, Leslie Starr, Ann Brash, and Christi Stanforth for their kindness and exceptional professionalism. Thank you also to Lyn Hejinian, who made it all possible.

Thank you to the University of Pennsylvania, and in particular to the wonderful community at the Kelly Writers House. When I first visited Philadelphia in 2009, I never imagined the many ways it would change my thinking and writing. Thank you to everyone I spoke to and heard speak—in the classroom, in a kitchen, on a train, off the record. Thanks in particular to Bob Perelman, Charles Bernstein, Al Filreis, and Rachel Blau DuPlessis for inviting me into their pedagogical spaces.

Early versions of this work were presented at the Whitehead Research Center at Claremont College, the Open Fields forum at Serial Space in Chippendale, the Critical Animals creative research symposium in Newcastle, the Blanket talk series in Philadelphia, ModCon at Sydney University, and the 2010 annual conference for the Society for Literature Science and the Arts. Thank you to everyone who hosted, fed, and talked to me in my travels. Thank you to the staff at the Mandeville Special Collections Library at the University of California San Diego for their assistance in my archival pursuits. Thank you also to my students and colleagues at the University of Technology Sydney and the University of Western Sydney—all the way through the writing process I was cheered along, encouraged, and nourished by classroom discussions.

Thank you to Tom Lee, Jason Childs, Elena Gomez, Kieran Daly, Trisha Low, Sam Moginie, Michael Farrell, Ella O'Keefe, and Ed Hopely for reading various versions and drafts of chapters. Thank you also to my doctoral thesis examiners—Charles Bernstein, Lyn Hejinian, and Lee Ann Brown—for their suggestions and encouragements. Thank you to the two anonymous reviewers who read for Wesleyan University Press and whose comments were most useful and insightful. An *enormous* thank-you to John Paetsch, a scholar and poet I admire, respect, and love, who kindly read the near-to-final version of the manuscript and whose suggestions, challenges, inquiries, and celebratory marginalia have finally brought this book to life.

There are many people dear to this project whom I haven't yet mentioned: Gordon Faylor, Václav Paris, Kaegan Sparks, Cecilia Corrigan, Laura Finch, J. Bret Maney, Gabriel Sessions, Jessica Cross, Lanny Jordan Jackson, Kristen Gallagher, Andrew Hao, Nathaniel Davis, Michael Halewood, Patrick Armstrong, Patrick Grant, Aden Rolfe, Stuart Cooke, Tim Wright, Kate Fagan, Peter Minter, Joel Scott,

Jacquie Kasunic, Zoë Sadokierski, Alastair Pennycook, Emi Otsuji, Liam Field, and Alex White. Thank you for advice, chats, wanderings, adventures, and vital oddities.

Thank you to my family for everything. Thank you to my dearest friend, Miriam Chatt, for a lifetime of love, and to Tom Lee, Tom Smith, and Nick Keys, for being alongside always. Finally, thank you to Ed Hopely, who walked into the middle of this book and with whom the future extends, brilliantly.

I dedicate this book to my mother, Patricia Magee.

ABT   *The Autobiography of Alice B. Toklas*

ASR   *A Stein Reader*

EA   *Everybody's Autobiography*

GP   *Geography and Plays*

GSS   *Gertrude Stein Selected*

HTW   *How to Write*

HWW   *How Writing Is Written*

I   *Ida: A Novel*

LA   *Lectures in America*

LB   *Lifting Belly*

LOP   *Last Operas and Plays*

MA   *The Making of Americans*

N   *Narration*

PP   *Portraits and Prayers*

TB   *Tender Buttons*

W   *Writings: 1932–1946*

WAM   *What Are Masterpieces*

The use of this is manifold. —Stein *TB* 8

Index

In the early stages of this project, I accidentally became a book indexer. Having no formal training, I approached the activity of indexing as a reader and researcher. I know how to use an index—indeed, I rely on indexes to follow conceptual and thematic threads across diverse texts. I have always considered the index a synthesis of two distinct inventories: on the one hand, a list that one searches for specific entries; and on the other, a list that one cruises for oddities and unanticipated connections. My own attempts to construct indexes have been with this synthetic goal in mind; I aim to write an index that functionally organizes conceptual and referential material in addition to documenting the contingencies and unexpected convergences of a text.

The concept of an index is ambiguous. An index is a paratext—auxiliary and derivative. It is also a kind of translation that presents an alternative version of a book's text. An indexer chooses specific concepts to act as categories, subcategories, and cross-references: these choices, implicitly, constitute editorial statements (and sometimes political propositions) via the emphasis or de-emphasis of certain relations. An index is often a reader's first point of contact with a text—it functions as an introduction, glossary, directory, map, or lexicon. Indexing is an inexhaustible activity; each index contains only an example of possible entries. The word "index" refers to various activities and occasions of pointing. As a book's index points to its content, an index finger points to objects of concern or interest;

so too does the index of a measuring instrument point to a reading on a scale, and the hands of a clock point to the time. The nose is an index, for it points out and away from the face, just as a singular vector points out away from a problematic and toward an approach for solution. In printing, an index is a typographical image in the shape of a gloved hand pointing. In mathematics, optics, computing, and economics, the index functions variously to denote different kinds of dependent, contextual, and indicative relations. An index is that which indicates, elicits a response, redirects gaze, diverts attention, shifts the conceptual terrain.

My study of indexes and indexicality is, in a very basic sense, connected to the foundational theories of C. S. Peirce. In Peirce's semiotic theory there are three categories of signs: icons are representational; indexes are correspondent; symbols are associational. Peirce's examples of indexes include "a guidepost, which points down the road to be taken, or a relative pronoun, which is placed just after the name of the thing intended to be denoted, or a vocative exclamation, such as 'Hi! there,' which acts upon the nerves of the person addressed and forces his attention" (2:5). Other typical examples offered in summaries of Peircian indexes include the relations between a footprint and a foot, smoke and a fire, and a symptom and a disease.

Mary Ann Doane writes in an essay on indexicality and contemporary art:

> Given the fact that Peirce applied the term "index" to such diverse signs as a footprint, a weathervane, thunder, the word "this," a pointing finger, a photographic image, it is not difficult to see why the concept has occasioned confusion. On the one hand, the term seems to specify signs in the order of the trace—the footprint, the death mask, the photograph (where the object leaves its imprint

on a light-sensitive surface). This type of index partakes of the iconic because the sign resembles the object. On the other hand, Peirce emphasizes that the shifter in language—a category including pronouns such as "this," "now," "I," "here"—is an exemplary form of the index. In this case, the index partakes of the symbolic. In both these instances, the index is defined by a physical, material connection to its object. (2)

Doane argues that the biggest question facing artists and critics in today's "post-medium condition" concerns the status of representation (3). Writing specifically about photography, Doane calls for a return to Peirce's concept of the index in order to rethink the complexity of reference in contemporary aesthetic practices. Indexes, she argues, point in several directions at once and thus problematize the efficacy of the categories of representation they serve to demonstrate:

> As photographic trace or impression, the index seems to harbor a fullness, an excessiveness of detail that is always supplemental to meaning or intention. Yet, the index as deixis implies an emptiness, a hollowness that can only be filled in specific, contingent, always mutating situations. It is this dialectic of the empty and the full that lends the index an eeriness and uncanniness not associated with the realms of the icon or symbol. At times, the disconcerting closeness of the index to its object raises doubts as to whether it is indeed a sign, suggesting instead that the index is perched precariously on the very edge of semiosis. (2)

For Doane, the indexical relation is also iconic and symbolic, and hence the index engages in all three categories of representation set out by Peirce (that is, the modes of representation correlated with icons, indexes, and symbols, respectively): resemblance, correspondence, and association. Her designation of the photograph as a kind of index shifts the problem of representation from a question of the ontological difference between an object and its image to a question of how certain relations emerge and come to be understood *as* relations. For the former, reality is taken to be that which is represented via photography; for the latter, reality is taken to be the emergent condition in which both objects and images coexist in a complex relation.

This present study is doubly indexical: it points to Stein's work from my position as a reader, and it points out the relations between her work and an open set of diverse texts and concepts. The index can be read as a selective guide to Stein as well as an intellectual history of Steinianism by other means. In reading and writing "with" an index—in reading and writing with an index as a search tool and scholarly reference guide—one uses the index to move laterally and variously across a network of affinitive texts. To the degree that this network becomes the material of a critical project, the index can be theorized as an alternative mode to literary criticism. This book is an attempt to practice the possibilities of this mode.

Stein

I'm often asked, *Why Stein?* It's not a question easily answered, but it's one worth thinking about. Most importantly, Stein's work is enduringly relevant. The questions she asks, the challenges she sets, and the concepts she develops continue to mobilize conversations around poetry, representation, and experience. Her work is endlessly generative—each engagement raises different and often vexing issues, and problematizes normative conceptualizations of both reading and interpreting meaning. Stein is funny, smart, obnoxious, obtuse, and incisive. Her vocabulary is basic—misleadingly so, for she writes complexly and innovatively. Stein's texts endure. Or, perhaps more exactly, Stein's readers endure her texts—for they do, undoubtedly, require a significant effort. Like her contemporaries Henri Bergson, Alfred North Whitehead, and William James, Stein was interested in the duration as a temporal manifold that includes coexistent, often incommensurable, events, objects, and experiences. Duration is what happens in time and not merely its measurement: a duration is *what is endured*. Stein was concerned with the durations of reading and writing, and with the broader, experiential ambit that contains them both. What is endured, she asks in her work, in an engagement with this text? What happens in the time of reading?

Her work points to some of the trademarks of modernism—the vacillating optic between the micro and the macro, the dogmatics of the avant-garde, and the mistaking of appropriation and neocolonialism for worldliness and bohemia. Her work shows the uneasy wobbles between psychology, neuroscience, sexology, sociology, mathematics, physics, and aesthetics. Hers is a twentieth century built by industrialism and razed by war, focused on the quivering atom and the measurement of the universe, bent by relativity and the fourth dimension, folded into new durations of philosophy, approached by perspectives and aspects outside the vanishing point, cut into film sequences, and segmented by nationalisms.

Here in the second decade of the twenty-first century, the distance from the turn of the last century seems oddly narrow. The same questions endure: how do we account for the experience of experience, for the consciousness of consciousness? And, for those engaged with literature: how do we read and write with enough mobility to adapt according to the constant movement of the problems of experience and consciousness? And, for those engaged in poetics: how do we talk about the problems of reading and writing? The historical, social, and cultural—and certainly political—vocabulary has changed for all of these Steinian activities of thinking and rethinking, yet their aims and difficulties are resonant. In beginning to answer the question *Why Stein?* I must first ask myself, *Why poetry?* Why is it poetry, and the critical orbit of poetics, that seems apt, if not *most* apt, to tackle such questions?

Stein's work endures because she engages with these questions and the problems that they generate. Stein's oeuvre, despite its generic crossovers, can be usefully called "poetry," and her poetics is stubbornly unassimilable to the fixing aims of literary interpretations for which meaning is the end goal (if not the implicit primary milieu). Stein is not the only one to avert fixity through obscurity; the aim of this study is not to argue that Stein is singular in this sense. But there is something particularly efficacious about Stein's obscurity, which exists not only despite of, but also *because* of, remarkably explicit and often axiomatic proclamations of compositional intention. Stein is not elusive or mysterious; she presents her work with the force of someone who (regardless of anxieties about her place in literary culture) is nevertheless frankly certain about her poetics. Stein's assertions can be contradictory, even counterfactual, but the force with which she builds them into theoretical systems for thinking, writing, and reading demands that their implications and provocations be taken seriously and enacted in conceptual experiments. Stein's obscurity, thus, is not only aesthetic; it's a philosophical attitude. It claims the right to be unobscurely obscure.

It is partly to do with this issue of obscurity that Stein's work has been the subject of endless critical debate. Scholarship has been, for the most part, overinvested in the argument of whether Stein is readable or not. Such an argument rarely questions what is meant by "readability"; instead it focuses on the efficacy (or inefficacy) of hermeneutical efforts to redeem Stein's work and assimilate her meaningfully into preexisting vocabularies. Sympathetic critics redeem Stein by pointing to hidden or possible meanings. Unsympathetic critics foreclose the reading of her work by labeling her with the worst kinds of modernist clichés: Stein is hermetic, difficult, stubborn, and purposefully nonsensical. At the heart of this critical impasse, there is a common problem: the dominance of hermeneutical approaches to reading writing. In the Anglo-American tradition, and in the last century or so (to set a time for my own study), interpretative reading strategies, whether informed by New Criticism, deconstructionism, or historicism, have each and in different ways been practiced as exercises in hermeneutics.

"The problem . . . with hermeneutical modes of interpretation," writes Steven Shaviro, "is that they reduce the unknown to already-known, the already determined. These theories assume that my not-knowing is only a contingency for myself, that ignorance is a particular state that I am in; while they imagine that the object I am seeking to know is in itself already perfectly determinate, if only I could come to know it" (*Without Criteria* 62). Even in the case of critics who read Stein's work according to a kind of "poetics of indeterminacy" (to use Marjorie Perloff's phrase), the indeterminacy of meanings is considered a determinate fact: the reader's task, then, is to negotiate the affect of indeterminacy and to consider the possibilities of reading language for its capacity to be multiply meaningful. Despite the (interesting and always illuminating) readings of polysemy in Stein's work, and even despite the intention to do otherwise, critical accounts of Stein depend on determinate notions of indeterminacy, such that the reading of Stein's abstraction is understood as a lesson on abstraction and little more. Once she is read for her lessons on the itinerancy of meaning, there is very little room left to talk about what else Stein's work *does*.

Examples of this kind of reading can be found in Marjorie Perloff's *The Poetics of Indeterminacy: Rimbaud to Cage* and Ulla E. Dydo's *Gertrude Stein: The Language That Rises*. Perloff and Dydo are two of the most influential and important scholars whose writings on Stein have brought her into contemporary relief. It is not my intention to devalue their critical responses to Stein but, rather, to point to the problem of reading Stein's work as concerned primarily with the possibilities of its own meanings. Such a reading, which takes Stein's work as a metapoetic exercise in demonstrating the plasticity of the relation between signifier and signified, relies on the very structural logics of meaning that it aims to radicalize: whether the aim is to declare Stein meaningless, to find the hidden meaning, or to claim that the meanings are manifold, the emphasis remains on "meaning."

Stein knew that it was impossible to write without meaning; meaning happens, irrevocably.[1] Her compositional aim was not to disrupt, dislocate, multiply, or cloud meaning, even if these things may happen for a reader when engaging with her work. What Stein's work proposes, and what I attempt to formulate in this study, is that the compositional practices of reading and writing are constructive experiences that produce and investigate the contexts and relations of language in a specific occasion. Although I am attempting a kind of critique of hermeneutics, my critique is aimed not at interpretation per se but at the primacy of interpretation in literary criticism. My reading of Stein seeks to de-emphasize the question of meaning in order to consider other perceptual affects: the vague, often paradoxical, sometimes troubling, and endlessly variegated constructions that constitute experience. Thus Stein's obscurity is not meant

---

1. Stein writes: "All this foolishness about my writing being mystic or impressionistic is so stupid. Every word I write has the same passionate exactness of meaning that it is supposed to have. Everything I write means exactly what it says" (cf. Meyer 229). Elsewhere, she writes: "There is no such thing as putting [words] together without sense . . . Any human being putting down words had to make sense out of them" (*HWW* 18).

in the sense of obscuring, as in blocking or covering up, but as an ontological position: for the most part, experience consists of partial, suggestive, and half-glimpsed entities. On this matter, I am indebted to Steven Meyer's landmark study, *Irresistible Dictation: Gertrude Stein and the Correlations of Writing and Science*. In this book, Meyer argues that Stein's work is constructively, incisively "opaque": "My use of the term opaque may seem puzzling, for I regard it as a positive quality, and aim in my readings to respect the integrity, or opacity, of these dense texts. Too often, readers of Stein have attempted to render her compositions transparent, to crack the code. Such interpretations merely invert the mistaken accusation that her writing lacks any sense at all. Operating in another register than ordinary communication with its ideal of transparency, these autopoietic compositions function as what James called 'irreducible and stubborn facts'" (xxi).

In 1978, *L=A=N=G=U=A=G=E* magazine, coedited by Charles Bernstein and Bruce Andrews, published a special issue of critical responses to three poems from Stein's *Tender Buttons*—"A Carafe, That Is a Blind Glass," "Glazed Glitter," and an excerpt of "Roastbeef." Michael Davidson's essay, "On Reading Stein," which functions as a kind of editorial for the issue, begins as follows:

> Stein has been haunted by two antithetical criticisms. One proposes that her writing is all play, that it derives strictly out of her early researches with William James and motor automism and was later invigorated by Cubist formalism. The other proposes that Stein is a kind of hermetic Symbolist who encodes sexual and biographical information in complex little verbal machines which contextualize their own environments. Both views operate on either side of a referential paradigm; one wants her to mean nothing and the other wants her to mean intrinsically. But what makes

> TENDER BUTTONS so vital is not the strategies by which meaning
> is avoided or encoded but how each piece points at possibilities for
> meaning. Unlike the Symbolist who creates beautiful detachable
> artifacts, Stein's prose is firmly tied to the world—but it is a world
> under construction, a world in which the equation of word and
> thing can no longer be taken for granted. (2–3)

Later Davidson suggests that if one is to take Stein's challenges seriously, one must

> learn to read *writing*, not read *meanings*; we must learn to interrogate the spaces around words as much as the words themselves;
> we must discover language as an active "exchange" of meaning
> rather than a static paradigm of rules and features. The question
> is not "what" she means but "how." (4)

For this book, December 1978 figures as a significant occasion in which Stein is reintroduced to critical scholarship in the context of contemporary poetics. Davidson's essay challenges early- to mid-twentieth-century scholarship for its tendency to speak dogmatically from either side of a fixed notion of meaningfulness. Such bifurcation, Davidson suggests, is not particular to the community of those writing on Stein but symptomatic of endemic assumptions about language, meaning, and representation in the tradition of Western literary studies. Bernstein and Andrews's editorial project—which invites responses from poets, artists, publishers, critics, and scholars, all of whom had previously or would go on to engage with Stein—marks an important attempt to break from these assumptions and to investigate different approaches to the activities of reading and writing.

The responses focus on the convergences of language philosophy, semiotics, phenomenology, politics, deconstructionism, critical theory, and poetics. They also demonstrate new approaches to critical writing—Larry Eigner's response is a four-paragraph prose-poetic attempt to record the perceptual/affective outcomes of engaging with Stein's language (and ends with the wonderful one-line conclusion "Nothing is too dull" [5]). Bob Perelman's is a frenetic study of the "continual athleticism" of Stein's poetics, again seemingly focused on perception as the signal unit of linguistic composition and reference (5). Steve McCaffery responds with a short poem about a "She" with "queer ones" in her verbal patterns (6). Peter Seaton composes a dense, short-sentenced prose stream that collects, by association, individual companion lines to *Tender Buttons* (6–8). Rae Armantrout writes "on from" Stein—naming Stein's capacity for sameness (repetition) and difference (constantly moving frames of reference) as simultaneously "an exception and a reestablishment" of literary convention (8). Dick Higgins rewrites the three poems and takes up the puns in play (8–9). Jackson Mac Low mounts a serious attempt to find a method of "close reading" to suit Stein's work—one that considers each word for its sonic and visual histories, resemblances, and obscurities (9–10). Carl Andre reframes a couple of key lines into a staggered, spare, projective-verse-esque lyric (11). Bob Grenier's essay engages with Stein more broadly than the excerpted *Tender Buttons* poems, considering her long-term attempts to frame and reframe her poetics (11–13).

Near the end of his study, Grenier inserts a paragraph, entirely in parentheses, that challenges the notion (whether it was actually implied or whether Grenier feared it would be implied by the magazine's collective effort) that Stein was a proto–Language poet. He writes:

(In this context, for $L=A=N=G=U=A=G=E$, I want to say that I think it's at best a "creative misreading" of Stein to take her work as a whole as a primary instance of "language-oriented writing." Not only her somewhat less arduous later work (*Autobiography of A.B.T., Brewsie and Willie*), but *The Making of Americans* (a history of her family & compendium of sketches of every possible kind of human being), *Lucy Church Amiably* (an "engraving" or romantic portrait of life in the French countryside) & her long poem "Stanzas in Meditation" (written shortly before the *Autobiography of A.B.T.* &, if anything, a prototype of confessional poetry) all are intent to make new ways to say something—show her thinking language not as object-in-itself, but as composition functioning in the composition of the world. With the exception of some verbal experiment, with Williams & Pound, Stein's basic concern as a writer was to confront the imperative MAKE IT NEW however possible—"IT" being, equally/simultaneously, sentience, world & language as relation between these. T.B., specifically, exists as such confrontation—& to take it as a variously interesting arrangement of words, alone, is to perpetuate the initial journalist-parody response to the work as "nonsense.") (13)

The diversity of responses—in terms of their critical and formal approaches—is a good indication of the variety of conversations gathering around the work of Stein at this period in the overlapping contexts of innovative poetries in North America. Such conversations continue today, and, at least in the context of Anglo-American contemporary post-avant poetries (including, but not limited to, language-focused, conceptual, flarf, ambient, and documentary writing), they continue to invigorate scholarship on Stein. My research is both informed by, and an effort to contribute to, the rich field of Steinian poetics as I find it today. My excursions into this archival moment take Davidson's lead-in and Grenier's lead-out statements as guiding principles: we need to keep finding ways to read Stein and to write about our reading.

Three moments prior to 1978 have largely been left out of the archive of scholarship on Stein, and they figure for this book as important moments of critical insight. Each is prescient in its reading of Stein's poetic innovations and provocations, and each represents an important contribution to the kind of critical responses that Davidson and Grenier called for decades later. They are, in chronological order, texts written by Mabel Dodge, Mina Loy, and Allegra Stewart. Mabel Dodge (known later as Mabel Dodge Luhan) was an exceptionally well-read, intelligent commentator on art, literature, philosophy, and psychology. After meeting Stein in Paris in 1911 (during which time she was based in Italy), Dodge became an enthusiastic reader and advocate of Stein's work. She returned to the United States the following year and settled in New York City, where she hosted salons in her apartment and was one of the organizers of the Armory Show in 1913, where she distributed a pamphlet publication of Stein's "Portrait of Mabel Dodge at the Villa Curonia." Also distributed at the exhibition was an issue of the magazine *Arts and Decoration*, which included an essay by Dodge on Stein's poetics. These companion pieces comprise the first works by and on Stein published for an American audience. Dodge's essay, "Speculations, or Post-Impressionism in Prose," is a critical text of scholarly insight into Stein's compositional contexts and affiliations. Her writing reveals the intellectual preoccupations of the time—the provocations of Freud and Jung, the influence of Bergson's *élan vital*, and the dominance of European painting on the symbolic vocabulary of the modernist avant-garde.[2]

---

2. Dodge's essay was reprinted in full in *"Speculations, or Post-impressionism in Prose": A History of Having a Great Many Times Not Continued to Be Friends: The Correspondence between Mabel Dodge and Gertrude Stein, 1911–1934*, ed. Patricia Everett. Everett reproduced one minor typographical error from the original which I have corrected here for clarity.

*

The essay begins:

> Many roads are being broken today, and along these roads con-
> sciousness is pursuing truth to eternity. This is an age of commu-
> nication, and the human being who is not a "communicant" is in
> the sad plight which the dogmatist defines as being a condition of
> spiritual non-receptivity. Some of these newly opened roads lie
> parallel and almost touch. In a large studio in Paris, hung with
> paintings by Renoir, Matisse and Picasso, Gertrude Stein is doing
> with words what Picasso is doing with paint. She is impelling lan-
> guage to induce new states of consciousness, and in doing so lan-
> guage becomes with her a creative art rather than a mirror of his-
> tory. (Qtd. in Luhan, "*Speculations*" 269)

Dodge is often cited in order to claim that Stein identified as, or
attempted to be, a literary cubist. To be sure, there is an affinity between Stein and Picasso in terms of approaches to composition—
specifically, their emphases on the constructive and generative effects of the activities of composition and aesthetic engagement.
Stein and Picasso, in different ways, conceived of composition as a
process (for both the one who composes and the one who engages)
that impels, or induces, to use Dodge's term "new states of consciousness." Dodge's argument positions Stein and Picasso as resonant in their attempts to think through and reconfigure the relation
between composition and representation—and, while it is important
to note that Stein and Picasso were far from the only two engaged in
such an attempt, and further, that Picasso was far from the only cubist, Dodge's critical assertion is perhaps the first to figure Stein as a
constructivist poet: a writer who *makes things happen.*

Dodge goes on to theorize Stein's compositional method according to the notion of Bergsonian intuition: "She does not go after the words—she waits and lets them come to her, and they do" (270). By her account Stein perceived abstract impressions, against which words were carefully measured until matched. The result, Dodge proposes, is a kind of vitalist poetics in which "every word lives" (272). Her emphatic insistence that Stein's work inaugurated a break with established literary modes and forms makes a historical claim— Stein is anointed the figurehead for the nascent and dissenting century:

> Many roads are being broken—what a wonderful word—"broken"! And out of the shattering and petrification of today—up from the cleavage and the disintegration—we will see order emerging tomorrow. Is it so difficult to remember that life at birth is always painful and rarely lovely? How strange it is to think that the rough-hewn trail of today will become tomorrow the path of least resistance, over which the average will drift with all the ease and serenity of custom. All the labor of evolution is condensed into this one fact, of the vitality of the individual making way for the many. We can praise the high courage of the road breakers, admitting as we infallibly must, in Gertrude Stein's own words, and with true Bergsonism faith— "Something is certain coming out of them!" (273)

The second moment came in the writing of Mina Loy, who met Stein through Dodge. During the 1920s, Loy wrote several short critical reflections on Stein, as well as a poem. Loy's critical prose is composed in short, eccentric, and dogmatic paragraphs. Loy, like Dodge, immediately invokes Bergson in her reading of Stein. Recalling her first encounter with the Stein of *The Making of Americans*, Loy writes:

> This was when Bergson was in the air, and his beads of Time strung on the continuous flux of Being, seemed to have found a

literary conclusion in the austere verity of Gertrude Stein's theme
—"Being" as the absolute occupation.

For by the intervaried rhythm of this monotone mechanism
she uses for inducing a continuity of awareness of her subject, I
was connected up with the very pulse of duration.

The core of a "Being" was revealed to me with uninterrupted
insistence.

The plastic static of the ultimate presence of an entity. (*Last
Lunar Baedeker* 289)

And then, describing the shift to Stein's later mode of "impressionistic" portraiture (the Stein of *Tender Buttons*): "In her second phase
. . . [she] entirely reverses this method of conveyance through duration. She ignores duration and telescopes time and space and the
subjective and objective in a way that obviates interval and interpo-
sition. She stages strange triangles between the nominative and his
verb and irruptive co-respondents" (291).

Loy's reading of Stein is feral and brilliant, roaming from axiomat-
ics to associational riffings and from psychopathologic to intergalac-
tic scales. Echoing Dodge, Loy declares Stein to have "tackled an aesthetic of analysis of the habits of consciousness in its lair," and with
characteristic oddity she concludes that "the uncustomary impetus
of her style accelerates and extends the thought wave until it can vi-
brate a cosmos from a ray of light on a baa lamb" (298). Perhaps most
importantly, and tucked rather subtly into infinitely quotable and excited prose, Loy writes: "It may be impossible for our public inured
to the unnecessary nuisances of journalism to understand this literature, but it is a literature reduced to a basic significance that could
be conveyed to a man on Mars" (291). What Loy emphasizes here,
contra Dodge's celebrations of the extraordinary, is the ordinariness
of what goes on in Stein's work. The "basic significance" that Loy

imagines as being lucid to the proverbial Martian refers to the minor shifts in affect and structure that typify the dynamics of Stein's work. Even in her later "impressionistic" mode, when her vocabulary is less "austere," Stein still writes of and with the smallest structural differentiations, mobilizing and mutating by increments. The difficulty of her work is not because of some inherent radicality but because of the considerable effort required to actually engage with the activity of reading. For Loy and Dodge, the key to Stein's poetics is in its demand for a new consciousness—a consciousness tuned to the actuality of reading. The "Being" that Loy finds revealed via "uninterrupted insistence" is, as I argue throughout this book, in fact a kind of becoming. Being insistently and with deviation is becoming: an emergent ontology.

By the middle of the twentieth century, literary criticism that focused on Stein had settled into two distinct modes. Biographical and historical accounts of Stein—often interested more in her friends and enemies than in her writing—were increasingly popular. So too were detailed, cryptographic readings that claimed to crack the Steinian code. Writing against both trends, Allegra Stewart's book-length study *Gertrude Stein and the Present* (1967) considers Stein's writing in the context of contemporary metaphysics. Citing Peirce, James, Bergson, Whitehead, Santayana, Heidegger, and Wittgenstein, among others, Stewart constructs an epistemic survey of the nexus of (brain-centered) psychology, language theory, linguistics and semiotics, and (time-centered) philosophy of the early twentieth century. Situating Stein very much in this scene—as student, reader, and writer—Stewart carefully considers Stein's poetics according to its closest metaphysical companions. She concludes that Stein was engaged with the work of her teachers James and Santayana, though she didn't remain committed to psychological and neuroscientific theories throughout her writing life; she was familiar with Bergson (who was giving very popular public lectures throughout Europe in her first years there), but she was not influenced by his philosophy; she did not engage with Wittgenstein, even though her work shares certain affinities with his notion of the language game; she was very much engaged with the process philosophy of Alfred North Whitehead, whom she knew personally.[3]

Stewart's thesis is that Stein's work is a "phenomenology of mind" that takes its lead from Anglo-American revisions of Hegelian dialectics (25). This includes, most importantly, the processual and pluralistic models set out by James and Whitehead. Ultimately, Stewart argues, Stein's metaphysical interests are less the result of directive study and emulation, and more indicative of her contemporary situation: Stein is, more than anything, a writer whose work is "a manifestation of the twentieth-century spirit" (26), a spirit of investigation into the temporality of transformation, differentiation, and emergence, and the potentialities and latencies of selfhood, language, and identity. As Stewart's book progresses, Stein is constructed as a writer with "genuine philosophical insight" whose work was an attempt to "break through literary patterns to affirm the openness of the universe against all determinisms" (28, 31). She evokes Freud and Jung in her discussion of *Tender Buttons,* a text she reads as a concerted effort to plumb and fiddle with language's roots and meanings. She reads *Doctor Faust Lights the Lights* as an important

3. Evidently, Stewart wrote to Toklas to ask about Stein's influences. Toklas replied: "Gertrude Stein didn't know Wittgenstein. She was a pupil of Santayana . . . She was under the influence of James and Whitehead of course, but not Bergson" (23–24). Bergson, who is immediately cited by Dodge and Loy in their critical accounts of Stein, is noted as not being an influence. Bergson's theories were in wide circulation at the time that Dodge and Loy were reading and writing about Stein, so their references reveal more about their intellectual milieu than Stein's own investments. Stein's work is distinctly *not* Bergsonian in its temperament and affect, even if they asked companionable questions to do with the experience of durations of time.

retelling of a European trope in the context of American Pragmatist individualism. She ends with an analysis of Stein's secular, cosmological ontology. In the last pages of the book, Stewart writes:

> Behind the fresh honesty of her language, however, we find a world view that is not only coherent but profound. When we consider her metaphysical vision of reality, coupled with her long practice of "spiritual exercises," Gertrude Stein ceases to be merely a representative phenomenon of her time. In theory and practice alike she speaks to the modern consciousness with a kind of hard-earned, astringent wisdom which, though stripped of all consoling "overbeliefs" and focused wholly upon the present moment of experience, is an irreducible condensation of the spirituality of the past. Her primary object is not to explain the cosmic creativity but to elucidate and evoke in others the groundless act of presence—an act by which man may realize at one stroke his own "human mind" and the beauty or meaning of some aspect of the cosmos. In this philosophy, "being existing" depends wholly on one thing—the selfless realization of the human mind in an act of freedom. (212–213)

Stewart takes Stein seriously—as a writer and thinker whose poetics makes a genuine attempt to do something new. And while Stewart makes a case for a hidden, complex, and somewhat encoded meaningfulness to Stein's work, an argument that is quite different to the one I make here, Stewart's painstaking historiography is one of the first accounts of Stein's work alongside philosophy: indeed, *as* a kind of philosophy. Following on from Dodge and Loy, Stewart considers Stein for her intellectual and aesthetic contributions (and challenges) to twentieth-century thought. In these three examples, a model of scholarship can be traced in contrast to the prevailing strains of literary criticism throughout the last century. Dodge, Loy, and Stewart are remarkably prescient in their reading of Stein's relevance to a poetics that would come to impress itself on future experimentalisms, conceptualisms, and interdisciplinary aesthetics—broadly speaking, the post-$L=A=N=G=U=A=G=E$ moment in which scholars and critics have taken Stein up in increasingly diverse and generative contexts.[4]

Affinities

Though this study is a reading of Stein, it does not argue for a specific interpretation of Stein's work. Where interpretation seeks to elucidate core meanings exegetically, I seek to explore itinerant modes of reading (rather than tracking Stein's itinerant modes of meaning), in which one reads *with* and *alongside* texts. Each "index entry" focuses on a specific abstract concern that I identify as relevant to Stein's poetics. The entries cross-reference each other and are designed be read in any order: it is a constructivist book and is designed for use. I am using the word "constructivist" in part with reference to Isabelle Stengers, who theorizes a constructivist reading approach in the context of Whitehead's major work, *Process and Reality*. Stengers argues that *Process and Reality* demands a particular kind of readerly engagement—one that "emphasizes the need to actively and explicitly relate any knowledge-production to the question that it tries to answer," a question that impels one to construct a meaningful relation to the

---

4. Of course, I do not mean to imply that these three examples are the *only* ones that present a compelling case for Stein in the first part of the twentieth century. Laura Riding's essay titled "New Barbarism" at the end of *Contemporaries and Snobs*, which I discuss in the "Contemporaneity" chapter of this book, is certainly part of this group. My choice here of texts by Dodge, Loy, and Stewart aims to (re)introduce less-known, under-read, or forgotten accounts of Stein.

text at hand by taking up and taking care of the conceptual material of the work ("A Constructivist Reading" 92).

A constructivist approach requires a rethinking of the function of abstraction. Abstractions in the constructivist mode are taken to be inevitable, necessary modes of thought that must be critically revised (to paraphrase Whitehead) in order to keep actively engaged in the task of doing thinking. At the end of Stengers's essay, which theorizes constructivist reading by example, she describes *Process and Reality* as a nonlinear network of related abstractions, each of which is "appealing for an imaginative leap" that in turn "cannot be abstracted from its relevance to other abstractions which are also calling for an imaginative leap" (108). "This is why," she concludes,

> you cannot read *Process and Reality* from the first to the last page, in a linear manner, but must zigzag, using the index, being lured to come back to something you recollect but which had remained mute and now takes on a new importance, taking the leap that you have just felt is possible. And it may also be why Whitehead's own writing zigzagged as well, why he abstained from a careful rewriting of the whole text each time he redesigned his own concepts. Each new insertion, each addition was to be understood as a partially explicit definition of what had, until then, been indefinable for him. And, it may be, finally, that the very fact that his text does not run smoothly like a steam engine which has to avoid clashes or bumps is as important as the content of the book. (109)

Here Stengers presents a poetics of Whiteheadian philosophy—the form and content are inextricable, turning the book into an event in which the reader finds herself compelled to get involved, in order to find a way to move through and around the conceptual material. The reader must construct her own methodology in order to make reading possible—to set up a temporary laboratory in which the text's propositions are experimented and played with. Both Whitehead and Stengers play key roles in this thesis, not only in terms of providing models of a constructivist philosophy and a constructivist approach to reading, but also for their sustained efforts, in different fields and contexts, to think and write rigorously on philosophical models of open systems.

I came to Whitehead through Stein. In *The Autobiography of Alice B. Toklas*, Whitehead is named as one of three geniuses known to Toklas in her life (the other two being Picasso and Stein). In the same book, the story is told of Stein and Toklas's first meeting with the Whiteheads at a dinner in London that led to a visit to the Whitehead's home, prolonged to a six-week stay because of the outbreak of World War I. Toklas narrates that during their six weeks together, Stein and Whitehead enjoyed daily walks around the lake, nattering together about philosophy and history. From this intriguing story, I looked up Whitehead's work, beginning with his earlier treatises on mathematics and ending with his later philosophical monographs. Whitehead is a wide-ranging and original thinker: a mathematician who never quite loses the propensity for heavy, algebraic definitions and redefinitions of terms; a philosopher who sets out to describe a world of experiencing subjects in which neither experience nor subjectivity is predicated on (or exemplified by) human consciousness, and who proposes that all objects are events and all relations objects; a theologian who secularizes and radicalizes the concept of god; a constructivist who argues for the actuality of novelty and creativity; a historian of science who wants to position science and scientific knowledge as a participant in, and not the authority on, the world. Whitehead's revisions to the philosophical conceits he inherits from Spinoza, Leibniz, Hume, Locke, and others contribute to his careful and detailed ontological platform, which in its various insights anticipates the work of Gilles Deleuze and Félix Guattari, cybernetics, autopoiesis, and several strands of digital and network theory. Despite the scope of his work, Whitehead is only recently being revived in philosophy, science studies, theology, and literary and aesthetic theory. Work by Stengers, as well as Steven Shaviro, Steven Meyer, Joan Richardson, and Michael Halewood, have opened up Whiteheadian theory to contemporary concerns—including ecology, sociology, economics, and the digital humanities.

Whitehead's theory of the "bifurcation of nature" is particularly important to the conceptual thrust of this book. For Whitehead, nature is bifurcated whenever the world is thought to be composed of two different sets of things: primary and secondary qualities, the former constituted by matter and the latter that which is added on to matter by the perceiving mind in order to make sense of material reality. In *The Concept of Nature,* Whitehead explains this bifurcation as a recurrent, endemic problem:

> The reason why the bifurcation of nature is always creeping back into scientific philosophy is the extreme difficulty of exhibiting the perceived redness and warmth of the fire in one system of relations with the agitated molecules of carbon and oxygen with radiant energy from them, and with the various functioning of the material body. Unless we produce the all-embracing relations, we are faced with a bifurcation of nature; namely, warmth and redness on one side, and molecules, electrons and ether on the other side. Then the two factors are explained as being respectively the cause and the mind's reaction to the cause. (32)

One way to read Whitehead's work is as a constant effort to challenge the bifurcation of nature in its countless forms in contemporary thought. In this study, I challenge the bifurcation of nature as it is mirrored in the habits and tendencies of literary criticism. The two irreconcilable interpretative frameworks that Davidson identifies in

Stein scholarship are symptomatic of a broader divide in literary studies: on the one hand, the notion that meaning is intrinsic to language; and on the other hand, the notion that meaning is extrinsic to language. In the first case, Stein is read as purposefully negating the meaningfulness of language by writing self-consciously nonsensical constructions that render each word impotent. In the second case, Stein is read as purposefully producing obscured meanings in language by constructing riddles, secrets, and cryptographs that yoke each word to an external referent. What is necessary, following Whitehead, is a critical approach that considers the "all-embracing relations" between language and meaning, signification and representation, materiality and sociality. This means constructing a methodology for thinking, reading, and writing that focuses on relations.

The correspondences between Stein and Whitehead are not immediately obvious. However, the relation between the two, and the activity of reading them together (or alongside each other), generates a lively field of resonances and conceptual affiliations. They are both concerned with objects, subjects, events, and nexuses, where these terms describe modes of being or experience rather than ontologically distinct entities. They are both interested in the emergence of objects, subjects, events, and nexuses in, through, and as temporality. In Meyer's study of Stein and science, Whitehead and Stein are considered together for their shared preoccupation with "rhythm," the multiple relations of an event in its temporal and durational continuation through which variations and modifications produce new states and conditions (*Irresistible Dictation* 182). For Whitehead and Stein, experience is rhythmic—not in any sense of cyclic patterning but in the sense of vibrational and harmonic intensities. Rhythm refers to both movement and the relation of things in motion: in music, the rhythm concerns the beat as well as the space between beats.

Rhythm, as a conceit with which to read Stein's differential repetitions and emphatic intensities, brings her work into dialogue with the aesthetics of Whitehead's philosophy.

In this study, I follow Whitehead in his rejection of the bifurcation of nature, and I take up his challenge to begin the task of rethinking philosophy as a task that proliferates more and more questions—questions that must be taken seriously but that may never be resolved. With Whitehead, I take language as "indeterminate" and "elliptical," an abstraction that is one aspect of engaging with the world and not the defining engagement (*Process and Reality* 12–13). With Whitehead, I take meaning as a vagueness and knowledge as approximation.[5] And, from Whitehead, I approach Stein's poetics as an attempt, by other means, to get at a theory of "rhythm," where rhythm is a kind of aesthetic mode of accounting for, and emphasizing, the temporality of experience, and where experience is not limited to or even exemplified by human consciousness, but rather describes the mode of perception by which a world perceives itself.

Like Stein, Whitehead can be a turnoff for readers. Stengers writes: "If Whitehead's work is hard to approach, it is because it demands, with utter discretion, that its readers accept the adventure of the questions that will separate them from every consensus" (*Thinking with Whitehead* 7). The same can be said for Stein. If she is hard to read, it is because she demands from her reader the kind of attention that takes time and requires significant effort. In order to read with Stein and Whitehead, because of and in dedication to their difficulty, I have recruited a constellation of coreaders whose work sup-

5. In *Essays in Science and Philosophy,* Whitehead writes: "In human experience, the philosophic question can receive no final answer. Human knowledge is a process of approximation. In the focus of experience there is comparative clarity. But the discrimination of this clarity leads into the penumbral background. There are always questions left over. The problem is to discriminate exactly what we know vaguely" (122).

ports, invigorates, and problematizes the results of my engagement with Stein's poetics in the key of Whitehead.

This constellation includes Epicurus, Democritus and Lucretius, G. W. Leibniz, William James, Gilles Deleuze, Félix Guattari, Michel Serres, Isabelle Stengers, Karen Barad, Donna Haraway, Eve Sedgwick, and Manuel DeLanda, as well as a number of contemporary poet-critics (many who work or have worked on Stein), such as Lyn Hejinian, Charles Bernstein, Harryette Mullen, Maria Damon, Craig Dworkin, Joan Retallack, Daniel Tiffany, Sianne Ngai, and Tan Lin. In different ways, these thinkers and writers emphasize the importance of emergence, convergence, affinity, and relation, as well as difference, divergence, transformation, and aberrance. They tend to argue for a philosophical or poetic mode that suggests and generates material of/for further thinking—as opposed to an approach that seeks substantive truths. Collectively, this group of thinkers demonstrates a critical interest in events, processes, becomings, and assemblages rather than essences, identities, origins, and coordinates.

The constellation here gathered is variously associated with experimental aesthetics, politics, queer theory, feminism, philosophy and history of science, poetics, affect theory, sociology, psychology, Pragmatism, pedagogy, and so on. The interdisciplinary aim here is to explore the vibrational field between different discourses and epistemologies by pointing to shared concerns while not trying to smooth over the differences. My interest is in variations of modes of thought, and in relations of association and dissociation, contrast and similitude. Reading alongside a diverse cell of thinkers affords me the space and material to continue this study into the future: the following ten "index entries" are the first attempts and the initial findings of a lifelong commitment to writing the reading of Stein.

Reading

In "Time in the Codex," an essay in numbered micropoems, Lisa Robertson writes:

> 11 I read garbage, chance and accident. I can't fix what materiality is. Reading, I enter a relational contract with whatever material, accepting its fluency and swerve. I happen to be the one reading.

> 12 I can't fix what materiality is. I act into happenstance. A codex is or accompanies what is otherwise an interpretive surplus suffered or enjoyed in my body. With this complicity arrives a world, and timeliness: form.

> 13 I read to sense the doubling of time: the time of a book's form, which pertains to the enclosure and topology of rooms, allegories, houses, bodies, surfaces; and the time of my perceiving, which feels directional, melodic, lyric, inflectional. Then, because of the book's time overlaying my own, reading opens a proposition. It receives in me the rhythm I didn't know I missed. (Nilling 5)

Reading "opens a proposition," by way of rhythm, generated because of a doubling of time. The one who happens to be reading is the one who also happens to be a relation. One comes to reading and then must carry it on, take it up, and move alongside its happening. Like Robertson, I take reading to be an active, constructive, affective process that involves the body and is itself a kind of writing—an inscriptive thinking.

In the last few decades, an emphasis on reading as a form of writing has been theorized variously. Alberto Manguel argues in *A History of Reading* that reading precedes writing, developmentally and conceptually. We learn to read, in other words, before we have an understanding of the writing that is being read. Reading is an activity informed by the apprehension of images, shapes, patterns, and rhythms, which come to be recognized through repeated encounters and remembered forms; the meanings that are made in reading are in excess of the meanings that arise from the interpretation of written language. Franco Moretti proposes "distant reading" as a strategy for diversifying the strictures of canonical criticism and scholarship (56–58). For Moretti, close reading, whether under the auspices of New Criticism or deconstructionism, depends on a very small group of core texts and tropes on which to build reiterative literary theories. This leads, inevitably, to the overrepresentation of canonical texts and the underrepresentation (or exclusion) of everything else. Moretti calls for a distant reading approach in which multiple, diverse networks of texts are engaged by way of roaming and traversing. Distant reading is a feral methodology—finding new habits and habitats in ever-broadening territories.

In a similar vein, in an interview with Katherine Elaine Saunders for *BOMB Magazine*, Tan Lin proposes an ambient reading practice, in which reading is considered an activity that is always only partially engaged by a wandering and multiply distracted attention: "I'm interested in the formats and micro-formats of reading, and their coupling to other things in the world, like restaurants, yoga mats, poems, former boyfriends or girlfriends, wives and husbands (and their photographs), and of course other books (and their photographs they contain within them)" (Saunders, "Tan Lin"). Lin equates these "micro-formats" of reading with boredom, here reconfigured as a constructive state in which the bored mind cruises for any potential thing to perceive—any little hidden treat or game.

One central tenet of this study takes reading as a practice that in its teaching and learning often depends on normalizing and habituating assumptions about both the function of language and the reality it claims to describe. I argue that poetry is one way of challenging the naturalization of such assumptions by focusing critical and discursive attention on the construction of language in noncommunicative contexts. To challenge the assumptions that make reading possible is also to challenge the limits of reading so that it includes other kinds of imaginative and cognitive activities—thinking, speaking, and writing, for example. Reading as writing is always writing in conversation. It is, by nature, experimental, in a literal sense of the word: to experiment is to experience by trialing; to essay; to make an attempt. Stephen Muecke, in "Motorcycles, Snails, Latour," writes:

> Experimental writing, for me, would be writing that necessarily participates in the world rather than a writing constituted as a report on realities seen from the other side of an illusory gap of representation. . . . The experimental writing I envisage is not about breaking free of convention, but is actively engaged in creating assemblages or compositions as it goes along. This engagement may be with different registers of reality, because "the world" is not seen as bifurcated, with the "text" mediating the "subject" and the "object," as in older communication models. (42)

For his own part, Bruno Latour explains why he prefers the word "composition" to other terms for written texts:

> What is nice [about the word "composition"] is that it underlines that things have to be put together . . . while retaining their heterogeneity. Also, it is connected with composure; it has clear roots in art, painting, music, theater, dance, and thus is associated with choreography and scenography; it is not too far from "compromise" and "compromising," retaining a certain diplomatic and prudential flavor. Speaking of flavor, it carries with it the pungent but ecologically correct smell of "compost," itself due to the active

"de-composition" of many invisible agents. . . . Above all, a composition can fail and thus retains what is most important in the notion of constructivism. . . . What is to be composed may, at any point, be decomposed. ("Compositionist" 473–474)

Composition, of course, was a word close to Stein, too. Here I take composition to include reading and writing and the relationship between them, as well as their temporal and durational contexts. Muecke rejects a bifurcated world; Latour calls for a model of relationality that recognizes difference. For both, composition is neither a solitary act nor the work of the inspired or genius. Rather, composition is a methodology—a way of dealing with the fact of experience. The following entries are compositions on composition: a reader's account and a suggestive companion for reading Stein. I practice a kind of distant or ambient reading, and I invite as much as possible the orienting and disorienting concepts of others. The modular design of this indexical study avails itself to future and further additions. As I continue to think and write with Stein I will add to the index, working to consider the implications and possibilities of its flexible form: the present structure is an elemental design.

The ten entries are arranged in alphabetical order, and each focuses on a different thematic: Bodies, Contemporaneity, Food, Grammar, Identity, Objects, Play, Queering, Repetition, and the United States of America. Any one entry may reference another; the relations between them are denoted in the right-hand marginal textbox and by cross-references to specific pages numbers (where relevant). The index can be read chronologically as a set of discrete yet conceptually linked essays, with the links read as metadata. Alternatively, the index can be read according to links and across the entries nonlinearly. Also, each entry is designed to be able to be read on its own and without following the indicative references. Footnotes index secondary material that I consulted but that is not directly treated in my analysis. Each entry considers Stein's work using its particular thematic as a conceptual starting place. Each reads Stein alongside a variety of other texts and ideas and attempts to construct an argument by way of accumulative, resonant, correspondent, and disjunctive relations.

This word—relation—is perhaps the most important in the study. Following on from the philosophy of Whitehead, the radical empiricism of James, the metaphysics of Deleuze, the theories of performativity of Barad and Sedgwick, the Lucretian evocations of Serres, and a nexus of critical poetics, I argue that the relation is an entity both virtual and actual, eventlike and objectlike, one and many, particular and social. With an emphasis on the relation, I have tried to avoid conclusive or determinate answers to the questions that this book raises. Instead, I write alongside and because of these questions, suggesting modes and approaches to their investigation rather than solutions. This is what makes the entries distinct from essays; they shy from synthesis. Collectively, this index is an archive of a reader's relational engagement with the poetics of Gertrude Stein, and under the auspices of a thoroughly antiessentialist politic.

As Gertrude Stein recognized in Tender Buttons, *which constitutes the first literary work on non-fiction to function like a blind index or (colorless) idea that has been typographically reset, the index is a poetical text and a fictional text it sits next to, like a caption in reverse, or a dining room in which someone else's writing took place.*

— Lin, *Selected Essays about a Bibliography* 75

Language as a real thing is not imitation either of sounds or colours or emotions it is an intellectual recreation and there is no possible doubt about it and it is going to go on being that as long as humanity is anything.

— Stein, *LA* 238

Whatever can be said about the complexity and ambiguity of the status of the "body" in various and often at-odds discourses, the fact remains that the body of Gertrude Stein was and is explicitly interpellated by readers in a number of ways. Hers was the body of a queer Jewish woman, its fatness often read as evidence of the overlay of otherness. The gendered, sexualized, and racialized readings of Stein's body correspond to a litany of paratextual overdeterminations, prejudices, and projections regarding her work and its perceived meanings.

In *Gertrude Stein Remembered* (ed. Simon), a collection of accounts by people who knew her, Stein's body is the ubiquitous preoccupation. Arthur Lachman writes that Stein was a "heavy-set, ungainly young woman, very mannish in her appearance" and "awkward with her hands" (4). Daniel-Henri Kahnweiler commends her "fine Roman head" (19), Sherwood Anderson admires her "red cheeks and sturdy legs" (62), and Samuel Barlow recalls her "massive figure" clothed in monkish robes (67). Carl Van Vechten goes into great detail: "She is massive in physique, a Rabelaisian woman with a splendid thoughtful face; mind dominating her matter. Her velvet robes, mostly brown, and her carpet slippers associate themselves with her indoor appearance. To go out she belts herself, adds a walking staff, and a trim unmodish turban" (42–43). Harold Acton, comparing Stein and Picasso, cites their similarities: "Both were rugged and squarely built; both had short hair and might have been taken for Aztec Mexicans"; then notes a (markedly gendered) distinction: "Whereas Picasso was muscularly mobile Gertrude was dumpily static" (113). Stein's bigness is the constant theme: Cecil Beaton re-members her "monumental" body (139), and Mabel Dodge famously celebrated the "pounds and pounds and pounds piled on her skele-ton—not the billowing kind, but massive, heavy fat" (25).

See also
Food
(pp. 81–82)

Stein's fatness is often read as evidence of her appetite, which is also mentioned variously. Sherwood Anderson recalls Stein's peren-nial desire for and appreciation of "handmade goodies" (61) and names Stein "the woman in the great kitchen of words" (62) who rep-resents "something sweet and healthy in our American life" (63). For Lachman, Stein's appetite for treats signified her appetite for fame and success; indeed, the two appetites share the same set of refer-ences. Lachman quotes Leo Stein, whose criticisms of his sister in-cluded the accusation that she was passionately vain (she "hungers and thirsts for *gloire*" [8]), and to which Lachman adds his own as-sessment: Stein demonstrates an "almost morbid craving for recog-nition" (8).

In "The Somagrams of Gertrude Stein," Catharine Stimpson reads this emphasis on Stein's body (both in place of and defining her writing) as symptomatic of broader anxieties about the female body: she argues that the female body is figured as a kind of "mon-strosity" by patriarchal designation, something to be both managed and pathologized (67). Stein's body, she continues, "presents an alarming, but irresistible, opportunity" for scrutiny, because "the size of it, the eyes, nose, sweat, hair, laugh, cheekbones" were all and at once "strange," "unusual," "special," and "invigorating" (67). Fur-ther, she argues, Stein's fatness functions as a signifier "capacious enough to absorb contradictory attitudes towards the female body" (67). On the one hand, according to Stimpson, Stein's admirers read her fatness as the physical analogue of her intellectual largeness, vi-tality, and achievement (67). On the other hand, Stein's detractors read her fatness as exactly the opposite: proof of a "hideous cultural and psychological overrun" (68).[1] For Carl Van Vechten, cited above, Stein achieves a victory of "mind over . . . matter," with her quick wit and mental acuity able to harness the greatness of her body; and for less sympathetic critics such as Lachman, who later in his recollection appeals to a speculative hypothesis by psychologist B. F. Skinner that Stein cultivated and was ultimately betrayed by a second "personality" that practiced automatic writing, Stein suffers the opposite fate: her mind is weak, suggestible, and inevitably dominated by her unthinking body. In both cases, a mind/body split is taken as a natural fact, and in both cases, the gendered implications are clear: a woman must manage her body in order to be intellectually impressive.

See also Grammar *(pp. 99–100)*

In *Volatile Bodies: Toward a Corporeal Feminism,* Elizabeth Grosz identifies a foundational "somaphobia" that underscores Western philosophical thought. For Plato, she writes, "it was evident that reason should rule over the body and over the irrational or appetitive functions of the soul." Here the body is a kind of "prison," which "interfere[s] in," is a "danger to," and "betrays" the mind. Its usefulness, she continues in her gloss, is in its delineation of a "natural hierarchy, a self-evident ruler-ruled relation" which "alone makes possible a harmony with the state, the family, and the individual." This, she concludes, is "one of the earliest representations of the body politic" (5). The designation of the body as a constraint—that which restricts

1. One of the most explicitly abject critiques of Stein's work is also quite abstract in its reference. Wyndham Lewis writes, in what is a markedly bodily reaction: "Gertrude Stein's prose-song is a cold, black suet-pudding. We can represent it as a cold suet-roll of fabulously reptilian-length. Cut it at any point, it is the same thing; the same heavy, sticky, opaque mass all through, and all along. It is weighted, projected, with a sibylline urge. It is mournful and monstrous, composed of dead and inanimate material. It is all fat, without nerve. Or the evident vitality that informs it is vegetable rather than animal. Its life is a low-grade, if tenacious one; of the sausage, by-the-yard, variety" (qtd. in Hoffman, *Critical Essays on Gertrude Stein* 55).

and regulates by limiting and delimiting the individual—has persisted variously throughout Western thought. As a result, the relationship between a subject's body and the rights afforded or denied it, on the basis of biological, medical, legal, social, and cultural institutions (institutions whose meanings are determined in part by designations of gender, race, class, sexuality, and age), have also varied significantly over time, yet in any given instance they have been taken as legislative in the determination of relative autonomy. In the twentieth century, different attempts were made to challenge philosophical somaphobia and the regulation of bodies according to essentialist determination. From a feminist perspective, these attempts can broadly be organized into the following categories: poststructuralism, corporealism, intersectionalism, and new materialism (here I am following, loosely, Jasbir Puar's breakdown in her essay " 'I would rather be a cyborg than a goddess': Intersectionality, Assemblage, and Affective Politics"; these categories are of course *not* mutually exclusive).

Judith Butler's *Gender Trouble* is perhaps the signal text for the first category. Here Butler argues that gender does not correspond to (what is taken to be intractably) biological sex but is constructed via repeated, performative gestures that adhere to, or can subvert, heteronormative expectations and naturalized assumptions about identity. A corporeal account, such as that from Grosz, argues for a critical theorization of sexual difference. Following on from Luce Irigaray, Grosz gives an account of the body as constitutive of, and engaged with, manifold differences—differences that are systematically effaced in order to reinstate the singular subject of patriarchy and to deny the autonomy of otherness. Intersectionalism (following the foundational work of Kimberlé Crenshaw) argues that the body constitutes complex and dynamic interrelationships between gender, sexuality, race, class, age, and other markers of identification that are legislated, designated, and denied by hegemonic order and colonial/ capitalist economies of power. For the new materialist and science studies feminists (such as Donna Haraway and Karen Barad), the body is not a definite or singular unity but, rather, constitutive of diverse *phenomena*. Both Haraway and Barad give a posthumanist account of the body: for Haraway, the techno-historical context of the era of the cyborg challenges the binaries of nature/culture, mind/ body, and male/female by troubling the distinction between human and nonhuman agency and corporeality; for Barad (as discussed in greater detail below), quantum physics presents a phenomenal ontology that does not assert a gap between the world and its representation. At the heart of this complex of feminist critiques and counter-critiques are genuinely difficult questions to do with what constitutes the body. Thinking-the-body requires a simultaneous attention to the philosophical and political claims of bodily life—engaging both the body as complex and the body as subject not as though the claims were either oppositional or identical, but differentiated sites of intense speculation and activity.

Barad began her academic career as a particle physicist in quantum field theory. She is now a scholar of feminist theory and philosophy, and her research considers the material consequences of quantum physics alongside contemporary feminist and queer inquiry. In the essay "Posthuman Performativity: Toward an Understanding of How Matter Comes to Matter," Barad outlines her theory of "agential realism," a philosophy that posits "phenomena" as the constitutive unit of the world. Everything in the world, including but by no means only human bodies, emerges via the complex "intra-action" of phenomena. *Intra-action* is to be understood "in contrast to the usual 'interaction,' which presumes the prior existence of independent entities/relata" (818). Matter materializes through the intra-actions of phenomena:

See also
Objects
(pp. 145–146)

The world is a dynamic process of intra-activity in the ongoing re-configuring of locally determinate causal structures with determinate boundaries, properties, meanings, and patterns of marks on bodies. This ongoing flow of agency through which "part" of the world makes itself differentially intelligible to another "part" of the world and through which local causal structures, boundaries, and properties are stabilized and destabilized does not take place in space and time but in the making of spacetime itself. The world is an ongoing open process of mattering through which "mattering" itself acquires meaning and form in the realization of different agential possibilities. (817)

In this complex ontology, there are a number of key tropes. *Performativity* refers to the processes through which matter materializes and acquires meaning—in contrast to representation, through which meaning is applied to matter independent of its material becoming. Performativity is necessarily *posthuman* because it does not privilege the human subject and does not argue for any essential difference between human and nonhuman bodies. And *agency* is not aligned with human intentionality or human subjectivity, nor is it an attribute; it is a "doing" or "being" and refers to the enactments of "iterative changes to particular practices through the dynamics of intra-activity" (827). Barad is careful to point out that since discursive practices are often confused with or taken as meaning linguistic expression, discourse is imagined as being specific to human experience. But, she continues, the agential realist position opposes any such conflation of discursivity and humanness. "If," she writes, "'humans' refers to phenomena, not independent entities with inherent properties but rather beings in their differential becoming, particular material (re)configurings of the world with shifting boundaries and properties that stabilise and destabilise along with specific material changes in what it means to be human, then the notion of discursivity cannot be founded on an inherent distinction between humans and nonhumans" (818).

Posthumanist performativity is a mode of engagement that is, first, not confined to human praxis, and, second, concerned with the coming-to-be, that is, the performative aspect of, intra-actions and processes of meaning making. Barad concludes her multiple definitions with a thesis statement of sorts: "*discursive practices are specific material (re)configurings of the world through which local determinations of boundaries, properties, and meaning are differentially enacted. That is, discursive practices are ongoing agential intra-actions of the world through which local determinacy is enacted within the phenomena produced*" (820–821, emphasis in original). In rethinking materiality as discursive practice, Barad is talking, in part, about both language and the body. Language is one kind of discursive practice; so too is the process through which one thinks and talks about/through/from/of the body. Further, the body, as phenomena (the plural here is intended), is neither a discrete entity nor a definite object. What counts as the body, and what accounts for the body in its specific, local determinations of "boundaries, properties, and meaning," will be necessarily "differentially enacted" (821). "All bodies," writes Barad, "come to matter through the world's iterative intra-activity—its performativity. . . . Bodies are not objects with inherent boundaries and properties; they are material-discursive phenomena" (823). Performativity offers an alternative to representationalism, shifting the focus, in Barad's words, from "questions of correspondences between descriptions and reality . . . to matters of practices/doings/actions" (802).

Sara Ahmed has carefully critiqued Barad for her tendency to overstate the perceived power of language (and therefore representationalism) in contemporary theory. Barad opens her essay by claiming:

"Language has been granted too much power. The linguistic turn, the interpretative turn, the cultural turn: it seems that at every turn lately every 'thing'—even materiality—is turned into a matter of language or some other form of cultural representation" (801). Ahmed argues that to posit language as more trusted than matter only serves to reinforce the notion that the two are somehow opposed—and that one or the other can be an "'it' that we can be for or against" (35). What is needed is an account of language and matter and their relation: words and things coexist in a world that exceeds/encompasses both; further, language is a kind of matter. To be sure, such a project seems at the heart of both Barad's thesis and Ahmed's critique—they are each invested in a feminist politics that accounts for the "material-semiotic" (to use Haraway's term, which Barad and Ahmed both cite) realities of contemporary experience. With the cautious amendments of Ahmed in mind, I read Barad as attempting a kind of alternative paradigm for reading the relation between language and matter—something that, as far as this present study is concerned, provides generous ground for thinking.

Recently, Michael Halewood has engaged with Barad alongside Whitehead's notion of *symbolism* in order to rethink the relation of language and the body in contemporary critical and sociological theory. By Halewood's account, Whiteheadian symbolism provides an alternative to theories of representationalism for which signification is the central mode of meaning making and through which the body is divided. According to Halewood (and here he is aligned with Barad), the body, despite its prevalence as an object of study in cultural and social theory, has nevertheless remained tethered to the long-held assumption that we live in a bifurcated world in which nature and culture are divided realms with discrete realities. This assumption figures the biological body as belonging to the "hard" sciences, and the social/cultural body as belonging to "soft" sciences of the humanities. "The further that social research uncovers and describes the very sociality of the body," writes Halewood, "the further such analyses both empirically and conceptually distance themselves from the 'biological' body." Therefore, he continues, "the 'natural' body is viewed more and more rigidly as either some kind of a fiction . . . or as an irrelevance to the varied levels of social and cultural meanings which are somehow attached or written upon the body" (105).

As Halewood notes, there have been significant attempts to write against this bifurcated model and to theorize the body as both a material and a social entity: in other words, to theorize the body as phenomena. Halewood names Barad as someone who has made such an attempt, and while he acknowledges Butler's significant contributions to such theory, especially in *Gender Trouble* and *Bodies That Matter*, he also identifies what he believes to be a key problem in her formulation—namely, that she conceives language and the body as being cleaved by a gap that might only ever be bridged via signification (106). In *Bodies That Matter*, Butler posits a split between the external and historical processes that produce and enforce gendered subject positions, and the internal, actual, and individual experiences of these subject positions. The materiality of the body is recognized as the interface between these historical, normalizing processes and individuating, experiencing subjectivity. This then posits the material body as the end result of these interfacing processes; that is, a surface on which such processes are registered and made legible. While Barad also acknowledges the importance of Butler's emphasis on the historicity of matter, she argues that Butler's matter remains the passive outcome of discursive practice; furthermore, Butler's bodies are invariably human. What is needed, according to Barad, is for the notion of matter to be further reworked, such that it "acknowledges the existence of important linkages between discursive practices and material phenomena without . . . anthropocentric limitations" (882 n. 26). Similarly, Halewood calls for "a theoretical account of the complex status of the body within existence, an account which is able to describe both the materiality of the body *and* its sociality" (106).

Whitehead defines a "symbol" in the broadest possible terms as anything that evokes or elicits a response from another thing. Halewood writes that Whitehead's symbolism "does not rely on consciousness, subjectivity, culture, meanings, humans; furthermore, it is not bound to notions of representation, correspondence, or reference" (116). Symbolism, therefore, very simply describes an occasion in which *something happens.* Language is one kind of symbolism, in which words and meanings elicit responses from each other. Furthermore, for Whitehead, "symbolic reference requires something in common between symbol and meaning which can be expressed without reference to the perfected percipient; but it also requires some activity of the percipient which can be considered without recourse either to the particular symbol or its particular meaning" (*Symbolism* 9). This "something in common" is the body; it is the body that registers the relation of symbol and meaning (Halewood, *A. N. Whitehead and Social Theory* 118). By Whitehead's account, there is no ontological distinction between a symbol and a meaning, and the relation between the two is unfixed: for example, the word "tree" symbolizes a tree and a tree symbolizes the word "tree"—the tree and the word "enter into our experience on equal terms" (*Symbolism* 11). Language, as a kind of symbolism, does not presuppose a nature/culture division, and so does not attempt to bridge any perceived gaps between external matter and discursive meaning. For this reason, language is understood to be and to function "on equal terms" with other modes of experience.

For Whitehead, two different modes of perception—presenta-

tional immediacy and causal efficacy—synthesize as *symbolic refer-*
ence, the "mixed mode" of perception that accounts for both the immediacy of experience (sense-data) and the concept of causality (the
continuity and context of sense-data as perceived). As Steven Meyer
explains, presentational immediacy refers to that which is perceived
as being clear and distinct, and causal efficacy refers to the "vast
quantities of impressions that hover at the edge of ordinary waking
experience" and that, however vague, nonetheless contribute to the
apprehension of the world ("Creativity" 16). For Whitehead, philosophy has for too long been overly invested in presentational immediacy and not enough in perception in the mode of causal efficacy—
it has not, in other words, been concerned enough with *vagueness*.
According to Whitehead, the vast majority of what constitutes experience is not available to the senses, nor reducible to any particular
sensation or perception. Where the specific example of human experience is concerned, he posits, perception always occurs in this mixed
mode through which the senses apprehend at once the vagueness
and specificity of the world and its phenomena. The mixed mode is
named "symbolic" because it is this dynamic interplay of perceptive
processes that accounts for meaning *and* the articulation of a meaningful response to that which is experienced. The site for this symbolic reference, the material that allows for the synthesis of immediate phenomena and its social, historical meanings, is the body.
Halewood writes that the body "gives rise" to the possibility of symbolism, indeed, is never separate from the activities of the body (115).

See also
Contemporaneity
(pp. 69–72)

To return to Stein, I want to look at *Lifting Belly*, which is often
claimed to be an especially "bodily" poem. This claim is largely to do
with the interpretation of the phrase "lifting belly" as descriptive of
a sex act—specifically, a celebration of Stein's own sex life. This biographical interpretation triply inscribes *Lifting Belly* as a text of con-

See also
Queering
(pp. 181–182)

fessional lesbian erotica: the poem is read as an account of queer intimacy, and so one of Stein's more definitively "out" moments. Despite my own tendency to read Stein's queerness in terms of formal, material, grammatical, and philosophical innovation rather than in terms of narrative, allegory, or seemingly autobiographical commentary, *Lifting Belly* can be read as a performative account of queer embodiment, as well as an account of the interplay of perception in the mixed mode as set out by Whitehead: here it is "with" an indefinite belly, or set of bellies, that lifting occurs, a kind of metonymic investigation a range of bodily activities and relations, all of which both constitute and describe the experience of having a body in a world that is vague and exact.

The poem was composed between 1915 and 1917 but not published during Stein's life. It was included in two selected editions (1953 and 1980) and then on its own in 1989, edited and with an introduction by Rebecca Mark. Mark's opening essay celebrates *Lifting Belly* as a landmark text of lesbian erotica, and she predicts that its republication as such will extend its appeal to a nonliterary queer readership. Mark identifies three subjects of the poem: Stein, Toklas, and the result of their sexual relationship (an entity variously referred to as "creativity" or "poetry," and always signified by the phrase "lifting belly") (*LB* xxvi). By her account, in *Lifting Belly* Stein "births" a queer aesthetics: in composing the work, she is "heavy with the weight lying in her. . . . She is heavy and full with love, with the desire to express her love. She is excited and she is pregnant" and "must create a place where she can make love and give birth" (xxii). For Mark, this queer aesthetics reimagines maternity as a kind of feminine creativity, not defined by or restricted to (heteronormative forms of) reproduction. Mark's reading of *Lifting Belly* celebrates "lesbian sex in the world," a mode of relationality that "transform[s] everything it encounters" (xix). In contrast to Mark's autobiographical interpretation, I read *Lifting Belly* as an open set of bodies, relations, modes, and activities irreducible to stock narratives of the couple form, the family unit, or the erogenous zone.

In *Lifting Belly*, there are the indistinct bodies associated with pronouns (I, we, he, "jerk"), as well as bodies of water, the bodies of dogs, fish, petunias, strawberries, and butter pats, as well as the (not necessarily human) bodies implied by proper names (the Ethel of "I do not like Ethel"). Put simply, it's a work occupied by bodies of ambiguous origins and qualities. The phrase "lifting belly" is less descriptive (a belly that is lifting or being lifted) than performative: "lifting belly" indexes bodily modality. A flower, fruit, boat, or dog can be a lifting belly—or, perhaps more exactly, flowers, fruits, boats, and dogs are metonyms for lifting belly, where "lifting belly" is understood as the capacity for bodily life. Bodies have a tendency simultaneously to change and to remain somehow (or somewhat) continuous. Thus lifting belly, here read as a performative gesture, refers to this general tendency: at once a lifting and a grounding.

In her introduction, Mark asks herself: "Every time I read this poem, I wonder how words which rarely mention a body part can make me feel so aroused" (xi). Peter Quartermain declares the work "one of the great referential poems of the twentieth century—one that almost entirely withholds reference from the reader" (29). Here both Mark and Quartermain are interested in the paradoxical effects of erotic reference: the erotic is that which is not named or is ultimately withheld. The pleasure of the text, so to speak, is aroused by the "almostness" that comes with the double movement of concealment and exposure. What these two accounts find explicit about *Lifting Belly* is the lack of explicit reference—every single word, it seems, is equally erotically charged by the mere fact of its abstraction. Mark and Quartermain associate the abstracted yet implicitly explicit erotics with queerness, but both rely on the assumed fact of the text's autobiography in order to make this association. The queerness, I argue, is in the multiply located bodily erotics: *Lifting Belly* tracks erotic agency (of diverse bodies in diverse relations, of speech, of an address, of dialogue, of small or fragmented textlets, of notes, of names, of victuals and curiosities) in its boundless opportunities and orientations.

> Come together.
> Lifting belly near.
> I credit you with repetition.
> Believe me I will not say it.
> And retirement.
> I celebrate something.
> Do you.
> Lifting belly extraordinarily in haste.
> I am so sorry I said it.
> Lifting belly is a credit. Do you care about poetry.
> Lifting belly in spots.
> Do you like ink.
> Better than butter.
> Better than anything.
> Any letter is an alphabet.
> When this you see you will kiss me.
> Lifting belly is so generous.
> Shoes.
> Servant.
> And Florence.
> Then we can sing.
> We do among.
> I like among.

Lifting belly keeps.

Thank you in lifting belly.

Can you wonder that they don't make preserves. (54)

These clipped, axiomatically punctuated sentences suggest a chorus of an unknown number; propositions, questions, descriptions, and single-word phrases run one after the other with little recourse to a definite narrative. Bodies appear and disappear, presenting for a particular instance the context for experience both dynamic and vague, explicit and indefinite.

For Félix Guattari, queer bodies and dancing bodies present a challenge to the dominant semiotics—a semiotics predicated on the repression of the body and the assumptions of heteronormativity. The queer/dancing body breaks with the dominant logic by virtue of being emphasized—the queer body is emphasized in its being queer, and the dancing body is emphasized in its performance of bodily potentiality. By Guattari's account, such emphasis affirms the specificity of a body in its emergent, contingent, and dynamic context— thus it posits a theory of bodily orientations and identities as similarly emergent, contingent, and dynamic. For Guattari there are only *See also* ever minor bodies and minor sexualities; a dominant semiotics of Identity the body (which in turn institutes a dominant sexuality) is a political *(pp. 127–134)* abstraction and does not properly attend to the complexity of bodies and relations.

Stein's portrait of the American dancer Isadora Duncan, "Orta or One Dancing" is a sustained experiment in scoring bodily emphasis. Orta is one insofar as that oneness is contingent; and if it can be said that Orta is one, then she must also be able to be other: "She was like one and then was like another one and then was like another one and then was like another one and then was one who was one having been one and being one who was one then, one being like some" (121). The ontological differences between *being one* and *being like one*, and between *other* and *another*, are investigated by minor shifts in and rep-

See also
Repetition
(pp. 206–211)

etitions of propositions. Here a dancer is at once the one who dances, the one who comes to dance, the one who is being a dancer, the one who is doing dancing, and the one who is like a dancer.

Each of the first eight paragraphs of "Orta" begins with the conditional "even" as if to try the limits of what might account for, and count as, the one's oneness and the dancer's dancing. "Even if one was one she might be like some other one" is followed by "Even if she was one and she was one," "Even if she was one being one," "Even if she was one being one and she was being one being one," "Even if she was one being one and she was one being one," and so on (121). From there, the remaining paragraphs meditate on her "being one," a condition that does not fix her but rather reinscribes her oneness at every turn; she is one who dances, but a dancer becomes in movement and cannot be reduced to any one moment, hence she is both one and not-one. As the portrait progresses, Stein steadily adds new

See also
Identity
(pp. 131–135)

verbs to the prose. These verbs include, in a chronology of their addition: *believing, existing, doing, meaning, showing, changing, feeling, thinking, finishing, fading, greeting, contradicting,* and *moving.* The dancer's dancing comes to include all these other actions, which appear as corollaries of the dancing body's experience of dancing. At the end of the portrait, Stein considers the dancer's oneness coming to be known by another, or by some others:

> In being one she was one and in being that one she was one some one was knowing was that one. In some knowing she was that one she was one who would be completing being one and she was completing being one and she was one who was resembling some and these were ones who were a kind of one which is a kind which is

completing being one who are completing being one, they being ones being one and not being ones being completed then and being ones then not any one has been completing.

She was one. She was one and knowing one, that one was being one she was knowing and it might be that they were going on knowing one another and if they went on knowing one another and going on knowing one another she might be one not going on knowing that one and not going on knowing that one she would come to be knowing some whom she would be knowing and who would not come to be ones listening and looking. She would be one telling something and she would be one being one. She was one. She was dancing. She was one. She had been one. She was one. She was being that one. She would be that one. (135–136)

Completion seems to refer to a material relation of reciprocal knowingness, in which one is recognized as other and by this recognition is able to know the other as one too. The dancer is one only insofar as she is recognized and known *as* a one, so the dancer's body is completed in dancing by the one who looks and listens and recognizes dancing. To make things more complex, the dancer, being other to herself by dancing, recognizes herself dancing—thus the dancer is one and another, (auto)intrapersonally involved.

Toward the end of the portrait, Stein writes: "She was then resembling some one, one who was not dancing, one who was writing" (120). Tellingly, Stein removed this sentence from later drafts (though Dydo keeps it in *A Stein Reader*). Her ambivalence in emphasizing the relation between dancing and writing, and the subsequent resemblance with "ones believing in thinking, believing in meaning being existing, believing in worrying, believing in not worrying, believing in not needing remembering that some meaning has been existing, believing in moving in any direction, feeling in thinking in

meaning being existing, feeling in believing in thinking being existing, feeling in moving in every direction, believing in being one
thinking, believing in being one moving in a direction, feeling in being any one, feeling in being that one the one the one is being, believing in feeling in being that one the one each one has been and is
being" (130) may have been to do with an anxiety about drawing too
neat a line between this portrait study and her own practice. To
metaphorize writing as a kind of dancing perhaps risked emphasizing metaphoricity over writing and dancing. Stein, it seems, was interested not in reducing the difference between the two activities, but
in suggesting that bodies become bodies through complex engagements with activities including, but by no means limited to, writing
and dancing.

Whereas Guattari points to the dancer as an exemplary radical
body, Stein points to all bodily experiences as equally and potentially
radicalizing. Hers is, perhaps, a more utopian politics: rather than
beginning with the body as a subject, Stein begins with a body as an
abstracted capture of phenomena. To read Stein's diverse oeuvre this
way is to read her alongside her contemporary Whitehead as well as
more recent philosophical scholarship to do with the body, bodies,
and the body politic. Stein's work argues, by way of example and emphasis, that the body emerges through its engagement with and in a
diverse world of other bodies—indeed, such engagements constitute
the world.

Contemporaneity

In her lecture "Composition as Explanation," Stein outlines a theory of composition in what is probably her most explicit and demonstrative statement of poetics. It includes—as such a statement necessarily must—a description of method as well as a theory of aesthetics. It is worth paraphrasing the core propositions of "Composition as Explanation," even though by doing so, the accumulative rhythm of argumentation is diminished. The lecture begins by stating that each generation "looks at something different"; this difference *is* composition. Thus what changes from generation to generation are modes of composition as well as modes of engaging with composition. Composition is an aesthetics and a philosophy: when Stein speaks of "composing" she is referring to both art practices and, more broadly, *modes of existence* (to borrow Latour's recent and evocative phrase). Difference, she argues, is to be found in the way that doing and seeing changes from period to period. Since difference is always only a difference of approach, no one is truly or radically different, that is, outside of, his or her time. Those who are perceived as such are in fact simply more attuned to their own particular way of being in time, that is, more engaged with what is happening as it is happening and less concerned with retrospection and classification.

The irony, Stein argues, is that an artist who is attuned to her sense of time will not be accepted in her lifetime. Acceptance is a belated gesture, so the contemporary artist is an outlaw in her lifetime and a classic after death. The designation of a "classic," she argues, is the outcome of aesthetic classification, a historical practice that is always retroactive. There is "hardly a moment in between" an artist being rejected as outlaw and accepted as classic (*WAM* 26). One key problem of this designation is that beauty is understood as inherent to classical works and thus cannot be associated with that which is contemporary. Against this assumption, Stein writes: "Beauty is beauty even when it is irritating and stimulating not only when it is accepted and classic" (29). To complicate matters, Stein considers the relation between aesthetic and military innovation—since war advances technology, wartime periods emphasize the contemporary and its compositional modes. Thus, she theorizes, an artist in the time of war may become classic in his or her life (to this category of the living classic, it seems, she adds herself). Her work, she implies, is contemporary insofar as she is committed to composing a sense of the time of her present. This is her poetics: composition is the differential of time (composition is that which registers time as difference), and difference is a "natural" phenomenon, therefore composition is a kind of natural—that is to say, necessary—response to the contemporary demands of existence.

See also
USA
(pp. 225–226)

Giorgio Agamben, writing on Nietzsche in a section of the essay "What Is Contemporary?," responds to the untimeliness of writing: "Those who are truly contemporary, who truly belong to their time, are those who neither perfectly coincide with it nor adjust themselves to its demands. They are then in this sense irrelevant [*inattuale*]. But precisely because of this condition, precisely through this disconnection and this anachronism, they are more capable than others of perceiving and grasping their own time" (*Nudities* 11). Here Agamben is saying something similar to Stein: to be contemporary is to be irrelevant, since the memorializing and fantasizing impulses of historicity and futurity cannot account for contemporariness. That which is contemporary does not fit into discourses of presentness. To be "truly" contemporary is to be disconnected from what is thought of *as* the present; this untimeliness, to use Agamben's use of Nietzsche's word, is, paradoxically, a kind of being in time. To experience contemporariness, Agamben writes later in the same essay, is to perceive obscurity. Clarity is always belated, whereas the immediate is always obscure. This is why, for Stein and Agamben (and perhaps for Nietzsche), to be contemporary is to be attuned to the obscurity of experience and to be considered obscure by conventional, which is to say belated, logic.

In Laura Riding's essay "T. E. Hulme, the New Barbarism, and Gertrude Stein," "Composition as Explanation" is read for its prescient and unassuming exemplification of a kind of contemporariness that Riding posits as the necessary development of modernist poetry. Riding begins the essay by outlining what she perceives as the problematic of the modernist moment, namely, the synthesis of creative and critical practices and the emergence of a self-aware and overly "civilized" literary culture that has produced poetry seemingly able to be written "by historical effort alone." Her hypothesis is that such manufactured sophistication and self-referentiality can only continue for so long before it reaches something like a return to a new beginning—a move she calls, anticipatorily, the "new barbarism." This new barbarism, she clarifies, must be different from "natural historical barbarism." Whereas the latter, by her designation, refers to an aesthetic and philosophical attitude in which "mass-time and mass-humanity are real and automatically fixed and absolute," in the "new" version there is "no mass-time or mass-humanity, time and humanity are personal sentimentalities" (*Contemporaries and Snobs* 142–143).

It's a complicated thesis and Riding's unusual, dense, and polemical prose is difficult to gloss. Nevertheless, what is important about this essay is the positioning of Stein as a writer who was already and without recognition (at least at the time of Riding's writing) practicing a kind of new barbaric poetics. In this way, Stein was far ahead of her contemporaries: "No one but Miss Stein has been willing to be as ordinary, as simple, as primitive, as stupid, as barbaric as successful barbarism demands" (183). Figuring Stein as at once the exemplary poet of barbarism *and* the object of derision by the poets that Riding suggests are in most need of barbaric reinvention is resonant with Stein's own sense of her uncertain place alongside her contemporaries. T. S. Eliot's dismissal of her work is read as symptomatic of something like an unconscious admission of her achievements—indeed, in many ways, his excoriating review of Stein makes basically the same point as Riding's celebration of its innovation. Eliot writes of Stein's work: "It is not improving, it is not amusing, it is not interesting, it is not good for one's mind." At the same time, he admits, "its rhythms have a peculiar hypnotic power not met with before. . . . If this is the future, then the future is, as it very likely is, of barbarians" (156).

Stein is thus the unacknowledged "large-scale mystic" and "darling priest of cultured infantilism" of her age—"if her age but knew it" (189). Ultimately, Riding suggests that something like a Steinian revolution is needed to break the modernists from their self-defeating program—by her account, the modernists had classic standards for art, incompatible with their desire for originality. The "perpetual embarrassment," to cite Jerome McGann's summary of Riding's critique, caused by such irreconcilable difference between classical standards and romantic pretensions produced endless irony (*The Scholar's Art* 55). Stein's work, on the other hand, is unencumbered by such anxieties and aspirations. "The ideal barbaric artist," Riding claims, "is superior in ordinariness rather than in originality": Stein embodies this ideal, indeed, she is "divinely inspired in ordinariness" (188, 189). Clarifying her own position in relation to her assessment of Stein, Riding writes: "What has been said has been said in praise and not in contempt. She has courage, clarity, sincerity, simplicity. She has created a human mean in language, a mathematical equation of ordinariness" (195). Riding commends Stein, and in particular "Composition as Explanation," for its demonstration of the dialectics of sameness and difference, time and composition. Stein writes:

> The composition is the thing seen by every one living in the living that they are doing, they are the composing of the composition that at the time they are living is the composition of the time in which they are living. It is that that makes living a thing that they are doing. Nothing else is different, of that almost any one can be certain. The time when and the time of and the time in that composition is the natural phenomena of that composition and of that perhaps every one can be certain. (WAM 29–30)

Crucially, "no one thinks these things when they are making when they are creating what is the composition, naturally no one thinks, that is no one formulates until what is to be formulated has been made" (30). In other words, the theory that Stein offers is one that is oddly guilty of the same retrospection that she critiques in the lecture. When one is actually doing the living one is doing, and so composing, one will not have a coherent sense of the composition's forms and tendencies. Such things are only apparent after the fact, and so not necessarily always relevant, since the composing will have always already moved on. On the other hand, and at the same time, since the act of composing and an account of composition exist in different time senses, they ensure that the work of composing is never done— the idea of composition belongs elsewhere to composing and so there is always something to be done, to be worked toward, to be rearticulated. For Stein, untimeliness is simply part of being in time.[1]

As "Composition as Explanation" progresses, Stein looks to her own practice, organizing works chronologically and in groupings corresponding to different compositional methodologies. By her own recollection, around the time she composed *The Making of Americans*, her compositional mode was characterized by a "groping" for a "prolonged" or "continuous" present (*WAM* 32). A "continuous present," far from signifying a smooth continuum of time, was for Stein a mode of composing that retained the constant repetitions, recursions, and disruptions of linguistic construction. In addition, this early work required another two modes to be engaged alongside the challenge of composing in a "continuous present": "beginning again and again" and "using everything" (31). Since "beginning again and again" acknowledges discontinuity and "using everything" acknowledges differentiation (while also emphasizing the potential mutual relevance of "everything" for composition), these two auxiliary methodologies problematize both the continuity and the presentness of the continuous present.

See also
Repetition
(pp. 206–211)

Critics tend to be fond of the phrase "continuous present" when it is abstracted from its specific (and limited) context in "Composition as Explanation" and applied as a wholesale description of Stein's compositional mode and aesthetics. Whether the continuous present

---

1. Later, in the lecture "Narration," Stein describes writing in terms of "achieving recognition of the thing while the thing [is] achieving expression" (*N* 60). Here, perhaps, is a kind of theory of the difference between writing and composition: writing is a practice that engages with its own thinking, as well as the emergent thought of the thing written. Composition, more broadly, refers to the entire event of coming to write and engaging with writing—that is to say, composition is that which contains the practice of writing, that which makes writing possible.

is argued as a kind of compositional ethos (the continuous present preserves the authentic machinations of thinking and writing) or political assertion (the continuous present opposes hierarchical power relations inherent in grammar and its temporal/relational convention), they serve to signify Stein's aesthetics as evidence of an investment "in" the present, often without critical consideration of what is meant by the present. In the first instance, Jacquelyn Ardam, for example, writes of Stein's *To Do*: "It feels spontaneous and unedited, and as if Stein is speaking to herself and telling herself how to write the book that she is writing," and she goes on to say that Stein "manufactures . . . a continuous present tense in which we imagine that we are reading her book as she wrote it" (580); and Kelley Wagers writes that Stein's mode of composition in the continuous present "defines a new relationship between past happening and present telling" (28). In the second instance, Lisa Ruddick claims that Stein's continuous present results in the "abolition of grammatical difference," and this abolition "disturbs the linear time, the sequence of past-present-future, that symbolically supports the ever-anterior father" and thus opens her texts up to "anti-paternal pleasure" (86). If it assumed that Stein's present refers literally to the duration of the composition of a particular work, there are problems (how many durations make a composition?) and risks (reading presentism as ahistoricism). Similarly, if it is assumed that Stein's present is largely a matter of grammar, in which presentness is an affect able to be "reactivated" in future readings by virtue of its syntax, the complexity of Stein's engagement with temporality is reduced to a matter of style.

See also
Grammar
(pp. 103–104)

I argue that Stein's interest in the present, as it is manifest in her description of the "continuous present," is more like a philosophical concept. And since it is constitutive of composition, we can consider her compositional theory as constitutive of a philosophical theory.

To complicate matters, I am opting to speak of the contemporary and contemporaneity in place of the present and presentness; contemporaneity, as a philosophical concept, affords considerable flexibility and reach in discussions of temporal relations. Discourses of presentness tend to be populated by specious metaphors and reified abstractions often mistaken for truths about temporality and experience: since, as Serres writes, "people usually confuse time and the measurement of time," the habit of abstracting, spatializing, and concretizing time easily "becomes" time (*Conversations* 60–61). And this time requires a "present" as its most real and readily experienced locus: the breaking experience of time's succession. Such a present privileges certain kinds of immediacies (for example, those inhering in sense-perception and cognitive function) while omitting others (for example, any vague, ambient, contradictory, or coexistent time-senses that might be said to be enduring in any particular duration but are not necessarily directly or cognitively perceived). Since the present can never fully attend to that which is happening even when it intends to include everything-at-this-moment, its usefulness in discussions of composition are limited: a composition is more than the sum or correlation of its being-made and being-engaged. A composition will come to include or suggest multiple temporalities and time-senses whose relation is more properly understood in terms of contemporaneity than presentness—a composition is indeterminately dimensional.

Stein plays with the ubiquitous but ultimately inefficacious "now" moment, the now that is always past by the time it is memorialized in utterance. In "If I Told Him: A Completed Portrait of Pablo Picasso" Stein engages with the problem of time in the capture of a subject. It is by one's rhythms and intensities—in other words, one's contemporaneity—that one comes to be known by the other. "If I Told Him" asks the question, How does a portrait endure? How can a portrait continue to be a portrait of a subject whose relation to the

See also
Identity
(pp. 122–128)

duration of composition is never fully available to representation? The refrain, "If I told him would he like it. Would he like it if I told him" further investigates the question of a portrait's temporality: can one, would one, "like it" if they were confronted with an object that claimed to be in relation to their present-continuous becoming? Would one recognize oneself in the portrait's rhythmic affect? If to "like" something is connected to "being like" that something, that is, to being engaged enough to imagine oneself in the same context or duration as that something else, then Stein's question seems to ask whether Picasso would feel positively and intimately toward her portrait of him if indeed he finds the portrait to harmonize with his own sense of the patterns and rhythms of his singularity:

> Now.
> Not now.
> And now.
> Now.
> [. . .]
> Exact resemblance to exact resemblance the exact resemblance as exact as a resemblance, exactly as resembling, exactly resembling, exactly in resemblance exactly a resemblance the exact resemblance as exact as a resemblance, exactly as resembling, exactly resembling, exactly in resemblance exactly a resemblance, exactly and resemblance. For this is so. Because.
> Now actively repeat at all, now actively repeat at all, now actively repeat at all.
> Have hold and hear, actively repeat at all.
> I judge judge.
> As a resemblance to him. (*GSS* 190–191)

Stein's portrait of Picasso (which is actually a speculative account of Picasso engaging with the portrait) at once makes a case for perceiving subjectivity as a kind of duration, as well as pointing to the diffi-

culty of representing subjectivity without effectively detemporaliz-
ing or fixing oneness in a singular capture. The way to approach these
questions, as I will outline below, is to reconfigure what is meant by
time.

In his conversations with Bruno Latour, Michel Serres makes the
case that Lucretius is a contemporary philosopher. He means this in
a number of ways. The theories set out in *On the Nature of the Universe* correspond, in terms of the questions asked and the hypotheses
constructed, to contemporary scientific theories of fluid mechanics,
turbulence, and chaos (*Conversations* 46). Rather than assuming that
the affinities between Lucretius and contemporary thought are affinities imagined by a "re-reading" of Lucretius "through" a contemporary lens, Serres argues that the affinities are evidence that Lucretius
was asking the same kinds of questions about chance, determinism,
and materiality that are being asked by scientists studying dynamic

See also
Objects
(pp. 147–149)

systems and chaos theory today. This means, then, that Lucretius can
said to be "contemporary" both to his time and to "this" time, which
in turn means that Serres engages with Lucretius as a contemporary
and not merely citationally. *On the Nature of the Universe* is relevant
not only as a historical text but also for its contributions to contemporary scientific and philosophical discussion.

"What things are contemporary?" asks Serres: "Consider a late-
model car. It is a disparate aggregate of scientific and technical solutions dating from different period. One can date it component by
component. . . . The ensemble is only contemporary by assemblage,
by its design, its finish, sometimes only by the slickness of the ad-
vertising surrounding it" (45). Likewise, he continues, books betray
a temporal dissonance by engaging in multiple temporalities and discourses. This is especially true of books that express innovation (say,
in science or technology) while remaining rooted in older philosophical systems. And so, says Serres, there cannot be a "truly" contem-

porary discourse or text. Scholarship studies the ways in which aggregates of texts come to be read as contemporaneous and, additionally, how the activity of reading constructs, deconstructs, and reconstructs these aggregates. In this present study, I am making a case for Stein's contemporaneity—not merely by insisting that she is relevant to present literary culture, but also by assembling a set of texts and by tracking the lateral relations within, such that affinitive propositions can be made and explicated. This method must be understood as being a constructive and therefore an occasional process, and must never assume a central or definitive position.

For Serres, "the word *contemporary* automatically takes two contradictory meanings. It means that Lucretius, *in his own time,* really was already thinking in terms of flux, turbulence, and chaos, and, second, that *through this, he is part of our era,* which is rethinking similar problems" (47, emphasis in original). Since "time alone can make co-possible two contradictory things," we can attribute the contradictions of contemporaneity to its temporal character (49). To give an example of the copossibility of contradictory things, Serres tells Latour, "I am young and old. Only my life, its time or its duration, can make these two propositions coherent between themselves. Hegel's error was in reversing this logical evidence and in claiming that contradiction produces time, whereas only the opposite is true" (49–50). This example bears a striking resemblance to Stein's line from "Sentences and Paragraphs" in *How to Write:* "He looks like a young man grown old" (25). Stein cites this particular line in her lecture "Poetry and Grammar," in which she explicates her theory that paragraphs are "emotional" and sentences are not (*LA* 223). Immediately complicating this theory, Stein discusses instances in her work in which her experiments to write an "emotional" sentence were successful. "He looks like a young man grown old" was one such sentence. One difference between a sentence and a paragraph is its

See also Grammar *(pp. 104–110)*

duration: even in the case of a single-sentence paragraph, or in the case of a very brief paragraph, a paragraph occupies a different duration than a sentence by virtue of its structural signification. Paragraphs are suggestive of assemblages, in which topical affiliations and internal transitions are understood to cohere as a thematic whole: a paragraph is one cohesive movement in a composition. In Stein's sentence, the temporal incongruence of young/old, which is nevertheless entirely "possible" (as Serres demonstrates in his sentence), occupies a duration that is synchronic as well as diachronic. Since the sentence contains within it a logical contradiction that also functions as an account of temporality, its duration bears witness to a subset of multiple, intersecting durations, and as such it has the capacity to "be" a paragraph and therefore "be" emotional.

Serres's problem with time, as a philosophical and scientific construct, is not that it has been imagined in terms of spatial metaphors, but that this spatiality is geometrical. When time is described in a schema of axes, planes, lines, points, and curves, its mobility is restricted to two very simple actions: stop and start. And since the most pervasive doctrine of time has it marching endlessly in one direction, the stop function isn't actually operable. It is used to describe the abstraction of a point-in-time, and as a result, flattens the mobility and "thickness" (to use Whitehead's word) of duration.[2] Serres's model is topological, "schematized by a kind of crumpling, a multiple, foldable diversity" (59). Objects and circumstances (space and time) are "polychronic, multitemporal . . . simultaneously drawing from the obsolete, the contemporary, and the futuristic" (60). Topology, a "science of nearness and rifts," assumes mobility and potentiality as the

See also
Objects
(pp. 149–150)

2. In *The Concept of Nature*, Whitehead writes: "A duration retains within itself the passage of nature. There are within it antecedents and consequents which are also durations which may be the complete specious presents of other quicker consciousness. In other words a duration retains temporal thickness" (56).

dynamic rules and understands fixity as a temporary or arbitrary abstraction (60).

Stein's "beginning again and again," "using everything," and "continuous present"—lists and series—together and in different ways
attempt to account for the mobility and multiplicity of time both as
it is experienced "in the living" and as it is experienced "in" composition. There is thus a tension between the compositional intention
and the compositional effect, arising from the disjunction of the
composition as the thing-done and composition as the thing-made.
This tension is manifest in the dynamic between the time-in and the
time-of composition: in other words, a composition's *rhythm*. John
Cage defines rhythm "in the structural instance" as "relationships of
lengths of time" (*Silence* 64). Correspondingly, Deleuze and Guattari
make a distinction between meter and rhythm: meter is *dogmatic* and
rhythm is *critical* (*A Thousand Plateaus* 313). Rhythm "ties together"
critical moments; it is the "in-between" that brings about a relation
that is durational, heterogeneous, and dynamic. The *difference* of relationality produces rhythm, not the repetition of the components of
a relation (314). Rhythm in poetry refers to this critical relation of the
"lengths of time" that cohere in/as composition; these "lengths of
time" include the formal, structural, grammatical, and syntactical
components of a poem's composition, as well as its historical and local circumstances. Relationships between these lengths of time are
not determinate, nor are they mutually dependent. In other words,
the rhythm of a composition is not the expressive manifestation of
relationships between different "lengths of time," but the *relationships themselves*. The external, expressive manifestation is what
Deleuze and Guattari call meter, and it might also be called measure
or beat. It is "dogmatic" because it assumes that there is a determinate (and thereby authentic) rhythm that organizes a composition in-
ternally and represents it externally.

Stein claims that she was preoccupied with the problem of "eliminating rhythm" while writing *Tender Buttons* (qtd. in Meyer, *Irresistible Dictation* 42). Here, following Steven Meyer, I take this claim as a critique of rhythm in the metric sense—rhythm as/via measurement. Stein attempted to compose in such a way that the dynamics of syntax were not determined by the strictures of a (continuous or consistent) beat. *Tender Buttons* is rhythmic in a sense quite apart from a metrical poem: its rhythms build, quicken, stumble, and break in patterns that are quite unpredictable. In *The Autobiography of Alice B. Toklas*, Toklas reports that Stein would "set a sentence for herself as a sort of tuning fork and metronome and then write to that time and tune" (*ABT* 223). Thus, for Stein, rhythm and writing are similarly and relatedly durational: rather than writing to an external measure, she wrote to the dynamics of her own composition.

In "How Writing Is Written" (an essay published in a collection of the same name) Stein begins with an axiom: "Everybody is contemporary with his period," and "the whole business of writing is the question of living in that contemporariness" (*HWW* 151). "The thing that is important," she continues, "is that nobody knows what the contemporariness is. In other words, they don't know where they are going, but they are on their way" (151). This resonates again with Cage, who writes in his "Lecture on Nothing": "I have nothing to say / and I am saying it / and that is poetry as I need it" (*Silence* 109). Here Cage's "nothing" is not an absence or lack. By having nothing to say *and* saying it, it is not the "it" that is key, but the "having-nothing" (that is, nonpossession) and the "and" (the capacity for simultaneity and contradiction). If one is "living in that contemporariness," they will not arrive to writing with an "it," but instead will come-to-it in the act of composition, the thing seen in the living one is doing.

And so, argues Stein, it is never the case that one is "ahead" of their time. Stein emphasizes the need to work out a way of being in one's time, since, as Charles Bernstein writes, "you can't help being in your time even if you never register this fact, if you are not in it you are out of it and even then you are in it, despite yourself " (*A Poetics* 143). Part of Stein's own attempts to write her contemporaneity was to experiment, during the period she was composing *The Making of Americans*, with "grammar-constructions" that would engage the "present immediacy without trying to drag in anything else" (*HWW* 155). The experiments yielded mixed results: she discovered that writing in this mode produces "resemblances" that activate memory (157). Stein conceived resemblance as containing "two prime elements": immediacy and memory. Resemblance occurs, in other words, when something in the present resonates with the memory of something in the past (157). From here, her aim was to try to write in a manner that did not induce memory. She changed her approach so that it was less concerned with tracking the continuation of an ever-shifting duration and more concerned with emphasizing the copresence of (often incommensurate) phenomena and activity in any given duration. Compositionally, this meant that she wrote less in the permutative-iterative mode of *The Making of Americans* (in which sentences' similarities caused too many memorial resonances in the language), and toward the more rhythmically and syntactically diverse modes typified in the portraits and *Tender Buttons*. To be sure, Stein's attempt to write in a manner that did not "induce memory," as I have called it, ought not be understood as an effort to somehow (as if it were possible) eliminate the function of memory in writing or reading. Rather, she was attempting to write in such a manner that the resemblances and affinities in her compositions did not determine, or depend on, certain memories or relations being made and maintained.

Stein's "present immediacy" is resonant with Whitehead's theory of *symbolic reference*. As outlined in the previous chapter, for White-

See also
Grammar
(pp. 96–99)

See also
Repetition
(pp. 210–211)

See also
Bodies
(pp. 46–47)

head symbolic reference is the synthesis of two distinct (but always mixed) modes of perception: presentational immediacy and causal efficacy. Presentational immediacy is analogous to what is often called sense-perception, though Whitehead is careful to point out that his thesis departs crucially from other theories. "Presentational immediacy," he writes, "is our immediate perception of the contemporary external world, appearing as an element constitutive of our own experience. In this appearance the world discloses itself to be a community of actual things, which are actual in the same sense that we are" (*Symbolism* 21). Through this mode of perception, one experiences the specific and local circumstances of their immediate context. This is something like what Stein calls "the thing seen . . . in the living" (*GSS* 218). Presentational immediacy "express[es] how contemporary events are relevant to each other, and yet preserve a mutual independence. This relevance amid independence is the peculiar character of contemporaneousness" (16).

But presentational immediacy is only *one* mode of perception, and the multimodality of Whitehead's theory of perception has a number of implications. First, perception is not restricted to humans: we can think of nonhuman affective relations as different kinds of modes of perception. Second, in the case of human subjects, perception most often occurs in a *mixed mode*, producing a heterogeneous dialectic (to use Meyer's phrase) of which presentational immediacy is one term (*Irresistible Dictation* 125). In *A. N. Whitehead and Social Theory: Tracing a Culture of Thought*, Halewood writes: "Whitehead insists that the mistake philosophy has made is in seeing presentational immediacy as primary when it is actually a specific and derivative stage of our perception and acquaintance with the world" (53). This mistake tends to over- or underdetermine the role that sense-perception plays in experience. If everything is perceived "as" sense-data, then sensation wholly determines experience. If this sense-data is secondary—that is to say, if it only refers to the attributes of an external primary reality, as they are perceived by the individual percipient—then they are mere "psychic additions" (Whitehead, *Concept of Nature* 29–30). To avoid both these determinations, Whitehead acknowledges presentational immediacy as a crucial mode of perception, but one that is most likely to be experienced in concert with another mode of perception—causal efficacy—in order to be registered consciously.

Causal efficacy, as Halewood explains, "provides us with more solid, lasting, data which emerge at a different rate, a slower pace; it situates us in a more settled manner, and in relation to past events" (54). It accounts for the awareness—however vague—of generative, connective, inherited, and/or enduring relations between things. In other words, it is a mode of perception by which one perceives things not apparent to the senses. Causal efficacy is a generalizing mode of perception, and presentational immediacy is a localizing mode. Whitehead's concept of symbolism can very broadly be defined as the process by which one thing evokes a response in another thing, where neither symbol nor meaning are fixed, and where the relation is not necessarily mutually recognized. Where human experience is concerned, symbolism requires—indeed, emerges from—the convergence of presentational immediacy and causal efficacy. A symbol is registered "with" the body and through the senses and is rendered meaningful by virtue of its "participation in the general scheme of extensive interconnection" (*Process and Reality* 168).

Stein's realization, despite her efforts otherwise, that writing in the "present immediate" invariably produced "resemblances," which in turn implied remembrance, seems to affirm Whitehead's schema. Resemblances, identified through remembrance, attest to the relevance of the past in the present and emphasize copresence rather than presentness as the condition of contemporaneity. Stein recognizes that the past will inhabit the act of composition; the question, therefore, is how to engage with the past without getting bogged in its pastness. One answer would be to follow Stein's lead in rejecting the concept of repetition. If there is no such thing as repetition (as Stein argues a number of times in multiple texts), since everything is always changing (in intensity, emphasis, etc.), then there is no op-

See also
Repetition
(pp. 206–207)

portunity to deny the mobility and activity of experience. By extension, contradiction and multiplicity will be part of any contemporary event. And contemporary writers—writers living in their contemporariness—will have to admit these disjunctions as part of the terms of contemporaneity.

Food

Stein's portrait of Christian Bérard—artist, set designer, and regular at the Rue de Fleurus salons—concentrates on the activities of a certain "She," sometimes called "Mathilda." Ulla Dydo suggests that Mathilda is Bérard (whose nickname, "Bébé," matches Stein's "Baby") in his drag persona (*Language That Rises* 339 n. 27). She further suggests that the portrait, which was written in response to Bérard's painting of Stein, is not only a portrait of Bérard, but also a portrait of Bérard's portrait of Stein: Bébé Bérard is Baby Stein, and the thing that "She" collectively enjoys most is *eating*:

> Eating is her subject.
> While eating is her subject.
> Where eating is her subject.
> Withdraw whether it is eating which is her subject. Literally while she ate eating is her subject. Afterwards too and in between. This is an introduction to what she ate. (*PP* 73)

"She" is the subject of the portrait, and eating is her subject. The poem continues with a good amount of eating: specifically, "pigeon and soufflé," "a thin ham and its sauce," "fish grouse and little cakes," and "breaded veal and grapes." Eating is not uncommon subject matter for Stein; food is one of the most persistent themes in her work. Not a lot has been written about this fact; if mentioned, Stein's culinary enthusiasms are usually assumed to be just that: *enthusiasms*. Stein evidently enjoyed thinking and writing about food. As a correspondent, Stein enjoyed the ritual of describing her daily eating, and in her autobiographical work, the details of what was being eaten and why is always pertinent to the action. I argue that food and eating contribute far more meaning to Stein's poetics than just evidence of her love for mealtimes—even though this fact, in itself, is by no means uninteresting. Her culinary emphasis is a critical aspect of her poetics, and in part it seeks to theorize, by example, the metaphysical concept *appetition*. My use of the word "appetition" comes from Leibniz, James, and Whitehead by way of Isabelle Stengers, Joan Richardson, and Steven Shaviro.

Leibniz's metaphysics challenges the basic assumptions of both materialism and Cartesian dualism. Leibniz rejects the materialist assertion that perception and consciousness can be described in terms of, and hence be understood as a kind of, physical process. He argues that perception and consciousness can only be attributed to an entity with a "true unity," that is, an entity that is a singular and indivisible *one*. Since materialism speaks of being in terms of mechanistic process, and since the constituent units of such processes are bits of matter, which are divisible, for Leibniz there is no accounting for oneness, being, and unity—and therefore, for perception and consciousness—in the concept of matter. Yet he does not opt instead for an idealist position, since he is also opposed to the mind/body bifurcation supposed by Cartesian dualism. Instead, Leibniz reimagines the conceptual terms of materialism, specifically, in regard to aggregation: he accepts that material bodies are aggregates, but posits that their constituents are indivisible, unextended, and indestructible. These "primitive unities" are called monads, and the world consists entirely of monads in aggregates. Each monad is different from another, and each is subject to change, but there is no external relations or interactions between them: in other words, any change in a monad must come from an internal principle, "because an external cause can have no influence upon its inner being" (*Discourses on Metaphysics* 69).

As well as the principle of change, a monad also contains a *man-*

See also
Objects
(pp. 137–141)

ifoldness. This manifoldness accounts for any change in the simple substance, which itself remains a unity: the monadic unity is a multiplicity, therefore there is always something that changes and something that remains the same. There is, in other words, "a plurality of conditions and relations" in a monad "even though it has no parts" (69). Leibniz calls this plurality of conditions and relations or, rather, the specific (and temporal) conditions that change the multiplicity of the unity of the monad *perceptions*. This, he cautions, should be considered quite apart from apperception or consciousness, as those terms are taken in Cartesian philosophy. Perceptions are not dependent on consciousness; a monad need not be conscious of its perceptions. Further, not all monads "have" consciousness, or, put differently, some monads "are" consciousness (that is, form the consciousness of conscious being) and some are not. Leibniz inverts the Cartesian arrangement: it is not consciousness that is necessary for perception, but perception that is necessary for consciousness.

Leibniz also introduces a second term, "appetition," to describe the "action of the internal principle which brings about the change or the passing from one perception to another" (69–70). Appetition is a kind of desire—the monad's desire for new perceptions. Leibniz proposes that it is via the movement (or striving) of desire that the monad reaches new perceptions, which may or may not correspond at all with the actual object of desire. Leibniz's emphasis on the disjunction between the object of desire and the object actually obtained is close to Deleuze and Guattari's post-Kantian conception of desire as a constructive force—in Leibniz's arrangement it is the actual process of desiring that is transformative. In other words, desire is something that creates its object.[1] Appetition refers not to the process by which a desire is fulfilled but, rather, to the transformation of the

See also
Queering
(pp. 201–204)

1. See "The Desiring Machine" in *Anti-Oedipus* (1–42) for Deleuze and Guattari's discussion of desire. See also Shaviro's discussion of Deleuze and Guattari and their relation to Kant in the first chapter of *Without Criteria* (1–19).

one who desires through the act of desiring. Thus a monad's unity, which is a multiplicity, is a manifold of perception and appetition, the relation of which both transform and maintain the monad. In Leibniz's summary:

> A monad, in itself and at a given moment, could not be distinguished from another except by its internal qualities and actions, which can be nothing else than its perceptions (that is, representations of the compound, or of what is external, in the simple), and its appetitions (that is, its tendencies to pass from one perception to another), which are the principles of change. For the simplicity of substance does not prevent multiplicity of modifications, which must be found together in this same simple substance, and must consist in the variety of relations to things which are external. Just as in a centre or point, although simple as it is, there is found an infinity of angles formed by the lines which there meet. (*Philosophical Works* 299, emphasis in original)

For William James, appetition is the "true, primordial, and continuous consciousness" that registers "the feeling of something in us that suffers and reacts" (*Works of William James* 458). This "movement towards the future" in fact occasions the future, since "the being who enjoys or suffers does not repeat himself continually" (458). One suffers, and so seeks to cease suffering; one enjoys and so seeks to prolong enjoyment. Although James is concerned specifically with human psychology, his notion of appetition as a movement toward the future that thus occasions the future corroborates with Leibniz's account of monadic appetition. Similarly, Whitehead defines appetition as the "principle of unrest" (*Process and Reality* 56). In *Process and Reality*, he writes, "[all] physical experience is accompanied by an appetite for, or against, its continuance" (59). Anything that can be said to be "living"—a broad category in Whitehead's ontology—must also be said to have an "appetite for difference." Indeed, as Shaviro writes, citing Whitehead, "an entity is alive precisely to the extent that it envisions difference and thereby strives for something other than the mere continuation of what it already is" (91).

Here Whitehead offers an important corrective to James's description of the subject who does not repeat: for James, enjoyment and suffering are taken as self-evidently desirable and not-desirable; the enjoying and suffering subject is taken as self-evidently invested in prolonging enjoyment and avoiding suffering. This construction relies perhaps too heavily on a universalized notion of both enjoyment and suffering, as well as on the certainty and mobility of something like free will or agency. Further, James's description only considers change, and hence difference, in terms of exceptional circumstances: a subject will change only when conditions impel change. For Whitehead, however, appetite for difference is of critical importance to subjective experience. Shaviro, citing Whitehead, writes that "appetition is the 'conceptual prehension,' and then the making-definite, of something that has no prior existence in the 'inherited data'" (91). In other words, appetition perceives difference *in*, indeed *as*, the future. The future, then, is both potential and actual, since it is experienced as real potentiality. Appetition, in its striving, actualizes potentiality; appetition is the "realization of what is not and may be" (Whitehead, *Process and Reality* 32). As Shaviro points out, this aspect of Whitehead's metaphysics can be read as a reworking of evolutionary theory: an entity experiences appetition in order to assure self-preservation; this then creates a counterappetition for "transformation and difference," since adaptability is a condition of self-preservation (95). Appetition is thus a kind of "thinking" through which a future is engaged in and as contemporary experience.

In *A Natural History of Pragmatism*, Joan Richardson reads proto-Pragmatist American philosophy in terms of appetition. For Rich-

See also
Repetition
(pp. 207–210)

See also
USA
(pp. 228–230)

ardson, appetition is explicitly connected to language: new forms of thinking, speaking, and writing, emerge alongside new forms of experience and situations of subjective reorientation. The New World experiment, according to Richardson, inaugurated a new language— one that attempted to account for the experience of being elsewhere and otherwise and to conceptualize the sudden displacements and alienations associated with settlement (3). Practically speaking, the old vocabulary was no longer workable, and at a metaphysical level, the old abstractions were no longer relevant. Richardson finds, in the New World context, a history of an emergent poetics, perhaps even a poetics of emergency. In such "frontier instances" she tracks the germ of Pragmatism, a mode of thought she identifies in the work of Henry James, Wallace Stevens, Stein, and Whitehead (1). Elsewhere Richardson writes of her subjects in *A Natural History* (which also include Jonathan Edwards, Emerson, and William James): "All [of them] shared two important characteristics: a ministerial function in wanting to provide in their language a vehicle adequate to belief of some kind—'spiritual force'—and an active interest in understanding, insofar as possible, the natural-historical and scientific facts of their moments, and in using that information in shaping the 'more than rational distortions[s]' of their styles, their thinking" ("Recombinant ANW" 117–118 [Richardson is quoting Wallace Stevens]).

Since, as she argues, the "signal, if implicit, motive of Pragmatism is the realization of thinking as a life form," thinking can further be understood as an entity "with" appetition (1); thus language, for Richardson, has an appetite for new forms of expression (8). Richardson reads Whitehead as reframing some of the key assertions made by James about language in *Principles of Psychology*—assertions that she argues come to James from a Darwinian-Emersonian context. In her essay, "Recombinant ANW: Appetites of Words," she writes: "Whitehead continued, centrally, to theorize the perception of lan-

guage articulated by James . . . a perception that James himself derived from his deep immersion in the work of Emerson and Darwin,
both of whom had realized language in its reciprocal relation to
thinking, to consciousness, as a life form, an organism like any other,
active and changing in response to 'the exquisite environment of
fact'" ("Recombinant ANW" 118 [Richardson is quoting Wallace
Stevens]). By Richardson's account, one of the important adjustments that Whitehead makes to James's theory is the shift in the
meaning of appetition. For James, as we have seen, appetition is the
"true, primordial, and continuous consciousness" of a subject: the
thing that impels a subject to continue toward the future. For Whitehead, appetition refers to far more than the base desire of subjects
with a certain kind of consciousness; appetition is the "motive force,"
to use Richardson's term, of an entity's striving for difference ("Recombinant ANW" 119). Thus appetition is both difference and continuity, differentiation and continuation: the Pragmatist position
posits a differential continuity, or continuous differentiation, as a
principle, perhaps even *the* principle, of existence.

Since for Pragmatism (with which Richardson aligns Whitehead)
both thinking and language are forms of life, appetition must be the
"motive force" of both, and the relation between the two must itself
be a kind of appetition, or, perhaps more accurately, an appetitive correspondence. For Richardson, Whitehead "grounded the most abstract of human activities in the most basic and sensual" by conceiving of thinking as having an appetite for difference and, further, by
conceiving of language as one of the ways that thinking achieves difference and newness in its adaptive and mutative projections ("Recombinant ANW" 119). Richardson takes care to point out that although Whitehead recognizes language as the nominated tool of, and
for, philosophy, he also recognizes the problems inherent in the expectation that language will perfectly articulate, let alone disclose, the

abstractions, obscurities, and vaguenesses of philosophical inquiry. This is not because of some unbridgeable gap, however, between language and the world: it is exactly the opposite, in fact. It is because language is always a part of philosophical inquiry ("Recombinant ANW" 126). Thus, for Whitehead, a different approach is necessary in thinking about language: rather than expecting language to exist apart from in order to articulate abstractions, obscurities and vaguenesses—in other words, rather than inserting a "gap" between language and the world—Whitehead suggests that language ought to be considered as a part of the world and, as such, something that is already coexistent in the things it is perceived to represent. As Shaviro writes: "Language, as a limited tool, is an empirical part of the world to which it refers, rather than a transcendental condition of that world. And there are other ways, besides the linguistic one, of prehending the world, or more precisely entities in the world" (151).[2]

See also ·
Bodies
(pp. 44–48)

Language is subject to mutations, adaptations, strivings, and differentiations, just like other entities. Following Richardson's lead, language can be thought in terms of appetition. But a clarification is necessary here: Shaviro notes that Whitehead uses "appetition" as a *technical* term and, further, that he warns against conflating technical and common usages of words. "In the case of 'appetition,'" Shaviro writes, "this can lead to the improper anthropomorphization of a process that applies to all entities" (91–92 n. 13). This may seem at odds with the prior assertion of language as inextricable with the world; in other words, it may seem contradictory to assume, and indeed uphold, a definite distinction between technical and common

2. Shaviro continues to say: "Whitehead does not deny the radical contingency that is inherent to language, and that has become a hallmark of all aspects of modern life. But he suggests that this contingency, this condition of groundlessness, is not a reason to despair. Rather, it should itself be taken as a sort of metaphysical ground" (*Without Criteria* 151).

usages of language. However, the important point is that so-called common usages of words are easily conflated with their specifically human contexts. If "appetition" is read as synonymous with "appetite," there is a risk of assuming that Whitehead is seeking to universalize phenomena by processing all entities through anthropomorphic metaphors. The key is not in trying to demarcate the technical from the common senses of *appetite*, but in recognizing that in the case of Whitehead's philosophy, "appetite" in the common sense would not be the root of "appetition" in the technical sense; rather, it is one example or instance.

Thus "appetition" as technical term and "appetite" as common term are related, but not by metaphor. In this chapter, I am attempting to find a way to theorize this relation in a manner apart from metaphoricity. In Stein's work, appetite and *appetition* symbolize each other—that is, one evokes the other, and in no definite order. I am using this verb, "symbolize," in accordance with Whitehead, to describe any event in which one thing elicits a response from another, in which something affects and is affected, and in which something *happens*. In the case of Stein, ordinary appetites evoke metaphysical appetitions. Thus when I say that Stein's food-oriented poetics exhibits a preoccupation with what Whitehead calls appetition, I am also saying that Stein's work exhibits a preoccupation with finding a way to write the relation of food and appetition. Her tendency to write about food can never be read apart from her project of defining and redefining the metaphysical implication of language and grammatical constructions. For this reason, a sentence "about" food is in fact a sentence in which food is the subject of philosophical inquiry. And food is a perennially relevant subject of philosophical inquiry, since eating provides quite an explicit example of how entities come to be in a relation with, or come to occupy, or come to be occupied by, other entities.

See also
Bodies
(pp. 38–39)

In "Stein Is Nice," Wayne Koestenbaum argues that Stein's writing is often read in relation to her fatness, where fat is understood as a kind of *affect* rather than an adjective.[3] Citing the title of Sedgwick's poetry collection *Fat Art Thin Art*, Koestenbaum writes: "To pursue a fat art is to pay attention to the food in front of you on the table. As Alice B. Toklas—and the meals she made—always underwrites Stein's production, so all of Stein's formulations can be reduced to food, to nutriment. To write a swelling prose poetry like Stein's is to confess that nourishment has been had" (*Cleavage* 322). The one who writes must also eat, and eating is not a neutral activity. Food production, distribution, preparation, and consumption are complexly political activities. The question of who cooks for whom is always important; so too is the question of *how easily* and *how well* one eats. It seems obvious that eating is often pleasurable, but eating for pleasure is clearly a very certain kind of privilege. Stein's work is oddly discomforting for this reason: one is never quite sure of the politics of her enthusiasm, or of whether her pleasure is in the ordinariness of food or in the extraordinariness of treats. Koestenbaum identifies this tension as the primary dynamic of Stein's work: a poetics concerned equally with banalities and luxuries. Stein uses ordinary language and a small vocabulary, and she is most concerned with small and unexceptional things, like dogs, apples, roses, tables, and mutton. Yet as Koestenbaum emphasizes, her work is also luxurious in its "profusion, repetition, and magnanimity" (315). Reading Stein requires energy—sometimes a great amount.

3. Koestenbaum writes further on Stein and fatness: "Stein's public persona was 'fat' and her writing, too, sold its own solidity and pulchritude—fat with densely typeset pages; fat with meaning, fat with the refusal of meaning; fat with privilege; fat with isolation, the tinned meat (confit, foie gras) of exile. When 'fat'—the word, the concept—appears in Stein, it signifies complacency, freedom, prosodic waywardness. To be fat is to be nice, cute, safe, and exempt" (*Cleavage* 321).

In his chapter on Stein in *A Poetics*, Charles Bernstein writes:

Reading a Stein poem I feel an enormous satisfaction in the words coming to mean in their moment of enfolding outward and a correlative falling away of my need to explain, to figure out. I find the work satisfying, self-sufficient. It makes me want to savor its words more than account for them.

I think this is the meaning of Stein's great discovery—call it invention—of "wordness" in the last section of *The Making of Americans* and in *Tender Buttons:* satisfaction in language made present, contemporary; the pleasure/plenitude in the immersion in language, where language is not understood as a code for something else or a representation of somewhere else—a kind of eating or drinking or tasting, endowing an object status to language, if objects are realized not to be nouns; a revelation of the ordinary as sufficient unto itself, a revelation about the everyday things of life that make up a life, the activity of living, of speaking, and the fullness of every word, *ofs* and *ins* and *ass*, in the communal partaking—call it meal—of language arts. (143)

Here food and language are cognate; Bernstein wants to "savor" Stein's words and so experience a kind of "satisfaction." But this is not simply an analogy, in which reading and eating are metaphors for each other. What Bernstein is suggesting is something more complex, namely, that "language arts" emerge from collective engagement. He calls this a *meal*, which is apt. Meals are collective engagements—events in which the becomings are circumstantial and local. (No matter how many times one might make or eat the same meal, or how many times one might eat a meal with another, each meal will be its own occasion.) As Bernstein suggests, the desire to savor is paradoxical: one wants to savor the anticipation of satisfaction as much as experience the satisfaction itself. Savoring is a temporal activity, a holding-off or holding-back in order to most thoroughly register an experience. Bernstein's "satisfaction" with Stein's language is bound up with his impulse to savor it; and his notion of savoring words is posited as an alternative to "accounting for them," say, assigning a final place for each word according to an interpretative framework. He goes on to say that Stein's "invention" is finding a way to write the "wordness" of words such that this wordness is the subject of the composition and the object of reading. Bernstein exemplifies, as a reader of Stein, the "pleasure/plenitude" of the reading occasion. Koestenbaum elsewhere describes the experience of reading Stein's wordness as a kind of "embarrassment" of not knowing what to expect (*Cleavage* 71). Bernstein's savoring finds pleasure in facing what is yet-to-be-known in a textual experience, and Koestenbaum finds a kind of pleasure in the embarrassment of that same unknowing. A couple of paragraphs later in *A Poetics*, Bernstein adds: "Stein's poems strike me dumb, are dumbfounding; not in the sense of being confusing but amazing: they are specifically designed not to send us *away from* the experience of the words happening in time" (144). This affect, whether it is called dumbfoundedness or embarrassment, and whether it is savored or experienced as a flash, is critical to the work's becoming.

Serres theorizes the meal in his parabolic study of relation, *The Parasite*. In French, "parasite" has three meanings. The first two correspond to the word's English meanings, namely, the biological parasite and its social analogue. The third, however, is not at all reflected in the English word, and is translated as "static," or "white noise." Further, in French, the one word, *hôte*, is used to describe both the "guest" and "host" positions of a parasitic relation. For Serres, this triply meaningful word, with its positional ambiguity, lends itself to a philosophy of relation, where the parasite accounts at once for differentiation, interference, deviation, and novelty. Serres writes: "The theory of the parasite brings us to miniscule evaluations of changes of state. It installs unexpected chains where small causes or very tiny differences are followed by zero effects or by effects of return and better resistance or by immense catastrophic effects," and, "[the parasite] multiplies wildly with its smallness; it occupies space with its imperceptibility" (194). As Cary Wolfe points out in his introduction to the English translation of *The Parasite*, Serres's study is resonant with systems theory, specifically the work of Gregory Bateson and Niklas Luhmann. Wolfe quotes Luhmann:

> The difference between meaning and world is formed for this process of the continual self-determination of meaning as the difference between order and perturbation, between information and noise. Both are, and both remain, necessary. The unity of the difference is and remains the basis for the operation.
>
> This cannot be emphasized strongly enough. A preference for meaning over world, for order over perturbation, for information over noise is only a preference. It does not enable one to dispense with the contrary. (Wolfe, introduction to *The Parasite* xii–xiv, emphasis in original)

Elsewhere Luhmann writes: "The excluded third, or the 'interpretant' in the sense of Peirce, or the operation of observing in our theory, or the 'parasite' in the sense of Michel Serres, or the 'supplement' or 'parergon' in Derrida's sense, is the active factor indeed, without which the world could not observe itself" ("The Paradoxy of Observing Systems" 46).

Thus the parasite—noise—is an essential part of any relation, message, transmission, or communication. In fact, the parasite is *the* essential relation of relations. Yet it is the "excluded third" often left out of analyses (of communications, politics, economics, biology) in favor of a simplified two-part transmission model. Dialogue is assumed to function when this third noise is excluded; Serres argues that in fact the opposite is true—the noise is what makes anything possible. Serres figures the parasite as the operator of all relations: the parasite is a "primordial, one-way, and irreversible relation," "where one eats the other and where the second cannot benefit at all from the first" (Wolfe, introduction to *The Parasite* x, 5). That the parasite is a one-way relation does not contradict the doubling of the guest and the host. One is both a guest and a host, but each relation is distinct and irreversible. Gifts and thefts are not interchangeable; each is its own particular occasion. Parasite: *para*, "alongside"; and *sitos*, "food." The parasite is the one who eats alongside, both the dinner guest and the host. Whatever the specific formulation, the parasite is a "little troublemaker"—literally, an "inclination toward trouble"—as well as a "deviation" and a "differential operator of change" (*Parasite* 198, 196). All relations emerge from a foundational disorder, which itself is composed from the most minor differences. Parasitism is a method of survival, and evolutionary theory is a theory of parasites. (I am reminded here of Whitehead in *Process and Reality*: "Life is robbery" [105].) In Steven D. Brown's summary:

> In informational terms, the parasite provokes a new form of complexity, it engineers a kind of difference by intercepting relations. All three meanings [biological, social, informational] then coincide to form a "parasitic logic"—analyse (take but do not give), paralyse (interrupt usual functioning), catalyse (force the host to act differently). This parasite, through its interruption, is a catalyst for complexity. It does this by impelling the parties it parasitizes to act in one of two ways. Either they incorporate the parasite into their midst—and thereby accept the new form of communication the parasite inaugurates—or they act together to expel the parasite

and transform their own social practices in the course of doing so.
... Here then is the origin of human relations: the struggle to in-
corporate or expel the parasite. (17)[4]

Analysis, paralysis, catalysis: what might such terms lend to a parasitic theory of the text? Craig Dworkin suggests, in his essay on Lyn
Hejinian's *My Life*, that while "conventional texts can be seen as attempting, always futilely, to suppress the parasite, minimize the
noise, and enhance the message; accordingly, one can read a text like
My Life as instead emphasizing the noise, as an investigation to *bid
chaos welcome*" ("Penelope" 77). Certainly, we could consider Stein,
too, as one who emphasizes noise and whose texts are emphatically
noisy. In fact, as Dworkin points out in his essay, Hejinian's writing
on Stein can be read alongside her own poetry; in *The Language of
Inquiry*, Hejinian sets out her compositional attitudes in a Steinian
context. In the chapter "Language and Realism," Hejinian describes
Stein's project in terms of a philosophical challenge to the primacy
of the noun: Stein's work, by Hejinian's account, argues that "states
of consciousness exist as full sentences; the topography of consciousness consists of a rich verbal landscape" (93). "In imagining it," continues Hejinian, "we have to bear in mind its porosity and observe
the range of activity on its surface. We must acknowledge our sensa-
tion of *of*, *if*, *the*, and *some*, as well as *tree*, *smoke*, *shed*, and *road*" (93).
Here Hejinian echoes Bernstein's designation of a Steinian poetics
that recognizes the "fullness of every word," including the "*of*s and
*in*s and *ass*."[5] And both Hejinian and Bernstein echo William James,
who calls for something similar in *The Principles of Psychology*:

See also
Grammar
(pp. 115–117)

4. *Analyze*, *paralyze*, and *catalyze* is a triad that Serres himself designates and refor-
mulates variously in *The Parasite*.

5. Koestenbaum, too, makes a similar point: "Stein relates to language as a cook (or
a hungry eater) relates to staples: her interest is not in the elite concoction, but in the ordinary ingredient, the it and and, the slice of nicely buttered bread" (*Cleavage* 323).

If there be such thing as feelings at all, then so surely as relations
between objects exist in rerum natura and more surely, do feelings
exist to which these relations are known. There is not a conjunction or a preposition, and hardly an adverbial phrase, syntactic
form, or inflection of voice, in human speech, that does not express some shading or other of relation which we at some moment
actually feel to exist between the larger objects of our thought. . .
. We ought to say a feeling of and, a feeling of if, and a feeling of
but, quite as readily as we say a feeling of blue, a feeling of cold.
Yet we do not so inveterate has our habit become of recognizing
the substantive parts alone, that language almost refuses to lend
itself to any other use. (1:245; emphasis in original)

This critical nexus of thinking around the relation, and relationality, set the scene for various twentieth-century poetries and aesthetic theories, with which Stein, Bernstein, and Hejinian are variously affiliated. What links these inquiries and practices, to each
other and to philosophers like Serres (and one could easily add
Deleuze and Guattari here too) is a shared concern with process, mobility, and orientation in the framing of cognitive, perceptive, linguistic, material, and social activity. In its ubiquity, the parasite
speaks to every instance of relationality—taking into account the unequal terms and unidirectional play of any given encounter, as well
as to the capacity for the parasite to infiltrate systems of power (to in-
terrupt or hack)—and further, recommends that the most minor and
ordinary objects, affects, and actions, are ontologically equal to the
most "major," in that they participate in the same parasitical relations
and are susceptible to further parasitic transformation.

For Serres, the signal site of and for the parasite is the mouth:
"The mouth is the organ of the parasite. Its polyvalence is admirable:
it is used for eating, speaking, yelling, singing, burping, hiccough-

ing, and gargling" (*Parasite* 243). Literally, the mouth makes noise. Serres's parasite encounters the world with its mouth, and it is the mouth, in its varied and often incommensurate activities, that establishes the terms of a relation. In Stein's poem "Eating" from *Tender Buttons*, eating and noise are closely allied too: "Is it so a noise to be is it a least remain to rest, is it a so old say to be, is it a leading are been. Is it so, is it so, is it so, is it so is it so is it so" (36–37). One of Stein's chief concerns, throughout her work, is the affiliation of eating and speaking—specifically, their relation to writing and reading. Eating and speaking are explicitly associated with the body and with social encounters (one must find the right balance of eating and speaking in order to share a meal with others). But writing and reading are often assumed to be somehow less embodied or social activities, and writing and reading are often considered apart from eating and speaking. Stein's interest, in part, is in a poetics that works on the four-way relation of eating, speaking, reading, and writing. This is perhaps why her work is so concerned with speech patterns and simple vocabularies, foods and meals, writing processes and grammatical formations, and the affects and experiences of reading. These concerns interface at the level of daily life, as well as at the level of complex philosophical considerations of being, knowing, and becoming. Stein quite rightly underscores the necessarily nourishing and materializing processes that ground daily living and metaphysical propositioning: *eating, speaking, writing,* and *reading.*

"Food," the middle section of *Tender Buttons*, comprises thirty-eight discrete poems. The titles for each poem, capitalized and separated by semi-colons, are listed at the beginning of the section. The titles include food-objects ("Roastbeef"; "Sugar"; "Milk"; "Apples"), food-objects in specific relations ("And Clear Soup and Oranges and Oatmeal"; "Salad Dressing and an Artichoke"), durations ("End of Summer"), actions ("Eating"; "Dining"), events that are also objects

("Lunch"; "Dinner"), and spaces ("A Centre in a Table"). Most often, the poems of *Tender Buttons* do not respond to the titles' designations, nor do they describe the titles' objects. The relation, or relations, between a poem and its title is thus ambiguous, disorienting, and riddlelike. "Food" is not simply what is eaten, nor even how or when or where eating occurs, but anything that can be thought and read alongside the event of the title. "Roastbeef" begins:

See also
Objects
(pp. 155–158)

> In the inside there is sleeping in the inside there is reddening, in
> the morning there is meaning, in the evening there is feeling. In
> the evening there is feeling. In feeling anything is resting, in feel-
> ing anything is mounting, in feeling there is recognition, in feeling
> there is recurrence and entirely mistaken there is pinching. (21)

The poem lists, via propositions and their negations, a varied collection of objects that might signify a meal: considerations of heat, taste, smell, division, tenderness, measurement, and regulation. Stein seems to suggest that any event—for example, a meal of roastbeef—involves an enormous set of related events: to think of roastbeef is to think of the many entities and systems that make roastbeef possible. And thus Stein's tendency to name and un-name phenomena serves to signify the ongoing relevance of the fact of difference: "It is so easy to exchange meaning," she writes in "Roastbeef"; "it is so easy to see the difference" (21).

The mouth is a crucial site of differentiation, for a mouth engages in a broad range of often incommensurate or oppositional activities. Freud posited the mouth as the critical link between the inside and the outside of the body and, hence, the site of an infant's worldly engagement and development. His thesis is that one comes to know first via the mouth. In one sense, the mouth forms language; in another sense, language forms the mouth: as Hejinian writes, "The mouth, certainly, bears the history of languages it speaks—its acquired habits of movement circumscribe the sounds it can make, whether mimetic (clickings, shushings, poppings, tootings, etc.) or descriptive (of the click and thump of horses crossing a bridge, water gushing from a pipe, fish snapping as it fries, a steam train in a park)" (*Language of Inquiry* 68–69). Both the mimetic and the descriptive functions "perform perception" in different ways, and bear witness to the language that shapes those very functions: language trains the mouth to move in certain ways (69). Hejinian, perhaps at her most phenomenological, suggests further that the perceptual performatives of mimesis and description are also perceived; that is, the performance of perception is itself a kind of perceiving of perception, or experience of perceiving. Thus the mouth affects and is affected by the sounds it makes, and by its capacity to both perceive and perform perception. In addition the mouth, though by no means exclusively, consumes. It is here, on the matter of consumption, that Stein's interest in food can be read in terms of contemporary aesthetics and commodity culture.

Sianne Ngai's essays "Our Aesthetic Categories" and "The Cuteness of the Avant-Garde," which form part of her recent and continuing study of *minor affects*, use *Tender Buttons* as a guiding example of *cuteness*—a key aesthetic category in the context of twentieth-century capitalism and commodity culture. According to Ngai's thesis, "minor" taste concepts such as cuteness, zaniness, and interestingness are key to grasping "how the concept of 'aesthetic' has been transformed by the performance-driven, information-saturated and networked, hypercommodified world of late capitalism" ("Our Aesthetic Categories" 948). This is because, she continues, such taste concepts "index economic processes." They also tell something of the "problems in aesthetic theory that continue to inform the production, dissemination, and reception of literature and art," such as "the close

See also
Grammar
(pp. 96–97)

relation between the form of the artwork and the form of the commodity; the ambiguous state of the avantgarde [. . .]; the relevance of
aesthetic to critical or other nonaesthetic judgments aimed at producing knowledge [. . .]; the relation between artistic production and
labor in a world where immaterial labor is increasingly aestheticized;
and the 'parergonal' relation between art and theoretical discourse"
(949).

The concept of cuteness, Ngai argues, indexes patterns and practices of consumption. The cute, as she defines it, is an "aesthetic dis-
closing the surprisingly wide spectrum of feelings, ranging from tenderness to aggression, that we harbor toward ostensively subordinate
and unthreatening commodities" (949). Cuteness describes a certain affect that includes both the pleasure and violence (and, to some
degree, the pleasure of violence and the violence of pleasure) that is
associated with consumption. Cute things are things that are desirable, and the desire for consumption is also a kind of desire for possession, occupation, or destruction. Cute things are therefore perceived as being vulnerable. Cuteness is not strictly a positive, nor a
negative, designation: it is ambiguous. As Ngai writes, cuteness is
easily dismissed as a "culinary" concern, and not at all relevant to discussions of art and theory (813). In particular, she adds, cuteness has
posed a "longstanding embarrassment" to poetry, at least in part because poetry is already often perceived as being small and vulnerable
(815). As a result, "cuteness" rarely enters critical discussions of contemporary poetics, despite obvious contemporary preoccupations
with "small, concrete, and everyday things: William Carlos Williams's
plums and strips of copper, Lorine Niedecker's granite pail, Robert
Creeley's rocks, John Ashbery's cocoa tins, Bernadette Mayer's
puffed wheat cereal, Thomas Sayer Ellis's balloon dog" (815). Such
anxiety, or self-consciousness, might explain why Stein's work is not
often considered for its cuteness, or else is designated as such in or-

der to dismiss it as frivolous, inconsequential, infantile, or overly domestic. Yet as Ngai argues, Stein's work, most obviously *Tender Buttons*, demonstrates precisely the complexity and ambiguity of cuteness and provides a good model for further investigations of the cute,
in terms of both aesthetics and consumption. Ngai writes:

> In addition to its capacity to convert a subject's veiled or latent ag-
> gression towards a vulnerable object into explicit aggression that
> seems to be directed toward the subject, cuteness names an aes-
> thetic encounter with an exaggerated difference in power that does
> something to ordinary or communicative speech. More specifi-
> cally, the concept names a relationship to a socially disempowered
> other that actively transforms the speech of the subject who im-
> poses the aesthetic quality on that other—abetting a fantasy of the
> cute object's capacity for retaliation. . . . Such a fantasy sheds light
> on why Tender Buttons features so many feminine and homey "lit-
> tle things"—a cup and saucer, a petticoat, a cushion, a shawl, a
> purse—described as "hurt" but also as "enthusiastically hurting"
> other objects of its own genre or kind. (828)

Stein, as read by Ngai, achieves an investigation of cuteness as
well as a cute poetry; her work is as cute as it is a serious consideration of the category of cuteness, inextricable as it is with the desires
and violences of relationality. Stein manages, in *Tender Buttons*, to an-
thropomorphize objects not in order to familiarize them, but to
demonstrate the peculiar fantasies inherent in anthropomorphism.
Far from simply writing cute poems, or writing about cute things,
Stein looks at what it might mean to attribute cuteness to objects, including food. Eating and consuming, here most fully cognate, bear
witness to the contradiction in wanting to savor *and* possess something. There is something cute about Stein's tendency to cite and list
food. If, as Ngai shows, cuteness emerges from the constantly mod-

ulating tension between pleasure and displeasure, tenderness and violence, submission and domination, then something is cute only after it is checked for its violability and thus considered in and as a relation. The cuteness of Stein's culinary conceits therefore might have something to do with the vulnerability inherent in explicit engagement in the aesthetics of the domestic and the culinary. The cuteness of *Tender Buttons* is doubly so: the poems are cute and their subjects (objects) are cute, too. Small poems about everyday things are especially vulnerable to gendered classifications, and hence might easily be dismissed as wifey chits. But Stein's poems are cute in a third way, too: by Ngai's account, *Tender Buttons* is cute in its thorough disavowal of any notion that cuteness is merely a label for sweet things. The pleasures of eating and mealtime are not without their violences, not least of which is the violence necessary in having food to eat. The question of how to engage with aesthetics, critical theory, philosophy, and the language arts in a cultural context so geared for *consumption* necessarily means reconsidering what is in fact meant by aesthetic experience and judgment, that is to say, *taste*. Works like *Tender Buttons*—an acquired taste, to be sure—are useful for showing up the critical importance of minorness. Stein's enthusiasm for food, which is no doubt genuine and particular, is indicative of her daily attentions to the smallest and most slight occasions: the parasitic relations, novelties, minor shifts, and material becomings of entities with appetites.

Following *Tender Buttons*, Stein's preoccupations shifted from objects and object relations to grammar and grammatical construction. She began a thorough investigation into the function of sentences and paragraphs, and she appraised language units according to their capacity to be *interesting*—a category she judged according to the potential for ambiguity. She directly associated interestingness with the likelihood of being mistaken: language is interesting if it is likely to be misrecognized, read as error, or read in error; inversely, language is uninteresting when it attempts the direct transmission of unambiguous fact. For Stein, the most interesting words are the words most easily mistaken, and the most interesting composition is the one that favors error-prone words. Her keenness for mistakes is syllogistic: she likes mistakes because they're interesting, and she is interested in the interesting because interesting things cause errors.

Stein argues that certain parts of language are more or less interesting by virtue of their grammatical function. This theory is explicated in the lecture "Poetry and Grammar" and later clarified in *Narration*. It can be summarized by the following: nouns and adjectives are not ordinarily interesting, because they claim to name and describe things directly; verbs are interesting because they are often indirect and so easily mistaken; adverbs, too, are interesting for their capacity to confuse (since adverbs qualify by modulating or transforming rather than simply clarifying or explaining); articles and prepositions are the most interesting of all because they are the least specific, the most context-dependent, and thus most easily mistaken; and punctuation (in particular, exclamation points, question marks, and commas) is generally uninteresting, because it tells a reader when to emphasize, inflect, and breathe—all of which ought to be done without guidance (*LA* 209–220).

In her essay "Merely Interesting," Sianne Ngai theorizes "interestingness" as an indefinite, indeterminate, and ambiguous designation—a concept with a "lack of distinguishing characteristics" and thus one that describes a kind of "aesthetic *without content*" (781, emphasis in original). Interestingness names an aesthetic judgment that includes (depends on) nonaesthetic features; in other words, interestingness "toggles," to use Ngai's word (788), between nonaesthetic and aesthetic judgments:

> *Interesting* always seems to come with this *merely* attached to it, as if to highlight its indeterminacy or what Hegel would call its lack of content. Yet . . . the aesthetic judgment of interesting *does* have a concrete and even "sensuously particularized" [this is Hegel's phrasing] content. Far from being an ahistorical abstraction, the interesting is a specifically modern response to novelty and change . . . and, more precisely, to novelty as it necessarily arises against a background of boredom, to change against a background sameness. It is moreover a modern aesthetic whose distinctiveness resides in its low or minimal affect, its functional and structural generality, its seriality, its eclecticism, its recursiveness, and its future-oriented temporality. (789–790)

Following Ngai, who flags Stein as a key figure invested in the category of the interesting, interestingness can be theorized as the *minimal affect* of aesthetic experience: because it is indeterminate, it suggests, or promises, future judgment, and hence describes the ongoing and indeed *endless* and diverse activity of aesthetic engagement. Stein's early novels—propelled by her preoccupation with classification, typology, and informational models of history and narrative—are examples of what Ngai refers to as the "sprawling encyclo-pedic works about ongoingness" that attempt to "discover what the absolute minimal conditioning of interesting might be" and which are typical of early-twentieth-century prose experimentalisms (791). Stein's portraits, plays, prose poems, essays, lectures, and novellas continue this engagement in various modes. The term "grammar" can be used to describe Stein's compositional investment in the aes-thetics of the interesting, where grammar refers to the total system— the modality—of language use and compositional practice. Stein's concept of grammar is founded on a primary interest in language *as* interesting, and in the activity of writing as an exploration of lan-guage's potentiality and flexibility.

Interestingness registers an important ambiguity in the experi-ence of aesthetic encounter. How one approaches and then deals with novelty is a critical question—especially, for Stein, when con-sidering the demands for newness and innovation of the various modernist avant-gardes that shared her compositional context. The novelty of Stein's experimental texts is not contained in their formal innovations but produced in the occasion of their encounters with innovative readers; Stein had high expectations of her readers, and this in part explains her ambivalence toward punctuation. Conven-tionally, punctuation scores syntax in order to designate sentence type (question, statement, and so on), rhythm, and tone. Stein's ideal reader is the one who comes to a text willing to wager and err on its tonal, rhythmic, and semantic nuances. Her model reader takes the initiative to pause, breathe, emphasize, speed up, and slow down without explicit instruction. She does not avoid punctuation marks altogether but uses them in nonconventional and ambiguous ways. At times this means leaving out commas or question marks, and at other times it means breaking up long tracts of language into clipped, phrasal quasi-sentences.

Stein insists that writing and thinking are simultaneous activities, and her compositional ethos required that she conceive the language of her writing in the sentence that she was composing and not beforehand; the language of her composition is the language of her thinking, as opposed to a *re*-presentation of thought. Consequently, it is not just her reader who is liable to mistakenly read a verb for a noun or fail to register an unmarked question: crucially, for Stein, the act of writing itself is equally liable to make mistakes and to be mistaken. If one is writing as one is thinking and not what one has already thought, the writing will register the dead ends, false starts, and discordances that are local to cognitive process. And if one is writing as one is thinking, one will be concerned with the modulating technology that allows for such (imperfect) simultaneity: *grammar.* Stein's compositional ethos, in which thinking and writing are necessarily coterminous activities, departs significantly from the "automatic writing" experiments that she conducted during her studies in psychology under William James at Harvard. Stein ultimately decided that automatic writing was a misnomer—she wrote that "writing for the normal person is too complicated an activity to be indulged in automatically" (qtd. in Meyer, *Irresistible Dictation* 221). Stein's ambivalence regarding the use of experiments in automatic writing for designating and understanding human cognitive process marks a break with James, who remained invested in experimenting with and observing the output of automatic writing exercises. Despite this break, critics have been quick to assume that Stein's compositions were in fact the result of automatic writing drills. A notable exception is Ronald B. Levinson, who in 1941 published a short paper in the *Journal of American Psychology* titled "Gertrude Stein, William James, and Grammar." In his account of Stein's grammatical innovations, Levinson considers the relation between

See also
Contemporaneity
(pp. 60–68)

·

Stein and James beyond the matter of automatic writing, anticipating contemporary discussions of Stein alongside Jamesian Pragmatism, neuroscience, and process philosophy.

Levinson responds to an earlier article by B. F. Skinner, "Has Gertrude Stein a Secret?," published in the *Atlantic Monthly* in 1934. Here Skinner argues that Stein composed in two distinct modes—automatically and nonautomatically—and attempted to synthesize the two modes under a singular authorial avatar, in which the "personality" of Stein and the abstractions of the automatic language present as the unified output of a literary innovator. Skinner dismisses Stein's work while commending her canny manipulation. As Meyer notes, Skinner's assessment was partly informed by "factual and interpretative mistakes" but is nevertheless a typical reading of Stein's work by her contemporary critics, many of whom were eager to find a quick reason to account for her work's apparent difficulty (*Irresistible Dictation* 224). Skinner's assessment is premised on the assumption that there can be a clear distinction made between conscious and nonconscious composition and that the former boasts a more authentic connection to the composer's subjectivity. In Levinson's account, Skinner figures Stein's automatic writings as the "cold and unmeaning products of [her] unhappy faculty of disengaging from her central self an 'elbow' with nothing significant to say and with no power to import interest into the saying of it" (125). In contrast, Levinson argues that Stein composed according to "quite definite stylistic doctrines . . . which are on the conscious level of her mind" and represent the "attempt to put into practice some notions of the ideal function of language" that were "in all probability" influenced by William James and were ultimately engaged with "the subtle issues, half psychologic, half philosophic, which turn upon the finer categoreal analysis of the creative world" (125, 128). Levinson

See also
Bodies
(pp. 38–39)

goes further, pointing out the affinities between Stein and James—not only in terms of language and language use, but also in terms of how language functions philosophically:

> [Stein's] accent on the more fluid and moving elements in language (the verbs and adverbs), her corresponding depreciation of the static moveless noun, what is this but the counterpoint of James' plea on behalf of "flights" as against the linguistic predominance of "perchings"? And perhaps most striking, though by no means the most fundamental, point of parallelism between them is the prominence they both accord conjunctions and prepositions, the often underappreciated parts of speech. It is perhaps not wholly fanciful to discern in this doctrine of verbal equality a remote variation upon the theme of sturdy American democracy which is characteristic alike of James' A Pluralistic Universe and Miss Stein's The Making of Americans. (127)

By her own account, Stein was interested in a philosophy of grammar that exemplified the kinds of principles that she perceived as central to the ideals of American democracy. In an interview, Stein describes how she attempted to democratize her grammar in order to emulate a republic: "I was trying to get . . . this evenness of everybody having the vote and that is the reason I am impatient with punctuation" (*WAM* 98). Stein celebrated, perhaps uncritically, a correspondence between the ontological equality of all the parts of language and the subjects of a democratic state. (I say "perhaps uncritically" since clearly not everybody had the right to vote when Stein was writing, and furthermore, her insistence on ontological equality is not articulated as a position against social and political inequality.) Similarly, James's insistence on the equal importance of the joining functions of language corresponded to his philosophy of relation. For both Stein and James, focusing on the movements and movabil-

See also
USA
(pp. 234–240)

ity of grammar was a key concern of a philosophy that did not prioritize the substantive.

See also
Objects
(pp. 141–149)

In metagrammatical works such as "Arthur a Grammar" from *How to Write*, Stein sets out a number of propositions whose ambiguities productively problematize their axiomatic formulation. Consider, for example:

> Whenever words come before the mind there is a mistake.
> This makes instant grammar. (66)

Here the phrase "come before" might easily mean either "prior to" *or* "occur to"; since Stein is already enthusiastic about mistakes, it is unclear whether this is a warning against preplanning composition or an endorsement of the easily mistaken and mistakable results of extemporaneous thinking and writing. Either way, the second sentence is also ambiguous: is it a follow-on sentence or a stand-alone, self-referential proposition? My point is not to try to clarify these issues, but to consider their important interventions in the reading experience. It is perhaps too obvious to say that Stein's notion of grammar is entirely apart from the rulebook kind that attempts regulation and enforcement in the interest of unambiguous signification. Stein's interest, very basically, is in how language is used, including, and especially, how language is tentatively or erroneously registered in its becoming, whether in/as thinking, speaking, writing, or reading.

Stein and Ludwig Wittgenstein are most closely aligned on this matter of the "how" of language use. After finishing the *Tractatus Logico-Philosophicus,* David Antin reports, Wittgenstein came to the conclusion that the problems of philosophy were problems of grammar rather than of logic (*Radical Coherency* 316). Antin characterizes this shift from logic to grammar as being like a shift from photography to filmmaking: Wittgenstein moves from attempting to capture *the thing* to recording the process of *things-in-action;* when Wittgen-

stein uses the word "grammar" he is referring to the "relation between a specific human practice and the use of a word within it" (317).
In other words, grammar describes the particular field of action
around a word, including its meaning-in-use and the consideration
of this meaning-in-use in terms of philosophical inquiry. In this way,
Wittgenstein's propositional philosophy—in which, as Antin writes,
"example was piled upon example" in performative and often contradictory formulations—can be read as a "poetic practice based on the
interrogation of the meaning of words in the context of life practices" (322, 324). Wittgenstein's "grammar," he continues, comes
close to "the Socrates represented in Plato's quasi-dialogues . . . the
improvising sophist in performance, exploring meaning by thinking
while talking" (324). The degree to which Wittgenstein is doing a
kind of poetry in his philosophy can be figured as part of a compositional methodology that includes—indeed, values—the coming-to-
be of speaking and writing.

Stein and Wittgenstein converge (and diverge) variously on the
matter of grammar, a concept that for each was roomy enough to include a range of movements in their respective philosophical accounts of language. The convergences are significant: consider
Wittgenstein's "grammar describes the use of words in the language"
(*Philosophical Grammar* 60) alongside Stein's blunt "Grammar in
use" (*HTW* 54); or Wittgenstein's notion of affinity as a kind of "family resemblance" (rather than direct lineage) (*Philosophical Investigations* 66–69) alongside Stein's assertion that "Grammar is the same
as relative" (*HTW* 49) and "Grammar is resemblance. They can be
indifferent" (59); or Wittgenstein's "Arithmetic is the grammar of
numbers" (*Philosophical Remarks* 23) alongside Stein's "Grammar
does make arithmetic" (*HTW* 93). Their divergences, which I will explore in more detail below, are most often to do with the roles and relations of sentences and paragraphs.

Both Stein and Wittgenstein conceived of language in practice, or, perhaps more exactly, language *as* practice. And though they both enjoyed writing axiomatically, as one reads through, for example, *Philosophical Grammar* or "Arthur a Grammar" one finds, rather than an accretive logical treatise, an affiliation of propositions that in their conflicts and resonances propose a philosophy of heterogeneity. The axioms participate in, are examples of, phenomena—as opposed to prescriptions or descriptions thereof. In "Arthur a Grammar," "Arthur" figures as a peculiar sort of subject: one might well read "Arthur" as a verb, in which case, (to) Arthur a grammar is to speak as Arthur, or else, a description of the way Arthur's language use is a grammar. When one considers Arthur, one must also consider the way Arthur Arthurs grammar; thus this poem is a portrait of Arthur Arthuring. He is joined, throughout, by other proper names, many of which are also introduced with "a grammar" following their names. There is no grammar that is external to language and thus no language *as such*. Rather, grammar as Arthur, Josephine, Ferdinand, Mary Rose, Antoinette, Florence, Alice, Simon, Winifred, and so on occurs when and because there is language-in-use: grammar is dependent on there being things to say, where speaking includes thinking, writing, and many nonverbal social encounters.

Recent scholarship on Stein has recognized Stein's revision of conventional grammar as a key achievement of her poetics. Juliana Spahr claims that the "real importance of Stein's work is in the alternate grammars they build. Correct grammar is most obviously one of society's more dramatic class markers" (*Everybody's Autonomy* 45), and Joan Retallack writes that "[Stein's] literary experiments were consciously framed investigations into the evocative powers of grammatical innovations" ("Introduction," *GSS* 9). Dydo argues that Stein's "rejection of the rigid conventions of language led her gradually to dissociate herself from all inflexible forms, including hierarchical thinking, authoritarian organization, prescriptive grammar, and chronological narrative—aspects of the patriarchy. In a sense, all her work is a demonstration of possibilities of grammar for democracy" (*Language That Rises* 16). Stein was interested in something other than rallying against "grammar . . . as we have inherited" like Olson does in "Projective Verse" (*Collected Verse* 224), and she was theorizing something more than the bare fact that "We very often . . . use utterances in ways beyond the scope at least of a traditional grammar," as Austin writes in *How to Do Things with Words* (3). She was interested in the *actual process of composing a grammar*, a process that considers all the contributing circumstances of compositional praxis, including, importantly, the dynamics of syntax and the structural category of the sentence.

See also
Contemporaneity
(pp. 65–66)

Stein repeatedly insists that paragraphs are emotional but sentences are not. As with the interesting/uninteresting split, the emotional/unemotional binary raises many questions: perhaps most explicitly, what Stein means by emotion; and then, what constitutes a sentence and a paragraph and how the two are related; and what happens when a paragraph contains a single sentence. Across her metagrammatical works, Stein proliferates definitions, explanations, and case studies in order to set out, and then obscure, the limits of her theory of the sentence/paragraph relation. In *How to Write*, three lengthy prose poems (that are very easily read as lectures, essays, or exegetical remarks) take the sentence as their subject. Her sentences-on-sentences often promise to follow subject-predicate convention— beginning with "A sentence is"—but then depart from the convention by failing to qualify the subject in a singularly meaningful way:

Think of sentences. What is a sentence. A sentence which they enjoy and she mends towels. (*HTW* 170)

A sentence is made with whenever they were however often it is very well for it and they do. (175)

A sentence depends whether they like it, they like it, along with it, as long as they like it they like it it is long and with they will with and without it not divide it they will go along with and without it. A sentence is dependent upon whether they open it again and again giving it for it and gave it to it. (181)

In *The Autobiography of Alice B. Toklas*, Toklas narrates:

Gertrude Stein, in her work, has always been possessed by the intellectual passion for exactitude in the description of inner and outer reality. She has produced a simplification by this concentration, and as a result the destruction of associational emotion in poetry and prose. . . . Emotion itself [should not] be the cause of poetry and prose. They should consist of an exact reproduction of either an outer or inner reality. (89)

And in the lecture "Portraits and Repetition," while reflecting on the period of time during which she composed *Tender Buttons*, Stein reports: "All this time I was of course not interested in emotion or that anything happened. I was less interested then in these things than I had ever been. I lived my life full of emotion and with things happening but I was creating in my writing by simply looking" (91).

It goes without saying that Stein lived a "life full of emotion and with things happening," but as Wayne Koestenbaum cheerfully concedes on behalf of all readers, such matters are "not our business" (*Cleavage* 314). "Your only business when reading Stein," Koestenbaum advises, "is the sentence before your eyes" (314–315). In other words, it ought not be the reader's aim to expect Stein to render her emotional experience legible in her writing—not least of all because it was not her wish to do so. Stein was expressly disinterested in the quest for direct representation of emotion in poetry and prose; she argued that it was not possible to compose a text in such a manner that there could be a perfect emotional correspondence between the act of writing and the act of reading. *Associational emotion*, the phrase she uses to describe this attempted transferal, suggests that Stein was aware of, and working against, the particular brand of associationism that posited consciousness in terms of a chain of discrete actions, feelings, and sensations that are able to be identified and represented unproblematically. William James argued that the "parts" of experience are in fact not distinct enough to be parts with such definite relations. Thus James's corrective to associational psychology, in which he emphasizes the indistinctness and nonlinearity of affective experience, brings him close to Stein on this matter, despite her flat rejection of association. As Meyer shows, Stein's objection is aimed at the *habituation* of association in language use: "Stein objected to association, whether lexical or syntactical, on two counts. First, it distracted from writing by removing one's attention from the object on the page and so breaking one's concentration. Second, and still more damning, it was entirely habitual. One had no control over one's associations—it was hardly possible to stop them—and as such they were a sign of one's dependence on habit" (*Irresistible Dictation* 239–240).

Stein is against the designation of emotion as the key currency of meaning in a text—meaning that is transmitted via direct passage from abstract reference to concrete realization. In distracting the reader from the immediate language event (the event of reading itself), such associational modes of textual engagement rely on habituated and generalized topoi. She attempted, in various ways, to compose in manners that self-consciously estranged the writing and reading processes from typically narrativized emotional set pieces. This required Stein to theorize the function of emotion in relation to the structural units of language—the sentence and the paragraph— in order to account for the "balance," as she calls it, of unemotional and emotional affects in writing and reading processes (*LA* 229).

When Stein theorizes the "unemotional balance" of the sentence and the "emotional balance" of the paragraph, she is not dismissing the sentence-unit for its lack of emotion—if anything, she is commending such a quality. But this does not mean that the paragraph is dismissed for its emotionality. The matter is more complex. Meyer proposes that Stein's notion of the individual sentence is something like an "idea," with the paragraph the equivalent of a "state of mind" (or, more exactly, coexistent multiple states of mind) (254–255). Thus the relation of the sentence to the paragraph is not merely one of part-whole complementarity, nor is it an opposition: the sentence-paragraph dynamic is "not a contradiction but a combination" (qtd. in Meyer, *Irresistible Dictation* 262). Paragraphs are composed of sentences, and it is in the broader context of the paragraph that sentences engage in, or demonstrate, a kind of sociality, and in doing so, achieve on behalf of the paragraph an "emotional balance." This emotional balance could also be called a *social context*, or the affinitive relation of sentential ideas. Here the paragraph is conceived, as in a landscape, as the total space and time, space of time, in which a complex of relations emerge. As Meyer notes, Stein's model of the sentence-paragraph relation is resonant with another of her axioms: namely, that in order to be "really and truly alive," one must be talking and listening at the same time, and hence acknowledging that they are "part of the same thing" (qtd. in Meyer, *Irresistible Dictation* 262). This resonance is key in at least two ways. First, these kind of logical constructions ("not only but also") exemplify Stein's commitment to heterogeneity and affiliative (rather than teleological, familial, and/or causal) relations. Second, they posit a critical aspect of Stein's compositional ethos and its philosophical import: by emphasizing the contemporariness of talking and listening, and the combination of sentences and paragraphs, Stein argues for a poetic theory in which there are always, and necessarily, coexisting and often seemingly contradictory events and entities in action.

Stein mythologizes the moment she realized the difference between sentences and paragraphs. According to *The Autobiography of
Alice B. Toklas*, it occurred while observing Basket, the poodle, lapping water with his tongue: "Listening to the rhythm of his water
drinking made [Stein] recognize the difference between sentences
and paragraphs, that paragraphs are emotional that sentences are
not" (268). In Stein's schematic, the sentence-paragraph dynamic
generates rhythm, and rhythm generates composition. In the event
of Basket drinking, the singular lap-unit collectively organized the
lapping; Basket's thirst was quenched, but the fact of quenching was
not achieved in any one tongue-lap. It was achieved in a duration of
drinking toward which every tongue-lap contributed. Stein equated
this rhythmic lapping with her own compositional method; elsewhere in *The Autobiography*, she writes that she would "set a sentence
for herself as a sort of tuning fork and metronome and then write to
that time and tune" (223). Time and tune, carried for the duration of
the composition, make the composition, and the sentence is the unit
that drives the rhythm.

See also
Contemporaneity
(pp. 67–68)

In the lecture "Poetry and Grammar," Stein reflects on her various
attempts to test the limits of sentences and paragraphs as she has
characterized them. She notes that while writing *The Making of
Americans*, she wrote paragraph-length sentences that achieved "neither the balance of a sentence nor the balance of a paragraph" and
that this was a failure of sorts "because after all you should not lose
two things in order to have one thing because in doing so you make
writing just that much less varied" (*LA* 224). By *How to Write*, she recalls, she was no longer concerned with what might be lost; instead
she was interested in what could be gained by trying to do two things
at once, so she tried to write sentences that could be both unemotional and emotional. She cites a small selection of her successful attempts, such as "He looks like a young man grown old" from "Sen-

tences and Paragraphs" (*HTW* 25). This sentence explicitly deals with relationships between lengths of time: the synchronic-diachronic rhythm of how "he" looks and the synchronic-diachronic rhythm of the syntax. Perloff reads it as a particularly Wittgensteinian sentence for its tendency to seem nonsensical unless, or until, a set of imagined circumstances are constructed around the sentence ("'Grammar in Use'" 41).

Perloff's methodology for reading Stein tends toward this recuperative mode, defending her work against charges of meaninglessness by finding ways to get meaning into the language. These efforts to assemble context for Stein's ambiguous sentences are endlessly fascinating, and they achieve much in the way of demonstrating the possibilities of a letter, word, or phrase. However, there must be another way of reading Stein's syntax: not just as potentially meaningful in context, but as occasioning meanings in the composition. It requires only the most minor adjustment to the analysis that Perloff engages, and in fact it takes her central thesis as a given: namely, that sentences, when read, proliferate narratives and suggest contexts. The difference is that for Stein, there is no definitive narrative or context—the proliferation of alternatives is interesting not because one might find the best fit or the true key to a text but because it is the material of language-in-practice and the construction of grammatical form. Rather than reading in order to find an occasion in which a sentence "makes sense," I argue that one can read every sentence of Stein for its *actuality*, for its being something that exists, in language, in an occasion of reading. "He looks like a young man grown old" emphasizes this complexity and obscurity—by Stein's account, so much so that its eventfulness and interestingness is that of both a sentence and a paragraph. I read Stein's designation of this sentence, among a select few others, as stand-out sentence-paragraph double-ups, not because of any specific emotional content or epic scale but simply because they are self-aware as conceptual-temporal event-fields. Thus as sentences they are protoparagraphic, and as paragraphs they are extrasentential.

In "The New Sentence," the title essay from his 1987 book, Ron Silliman outlines a compositional mode with the sentence as its primary unit that he claims as more or less the innovation of a small group of writers in the Bay Area of California in the 1970–1980s (and with the Stein of *Tender Buttons* and the William Carlos Williams of *Kora in Hell* as indirect predecessors). Silliman claims that the group focused on poetry written in prose while moving away from established conventions of the prose poem. For these writers, the sentence is a "unit of measurement," and when grouped in paragraphs, sentences achieve a "unity of quantity"—as opposed to a unity of logic or argument (91). "New sentence" compositions mark "the first prose technique to identify the signifier (even that of the blank space) as the locus of literary meaning," effectively reversing the "tyranny of the signified" (93). By Silliman's account, this is achieved at least in part by emphasizing the making and shifting of meanings at the level of interior arrangements, rather than by redirecting meaning out of the poem via exterior reference. One sentence is never entirely connected—causally or syllogistically—to another. Rather, sentences work with clauses (themselves pseudo-sentences); through their shifting, torqueing, and modifying movements, clauses engage the processes through which meaning is constructed.

Perhaps despite Silliman's attempt to periodize a new sentence poetics, he problematizes, more broadly, the grammatical foundations of the methods for and habits of reading poetry, and he calls for the critical review of what a sentence actually *is* and *does*. He begins his essay with a historical survey of the sentence as theorized in linguistics, language philosophy, and literary criticism. Immediately he finds that there is little consensus on this topic. Silliman notes that in Saussurean linguistics, the sentence is considered to belong to the domain of speech (*parole*) and is thus not treated to proper analysis. The conflation of the sentence with speech—the sentence as minimum utterance—tends to dominate linguistic theory, such that there is little analysis of the sentence in the context of writing. At this point in his analysis, Silliman states:

> The sentence is a term derived from writing that has been taken to refer to speech; in spoken language, the "utterance" is sentence-like in its construction, but it differs from a sentence in that it is infinitely extendable, whereas a sentence is fixed by the full stop; the emphasis on *langue* and *parole* in linguistics that somehow fails to address to the question of the act of writing, has resulted in a lack of critical treatments of the sentence and its operations in a poetics. (69)

Stein was similarly interested in the full stop—specifically, in its marking of the end of a duration. Silliman cites the following passage from "Poetry and Grammar":

> What had periods to do with it. Inevitably no matter how completely I had to have writing go on, physically one had to again and again stop sometime and if one had to again and again stop some time then periods had to exist. Besides I had always liked the look of periods and I liked what they did. Stopping sometime did not really keep one from going on, it was nothing that interfered, it was only something that happened, and as it happened as a perfectly natural happening, I did believe in periods and I used them. I never really stopped using them. (*LA* 217)

The full stop, as Stein says, is a "perfectly natural happening": one must inevitably stop and rest. At the same time, clearly, one does not only use full stops when one needs to stop; sometimes one does so also when one simply chooses to stop. It is not, in other words, an arbitrary notation of written language; it is a part of writing. The use of a period is compositional, and its function demonstrates a key difference between speaking and writing: in writing, language is organized conceptually and structurally into definite units.

Silliman's contribution to scholarship on Stein is his emphasis on the sentence as a compositional construct. His inquiry considers a poetics of the sentence: a methodology for composing and reading the sentence as an autonomous unit. Similarly, Meyer names Stein's "lasting accomplishment, at once scientific and literary" as her success in "rendering the organic mechanisms that operate in all sentence composition and comprehension" (*Irresistible Dictation* 270). For Stein, the central structural question of composition is, very simply, *how* a sentence becomes:

> Why can almost any word and any word which they know they can go and they can put it into any sentence in this way. In what way can they put any word that they know into any sentence which is what they allow. Any sentence. A word which is in any sentence is made to be confused with elegant and with inadvertence. But not with speed nor with mainly. A word which is allowed is for them and for them alone which they must with reluctance prepare in the remainder of the time which is at their disposal. What is a sentence. A sentence has hammered it as much as they are pleased alike. (HTW 198–199)

How to Write and *How Writing Is Written* explicitly evidence Stein's enduring interest in the "how" of composition. Her writing-on-writing emphasizes method; as such, Stein's methodological inquiry into the activity of writing might be said to be *adverbial* in the sense that it focuses on the specifics of becoming, emphasis, and orientation. An adverb, very broadly, is any grammatical unit that modifies language. Adverbs are not always in the service of clarification—they can cause ambiguity by generating modifications that negate, confuse, or obscure. I want to suggest two things: first, that writing is adverbial in the sense that it is acted out, negotiated in process, modified in becoming; second, that the adverb, as a grammatical function, is a key concern of Stein's poetics and provides a model for reading her work in order to engage with its philosophical inquiries. Stein's how-to texts, which would flummox the writer eager for a guide to writing communicatively, champion the adverb for its capacity to emphasize the mobility of language precisely by mobilizing language. Stein's adverbial compositions produce and modify phrasal, clausal, and syntactic relations.

Stein's fondness for adverbs again brings her into relation with Whitehead and James, as well as recent work by Bruno Latour. Halewood discusses Whitehead's conception of existence and its focus on the "how" of "becoming" (*A. N. Whitehead and Social Theory* 29). With an emphasis on the "how" and not the "what" (or the "why"), Whitehead's philosophy privileges manner, character, quality, and disposition over substance, essence, and identity—in other words, as Halewood argues, it is *adverbial*.[1] Working in similar (and more contemporary) terrain, Latour, in "A Plea for Earthly Sciences," considers the two senses of the word "social": in the first instance, "social" refers specifically to humans and human relations; and in the second it refers to the concepts of relation and relationality (4). Emphasis on this second sense of the social, he argues, is necessary for a philosophical position that properly attends to the relation of humans and nonhumans, especially where eco- and bio-crises are concerned. This would require, according to Latour, the social sciences reconceptualizing the notion of experience in terms of *adverbiality*.

1. Shaviro makes a similar claim, citing Whitehead from *Process and Reality*: "*How* an actual entity *becomes* constitutes *what* that actual entity *is*. . . . Its 'being' is constituted by its 'becoming'" (*Without Criteria* 55).

For Latour, as for Whitehead, *bifurcation* is the endemic problem of contemporary thought, not only in terms of a perceived nature/culture divide, but also in terms of the subdivisions of experience and knowledge into apparently independent domains, discourses, and disciplines. As a result, we think about how a certain concept or problem is attended to in different domains—science, law, or religion—and how and where these domains might intersect or conflict. Latour's point is that these domains are not independent, and the critical question for a contemporary philosophy (and politics) is *how* ideas and problems are engaged and *how* concepts are framed according to the points of contact and relation across modes of thought: "It makes a huge, a lasting, an enormous difference whether a connection is made legal*ly*, scientifical*ly*, religious*ly*, artistical*ly*, political*ly* or technical*ly*. It's the adverb that designates a really major ontological nuance even though there is no such thing as a substantive definition to be given. . . . The whole attention should shift to modes of connections, or 'modes of existence'" (7).

This is the paradoxical achievement of the adverb: it describes the particularity of what it alters, but more than that, it is copresent in the construction of what it alters. There is no realm of unaltered substantives, waiting to be modified; an adverbial philosophy theorizes the cobelonging of objects and qualities. Latour's "plea" corresponds to the tenets of James's *radical empiricism*, which is defined as follows:

To be radical, an empiricism must neither admit into its constructions any element that is not directly experienced, nor exclude from them any element that is directly experienced. For such a philosophy, the relations that connect experiences must themselves be experienced relations, and any kind of relation experienced must be accounted as "real" as anything else in the system. (*Radical Empiricism* 20)

This is echoed elsewhere by James in *Principles of Psychology*:

There is not a conjunction or preposition, and hardly an adverbial phrase, syntactic form, or inflection of voice, in human speech, that does not express some shading or other of relation which we at some moment actually feel to exist between the larger objects of our thought. . . . We ought to say a feeling of *and*, a feeling of *if*, a feeling of *but*, and a feeling of *by*, quite as readily as we say a feeling of *blue*, a feeling of *cold*. (245, emphasis in original)

Conjunctions and prepositions can be said to operate adverbially, since they emphasize relationships of context. Michel Serres argues that while contemporary philosophy has tended to fix on certain prepositions (*on, of, in*), it ought to engage with other kinds of prepositions—in particular, those that do not assert an inherent fixity of relation. Serres discusses prepositions in *Atlas*, which Steven Connor excerpts in his essay "Topologies: Michel Serres and the Shapes of Thought." Connor's translation of Serres reads:

Has not philosophy restricted itself to exploring—inadequately— the "on" with respect to transcendence, the "under," with respect to substance and the subject and the "in" with respect to the immanence of the world and the self? Does this not leave room for expansion, in following out the "with" of communication and contract, the "across" of translation, the "among" and "between" of interferences, the "through" of the channels through which Hermes and the Angels pass, the "alongside" of the parasite, the "beyond" of detachment . . . all the spatio-temporal variations preposed by all the prepositions, declensions and inflections? ("Topologies" 3)

In its hinging faculty, a preposition moves toward, or comes to be, an arrangement: it is locating rather than located. Connor suggests a list of especially "prepositional prepositions"—*along, between, amid, around, while, during, through,* and *throughout*—all of which readily admit the potential, possible, future and virtual into the conception of the actual ("Topologies" 3).

Since Stein's work is explicitly aware of the difference between spoken and written language, the adverbiality of her work can be registered in at least two ways: in the first instance, the written adverb modifies syntax; in the second instance, the adverb both establishes and modifies the tonal and intonational orientations of speech. When one reads aloud, one follows or disobeys adverbial cues and, in doing so, negotiates meaning in the text. The script of a play, as a written text, synthesizes these two registers when it provides explicit directions for a character's dialogue; a character might be instructed to speak angrily, or quietly, or drunkenly. Such instruction sets up an expectation between the general (a mood) and the particular (a line of dialogue). But the expectation is fraught with a good number of possible failures: what does it mean, for example, if a character is said to be speaking "dreamily" or "bitterly" or "meditatively"? And what does it mean if the subsequent dialogue is seemingly *not* dreamy or bitter or meditative? Stein was perennially interested in language's ability to be mistaken, and in its potential for ambiguity. Also, Stein was perennially disinterested in anything that would overexplain or overdetermine language. Thus Stein's fondness for adverbs has to do with their potential for movement and confusion.

See also
Play
(pp. 160–162)

In the case of her plays, Stein sometimes gives cues (*dreamily*); at other times, she erases all script directions. In the first case, these cues are often untrustworthy or perplexing (in the sense that they do not necessarily or immediately correspond to the following dialogue), and in the second case, their absence is loud: what is one to do with a directionless script? How is it to be played? In her prose and verse writing, similarly, Stein works in both adverb-rich and adverb-poor modes. The two modes work in different directions to suggest that directional and gestural cues in language (or their absence) are never neutral devices. The quality, manner, character, and local conditions of a relation are exemplified, and often obscured, by adverbs. The adverb, for its capacity to index and invoke syntactic, semantic, and tonal modifications, is the signal grammatical conceit of Stein's poetics, which in its foregrounding of the shifting contexts of textual meaning, necessarily emphasizes the conditions for shifts to occur: by way of variations, intensifications, and deviations.

"I have told you," Stein writes in "Poetry and Grammar," "that I recognize verbs and adverbs aided by prepositions and conjunctions with pronouns as possessing the whole of the active life of writing" (*LA* 220). This active life of writing was complicated, error-prone, confused and confusing, exciting, ordinary, and above all *interesting*. Stein's theories about grammar are inextricably tied to her commitment to the activity of writing. She wanted, at all times, to emphasize the becoming of writing in terms of the practice of language. Her writing on writing is always and emphatically adverbial, dealing with the "how" of language in use and the emergence of grammar. Even in her axiomatic moments, Stein's claims are performative rather than substantive—they do not assume to prescribe a set of rules for language; rather, they investigate the possibilities of thinking and writing. To think and write, propose and modify, begin again and again—this, for Stein, was both the life and the liveliness of the one who comes to use language.

Identity

Speculation about Stein's biography tends to dominate critical responses to her work. Such comments enjoy the gossipy intrigue of Stein's identity: Stein is a queer Jewish woman, writing abstractly and mostly without support from readers and publishers. Yet Stein resists easy assimilation into discourses of queerness, Jewishness, feminism, and experimental practice—in part because at the same time, she was also capable of expressing a politics variously associated with Anglo-American nationalism, social conservatism, and aspirations of mainstream celebrity. The fact of her survival in German-occupied France during World War II has resulted in accusations of collaborationism and treason.[1]

Scholarship that focuses on Stein's identity often minimizes the aberrant aspects of her complex output and maximizes singular texts that represent a coherent subject position. Critics who want to frame Stein as a queer author often point to the seemingly explicit content of *Lifting Belly*.[2] Critics who want to frame Stein as a figurehead for

See also

Bodies

(pp. 45–47)

1. In 2012, the issue of Stein and Toklas's survival of Nazi-occupied France was raised in the mainstream media, following an article by Alan Dershowitz in the *Huffington Post* which claimed that an exhibition at the Metropolitan Museum in New York showcasing the Stein's art collection had purposely suppressed the fact of her collaborationism with the Vichy government. In response, Charles Bernstein edited a dossier for *Jacket2* ("Gertrude Stein's War Years: Setting the Record Straight") featuring excerpts and essays from Edward Burns, Joan Retallack, Marjorie Perloff, Ulla E. Dydo, Václav Paris, and Christopher Sawyer-Laucanno. Each argues against the accusation of collaborationism and offers more complex readings of Stein and Toklas's survival. For an earlier, excellent essay on this same matter, see Maria Damon's "Gertrude Stein's Jewishness, Jewish Social Scientists, and the 'Jewish Question.'"

2. See Rebecca Mark's introduction to *Lifting Belly*.

an antipatriarchal poetics often engage a psychoanalytic-linguistic reading of her syntax in order to claim that her work operates at a pre-Oedipal level of semantics and in doing so anticipates contemporary feminist literary-deconstructionist efforts.[3] Critics who want to dismiss her work as bourgeois or banal often cite repetitive or doggerelesque lines to argue that she's disingenuous, inauthentic, or unintelligent.[4]

In his essay "Stein's Identity," Charles Bernstein reads her short play "Identity a Poem" as a play on the notions of identity and poem: the poem is a play in which identity is a poem; hence *identity is a play*, an "acting out" rather than an "inner state" ("Stein's Identity" 485). Bernstein figures Stein's playful attentions to identity-acting as reflective of her "triple distance from the ascendant culture"—her queerness, Jewishness, and womanness (485). Stein is always already at least triply other, and by her otherness, as it is registered in her consciously non-normative grammars, she emphasizes the constructedness of subject positions and designations. Her work is not radical *because* it deviates; it is radical because it shows that *everything is deviant*—certain deviations have simply been naturalized. As Bernstein writes: "In our current poetic landscape, identity is something the poet asserts the better to celebrate. Stein celebrates her sus-

3. See Marianne DeKoven's *Different Language* and Lisa Ruddick's *Reading Gertrude Stein: Body, Text, Gnosis*.

4. Michael Gold, for example, writes: "In essence, what Gertrude Stein's work represents is an example of the most extreme subjectivism of the contemporary bourgeois artist, and a reflection of the ideological anarchy into which the whole bourgeois literature has fallen. . . . In Gertrude Stein, art became a personal pleasure, a private hobby, a vice. She did not care to communicate because essentially there was nothing to communicate. She had no responsibility except to her own inordinate cravings. She became the priestess of a cult with strange literary rites, with mystical secrets. . . . The literary insanity of Gertrude Stein is a deliberate insanity which arises out of a false conception of the nature of art and of the function of language" (qtd. in Hoffman, *Critical Essays on Gertrude Stein* 76–77).

pension of identity, this holding off naming to see what otherwise emerges. Her writing becomes a state of willing, of willed, unknowingness" (487).

"Identity a Poem" was written as a marionette play and on request. Stein had met Donald B. Vestal, a puppeteer, in Chicago in 1935 during her American lecture tour. Vestal subsequently asked for a script from Stein; Stein promptly sent "Identity," and Vestal's production (with music by the young composer Owen Hayes) opened in July 1936 at the National Puppetry Conference (*Letters of Gertrude Stein and Carl Van Vechten* 2:461). As Dydo notes, "Identity a Poem" is in fact composed from excerpts of *The Geographical History of America*, a monograph on identity in the contexts of nationhood, war, politics, and memory (*ASR* 558). "Identity a Poem" can be read as a contribution to this theme. The short text, collated for the play of marionettes, speaks to the microactivities of identification and nonidentification—the activities of marking oneself as a one (that is, marking oneself as a provisional one, or as one provisionally). The text meditates on the line "I am I because my little dog knows me," which is also the refrain of *The Geographical History*. Identity is a relation, between one and a dog, and so a form of play, since the nature of the relation between one and one's dog is an ongoing (re)negotiation.

Part of Stein's attempt to come to terms with the problem of the relation of the *outside* of one's self (what others perceive) and the *inside* of one's experience (what one perceives) was to come up with a theoretical construct to problematize identification, or at least, to foreground the inherently problematic act of identification. She proposes "entity," roughly corresponding to the inside of experience, as a term distinct from "identity," which refers to the subject as perceived and constructed in/through relation. Entities are what the human mind perceives; identities are what human nature conceives about itself. Entities are largely dissociated from temporalizing and

memorializing processes, whereas identities are more or less dependent on such processes—that is, dependent on time and memory. While she asserts in "Identity" that "a dog does not know what
the human mind is," (59); nevertheless, Stein also seems to be attempting, throughout *The Geographical History*, to theorize the relation between a human and a dog. The answer, it seems, is *play*. Stein's
tautological propositions "A dog plays because he plays again" and
"The human mind plays because it plays" (92) suggest a critical affinity between dog and human subjects, and in dog-human relationships. Another way of understanding this relation is to say: a dog is
not invested in the collective and cultural memories of human sociality; a dog engages with human modes of being and playing.

Stein's little dog's knowing her both *is* and *is not* a relation of "identification." Her dog's formulation of her "as" her engages with the
notion of identity in its unfixed and playful form: the shared knowledge of a relation. In other words, the dog identifies Stein's *entity*.
Stein's insistence on rewriting and reworking the line "I am I because
my little dog knows me" (which in its first iteration is a paraphrase
of a nursery rhyme in which a woman whose petticoat is torn is no
longer recognized by her dog) betrays an anxiety that is partly bound
to the inside-outside dialectics she is concerned with, and (relatedly)
partly because of her sudden fame following the success of *The Autobiography of Alice B. Toklas*, the very premise of which problematizes the notion of Stein as "having" a singular identity. Dogs figure
throughout Stein's work as agents and examples of immediate experience: dogs, for Stein, seem especially capable of occupying the immediate space and time of experience. Maria Damon writes that dogs
are the "guardian spirits of experimental writing" in Stein's work:
guides, perhaps, to the continued experiment in writing apart from
the self-concerns of human nature (*Dark End of the Street* 211). Dogs
exemplify a mode of immediate being that best corresponds to the

See also

Play

(pp. 173–174)

human mind when it is writing in a manner dissociated from the constraints of the socialized and historicized ego. The human-dog relation that Stein so evidently values is not a communication but a correspondence of mutual recognition. Stein's writing emerges from her relation with her dogs and with her thinking through a dog's relation. Ultimately, she inverses the tragedy of the nursery rhyme's outcome: Stein insists that she is knowable to her dog despite her external knowability and despite any crisis of self-identity that she may experience.

In Stein's 1936 essay "What Are Masterpieces and Why Are There So Few of Them," she reworks the key problems of identity yet again:

> The thing one gradually comes to find out is that one has no identity that is when one is in the act of doing anything. Identity is recognition, you know who you are because you and others remember anything about yourself but essentially you are not that when you are doing anything. I am I because my little dog knows me but creatively speaking the little dog knowing that you are you and your recognizing that he knows, that is what destroys creation.
> (*WAM* 84–85)

So, one recognizes the other and recognizes that the other recognizes: this recognition and recognition-of-recognition is identity; identity is not *what* is recognized by the other but the *fact of being recognized*. When one is "in the act of doing anything," one has no identity: one will have identity only during the event of recognizing in oneself what the other recognizes. Stein is Stein because her little dog knows her, but it is her knowing the dog's knowing that "destroys creation" and precludes the immediacy of the relation. Thus identity is a feedback loop, ultimately returning one to one's own self-concern. When the dog recognizes Stein, Stein is not strictly Stein = Stein, equivalent only to herself; she is an activity of being Stein, a Stein with a specific relationship to the dog. The relation is remembered and the dog recognizes Stein at each moment of play: hence, the dog is attuned to the activities of Stein's "entity."

In *The Geographical History of America* Stein theorizes the "human mind" and "human nature." Put simply, the human mind refers to the immediate activity of human consciousness and human nature refers to the historicizing, temporalizing, and narrativizing habits of human sociality. The human mind has no identity, no time, no remembering, and no forgetting. Thornton Wilder, who appears as a character in the text and who corresponded with Stein throughout its composition, claims that the human mind "gazes at Pure Existing" (*Letters of Gertrude Stein and Thornton Wilder* 362). It can be in contact with other things but not connected to other things. Conversely, human nature is connected to other things but is not in contact with them. And since "to understand a thing means to be in contact with that thing" the human mind has the capacity to "understand" whereas human nature does not (*W* 380). The human mind is that which apprehends experience, and human nature is that which identifies and memorializes the effects and traces of experience.

In glossing Stein's schema, it is important to note two things. First, although she appears to construct a binary, Stein's oppositional definitions are never logically watertight. She writes, for example:

> Any minute then is anything if there is a human mind.
>
> Any minute is not anything if there is human nature.
>
> But any minute is anything so then there is a human mind.
>
> Think of how very often there is not, there is not a human mind and so any minute is not anything.
>
> Any one can see that human nature can not make any minute be anything. (*W* 380)

A minute is surely a principal invention of human nature. Parsing these propositions, it seems that one difference between the human mind and human nature is that in the former, clock time is irrelevant.

On the other hand, minutes represent a meaningful and functional metric of human nature's enterprises (politics, war, media, labor, history, celebrity). One minute of clock time cannot be any other minute of clock time in the context of human nature. Despite this explanation, Stein's definitional distinctions lack specific examples and rules. The difference she articulates is not ontological but representational: immediate experience of conscious perception is unrepresentable; nevertheless, human nature represents itself by way of identification, historicization, and memorialization. The second thing to note is that in her sketchy binary, though she seems more interested in the human mind's activities than in human nature's narratives, she does not, as Claudia Franken points out, "imply the sovereignty of the human mind towards reality" (*Gertrude Stein, Writer and Thinker* 87). In other words, Stein does not argue that the more authentic self is to be found in the activity of the mind. In fact, she posits the very concept of "self" as the product of human nature and its representationalism. Stein's model of the mind is as an emergent system—a dynamic and continually altering experiential field.

By the end of the *Geographical History*, Stein reconfigures her dog refrain yet again. This time she abandons her attempt to theorize her dog's recognition as a kind of identification—that is, an identification of entity. Seemingly, she decides that such an attempt is useless, since identity, no matter which way it is framed, is a construct of the human ego. Her updated position is as follows: "The little dog knows that I am I because he knows me but that is not because of identity but because he believes what he sees and what he hears and what he smells and so that is really superstition and not identity because superstition is true while identity is history and history is not true because history is dependent upon an audience" (*W* 426). In this version, Stein dissociates identity from the relation between her and her dog. The dog's recognition of Stein is not identification but *supersti-*

tion. With this shift, Stein posits identity as a self-conscious (that is, dependent on an audience) habit of human nature. Stein's sense of self, which she recognizes in her dog's superstitious investment in her singularity, may be read as a stand against other kinds of identifications. Stein clearly did not identify in ways that were expected of her in terms of her Jewishness, queerness, or womanness. Partly, this might be because Stein was suspicious of overstating collective experiences of subjectivity. She did not believe it was possible to "enter into anybody else's mind": the relation of subject and other occurs only via "slight contacts"—"You may touch, but you do not enter into each other's mind. Why should you?" (qtd. in Meyer, *Irresistible Dictation* 65).

Here Stein comes into contact with Leibniz, Whitehead, and Deleuze. To begin, a brief survey of the convergence of these three thinkers' diverse (but thoroughly affiliated) ontological projects is necessary. According to Whitehead, the world is made of experiencing subjects. As Shaviro writes: "There is nothing outside of experience; and experience always happens to some subject or other" (*Without Criteria* xii–xiii). Anything can, and indeed is, a subject (not just those endowed with what is called consciousness). Further, a subject is a subject because it experiences—is affected by—objects in the world. Thus a subject is that which is affected by an object and an object is that which affects a subject in an occasion of becoming. This means that subjects are always objects and objects always subjects in countless and often nonreciprocal relations: there is no ontological difference between subjects and objects. A subject is singular; it is unlike anything else in the world. As such, it contributes something new to the world, even though it is made from data of the world. Further, a subject is a subject only in its moment of becoming. After a subject becomes, it becomes the datum of some other subject's becoming. Occasions refer to a single instance of this becoming; events

See also
Objects
(pp. 136–141)

are nexuses (multiplicities, series) of occasions. Thus a process philosophy posits that "everything" is a relational complex of eventful
experiences. In this way, Whitehead's broad category of the "subject"

See also

Food

(pp. 74–76)

is very close to Leibniz's "monad."

Subjects and monads play the central role in both Whitehead's and
Leibniz's atomistic ontologies. Relationality, in both cases, is key, but
crucially, relations are to be understood as things-in-themselves,
rather than merely the passage of two correlatives. Leibniz's monads
have relations "without causal interaction" (Tiffany, *Infidel Poetics*
99), and Whitehead emphasizes the singularity and novelty of a subject in its becoming. In other words, monads and subjects have relations but are not substitutable or exchangeable with other monads
and subjects. Here we have something approaching Deleuze's *multiplicity*, a concept that he constructs from his reading of Bergson and
that attempts to foreclose the problematic of the one and the many.
A multiplicity speaks precisely to this form of relationality because
it does not collapse difference; rather, it comes from and is produced
by difference. A multiplicity is a differential modality by which things
(subjects and objects, for example) *become;* multiplicities are events
that mark the differentiating passage from the virtual to the actual,
from what was not to what is, from the past into the contemporary

See also

Contemporaneity

(pp. 66–67)

moment.[5]

Considering all three philosophers and their resonant conceptual
vocabularies, a philosophy of process emerges and can be engaged
alongside a process poetics. Stein's work "is" a kind of multiplicity—
composed of intensive variations in language—and the experience
of reading Stein affords the opportunity to consider the process of
becoming-subject and becoming-object in the event of a relation.

5. Deleuze outlines his theory of multiplicity in *Bergsonism*. See also "Dualism,
Monism and Multiplicities (Desire-Pleasure-Jouissance)."

Stein's differential grammar investigates the subject-object relationality and the multiplicity of becoming in part by problematizing subject-predicate conventions of representational signification and by confusing or obscuring the identities of the speaking subject's claim (even, or especially, when the subject is speaking axiomatically). In Stein, there is the sense that the dialogue—I mean this in a specifically philosophical sense—occurs between unidentified or trans-identifying subject-object event nexuses that speculate across critical questions of experience.

In *What Is Philosophy?*, Deleuze and Guattari theorize "conceptual personae," the dialogical others to and from whom philosophical questions and claims are constructed and argued.[6] Stein's most intimate conceptual persona is the dog, whose particular kind of relation affords Stein the room to consider the subjects and objects of her own poetic ontology outside the specific contexts of human praxis. The dog friend, for Stein, is the ideal other of philosophical inquiry: a creature whose precise modality—whether it is conceived as consciousness, experience, or anything else—remains obscured or undisclosed. The dog functions as a "condition for the possibility of thought" and does not require that Stein argue her philosophical claims against the conventional rhetorical apparatuses of dialogue. As a result, Stein's concepts—often vague or contradictory—roam throughout and across her wide body of work while effectively precluding their assimilation into structured argumentation. (If I am guilty of overhandling her axioms in this study, it is at the very least in full support of their capacity to undermine my investments at any point.)

In *Intensive Science and Virtual Philosophy*, Manuel DeLanda ar-

6. For extended discussions of "conceptual personae," see chapter 3 of part 1 of *What Is Philosophy?*.

gues that a Deleuzian ontology is to be found not in Deleuze's texts or readings, but in the fact of his ideas being so thoroughly "robust to change," that is, able to be redirected to a new set of materials in order to find the same conclusions (4). This, says DeLanda, is fitting considering Deleuze's commitment to a concept of multiplicity in which difference is conceived productively "as that which drives a dynamical process" (6). Ontology, as DeLanda frames it, refers to the set of things that are assumed to exist in reality: one's ontological position proposes the existence of a certain set of "stuff" and thus for a certain kind of reality. Deleuze's ontological entities are multiplicities—not essences, but *processes*. If entities are processes, affinities between entities must also be processual; and if one entity should resemble another, the resemblance is in the processes that produced the entities, rather than in the essential characters of the entities (10). Thus Deleuze's entities have contact without being connected, just as Stein's human mind cannot be "entered into" and Leibniz's monads cannot enter into each other. Their mode of relation is lateral—alongside.

Accordingly, and as Stein asserts, a portrait never "gets" its subject. Portraiture is a *tuning*: a practice that attempts to find the rhythm between the composer and the subject. Stein explains her compositional method in "Portraits and Repetition": "I must find out what is moving inside them that makes them them, and I must find out how I by the thing moving excitedly in me can make a portrait of them" (*LA* 183). The *objectality*[7] of the subject in a portrait is not achieved by representation but suggested by resonance. I am reminded here of Daniel Tiffany's description, in *Infidel Poetics*, of monadic relations as "expressive correspondence[s]":

7. "Objectality" is Tomlinson and Burchell's translation of the term *objectité*, used by Deleuze and Guattari (*What Is Philosophy?* 4).

Monads have no direct, or causal, interaction with other monads
or with the phenomenal reality designed—and perceived indi-
rectly—in concert with other monads. Hence perception, the very
substance of monads, occurs without external influence: a paradox defining the essential lyricism—that is, the obscurity—of
monadic being. Monads do, however, have relations, in a manner
of speaking, with other monads, though such relations consist
solely of expressive correspondences, or *harmonized perceptual
states*. (99–100, my emphasis)

Tiffany evokes the monad during his investigation into the metaphysics of obscurity. Tiffany's thesis is that poetry is constitutively
obscure—thus by looking to constructivist theories of metaphysical
obscurity such as *Discourses on Metaphysics and the Monadology*,
Tiffany seeks a way of reading poetry that does not assume, on principle, that obscurity is a problem that must be fixed. By Tiffany's account, even criticisms that reject the clarifying program of hermeneutics nevertheless tend to assume that reading is a practice that
yields meaning (even if plural, temporary, or radicalized). The problem here, for Tiffany, is that obscurity tends to get read in one of two
ways: as a secret that must be disclosed or as a quality that indicates
multiple or hidden meanings. If, as Tiffany claims, the obscurity of
a poem is not intrinsic but is a fact disclosed via reading, then the
event of reading—including the event of becoming-meaning—is the
site of obscuring, in which language obscures the exact terms of its
actualization, not merely *during* reading but indeed *because of* reading.

See also
Queering
(pp. 183–185)

Thus it is not the meaning of a poem that is obscured, but the obscurity of reading, that problematizes the concept of meaning. "Setting aside the question of meaning," Tiffany proposes that "lyric obscurity might be regarded principally as an event or deed, as a way of

doing things with words" and argues for a theory of *meaningfulness* that posits the "-ness" as the site of meanings, rather than the "-ful" as the condition of a unified meaning (*Infidel Poetics* 8, emphasis in original). If meaning is an event and not a thing, it is *obscure*, since anything that is eventful is necessarily dynamic. I am taking this word "event" in the sense that Whitehead uses it, which is to say, as a concept that constitutes everything. Shaviro writes: "Whitehead marks an important turning point in the history of philosophy because he affirms that, in fact, everything is an event. The world, he says, is made of events, and nothing but events: happenings rather than things, verbs rather than nouns, processes rather than substances. . . . Even a seemingly solid and permanent object is an event; or better, a multiplicity and a series of events" (*Without Criteria* 17). In the chapter "What Is an Event?" from *The Fold*, Deleuze considers Whitehead alongside Leibniz on the matter of the concept of the event. Deleuze theorizes the Whiteheadian event as comprising five components: extensions, intensities, individuals (*prehensions*), and eternal objects (*ingressions*). Extensions refer to the different elements of an event, which exist in infinite part-whole relations and which "stretch" over and across each other in durations, such that the event itself can be conceived as a "vibration with an infinity of harmonics or submultiples" (87). Intensities are the qualities and conditions of the elements and their emergent extensions. The individual is the *subject*, the concrescence of elements that become from the existing data of the world and subsequently become the data for future becomings. Finally, eternal objects refer to the elements that remain the same and so achieve continuity and successiveness (87–90). Deleuze reads Whitehead's theory of the event as largely coincident with Leibniz's monadology—but with one important difference. Where Leibniz insists on the unconnectedness of monads, Whitehead emphasizes the connectedness of subjects' perceptions (which he calls "prehensions"): every individual prehension draws on others and/or excludes others, thus even if the relation is nonreciprocal, it is still a relation of connection. Deleuze suggests that Whitehead's model attends more directly to relationality; from Whitehead we can conceive of the relations between subjects and objects, subjects and subjects, objects and objects, as events *and* as elements of events. "A new entity," writes Shaviro, "comes into being by prehending other entities; every event is the prehension of other events" (29). Continuing, Shaviro notes that this applies to a subject's self-prehension: "Self-identity, the relation of a subject to itself, has the same structure as the relation of a subject to an object. They are both grounded in prehensions. . . . I continually prehend myself; I renew myself in being, at every instant, by prehending what I was just a moment ago" (29).

Coming back to Stein via the event-nexus of Whitehead, Leibniz, and Deleuze, and considering Tiffany's thesis on the obscurity of poetry, I propose that in Stein's engagement with the concept of identity across her work and in her critical gestures, she argues for something close to a Whiteheadian ontology while also emphasizing the nondisclosure of Leibniz's monadology. In other words, Stein is interested in the becoming of subjects and objects, and in the event of the prehension of the self, *as well as* in the problem of dealing with these becomings in language. The question of how an event is registered in language (that is, how language participates in, as well as processually registers, evental occasions) coexists with the question of how identity is made. One must continually and actively prehend oneself; also, one must continually and actively prehend what is *not* oneself, even when the distinction is unapparent. Poetry, which in Tiffany's account is by definition *obscure*, offers one model for writing alongside the prehensions of self and not-self such that there are no definite identifications. This is because the event of reading a poem obscures its language and thereby brings the poem into being; thus the language remains, to some extent, undisclosed in its operations. To put it another way: a poem neither preexists nor "survives" the occasion of its reading—the obscuring of language is the condition for a poem's becoming. There can be no definite argument mounted for the identification of either a self or a not-self in a poetic text.

To consider this more closely, I want to look at *Ida*, a novel that Stein began to write in 1938 and published in 1941. Evidently, Stein found it difficult to finish the text. Her correspondence with Carl Van Vechten tracks her unease with the drafting process; nevertheless, she was excited by the notion of an "early American novel" and worked on numerous versions of the manuscript (*Letters of Gertrude Stein and Carl Van Vechten* 2:601). *Ida* is a novel occupied by refugees, race relations, unemployment, homelessness, religion, beauty pageants, regional politics, bureaucracies, marriages, and divorces. It is a historical account of wandering, settling, and unsettling. Ida moves between states and cities, dog friends and husbands. She seems to suffer from some sort of perceptual vagueness, and she finds herself in a state of constant relocation and disorientation. "Funny" is a word that runs through the novel: "funny" things happen to Ida, and Ida often has "funny" feelings. *Ida*'s funniness (which is also Ida's funniness) is a particular kind of dissociation: the affect of being or becoming dissociated from oneself. The funny feelings that Ida experiences are almost always objectless, untraceable, ambient, and only ever partially perceived. Funniness is felt as something like anxiety, desire, or memory.

The novel begins with Ida's birth and the birth of her "twin": "There was a baby born named Ida. Its mother held it with her hands to keep Ida from being born but when the time came Ida came. And as Ida came, with her came her twin, so there she was Ida-Ida" (7).

When Ida is a teenager, living with her blind dog called Love, Ida "makes" Ida-Ida again. She tells the dog her plan for manifesting her twin:

> You have always had me and now you are going to have two, I am going to have a twin, yes I am Love, I am tired of just being one and when I am a twin one of us can go out and one of us can stay in, yes Love yes I am yes I am going to have a twin. You know Love I am like that when I have to have it I have to have it. And I have to have a twin, yes Love. (10–11)

Ida achieves her doubling by writing her twin a letter. Once she is supported by the presence of her twin—a presence acknowledged entirely in and by the act of letter writing—she begins to "win." In one letter from Ida-Ida to Ida, her twin writes: "So pleased that you are winning, I might even call you Winnie because you are winning. . . . I will call you Winnie because you are winning everything and I am so happy that you are my twin" (23). For a short time, Ida and Ida-Ida are joined by Winnie, the one who wins. Presumably, she wins because she is fortified by the event of Ida's doubling: Winnie is equal to the excess of Ida's twinning. Initially, Ida, Ida-Ida, and Winnie seem to form a neat Freudian psychic trinity. Ida is the disorganized, vague, and nomadic id. Ida-Ida is the organizing, reflexive ego. Winnie, Ida and Ida-Ida's successful social avatar, is their collective superego: Winnie is the name everyone remembers. Yet Stein does not allow such an easy correspondence to stick. Soon after the Idas are united, they are suddenly alienated from each other, and Ida is alone again. At this point, she wonders whether she is one or many. The plurality of her existence, once so apparent, is now a disorienting question. She is not quite one and not quite multiple, and so she reconciles her ability to be both alone and with herself by talking to herself and by saying her own name. Ida's experimental doubling and tripling only ever achieve a temporary sense of a complete identity; what Stein's Ida-mass achieves in the novel is a vague and catastrophic theory of becoming-identity. Ida imagines that there is another step after the confusing experience of being recognized and named by the other: recognizing and naming oneself from a set of selves. It is the very notion of an authentic or original self that Ida disproves in her multiplications and imitations.

In the middle of the novel, Ida reflects at length on all the dogs she has known in her life. (At this point, the narration changes temporarily to a first-person account.) Her relationships with dogs are evidently a critical function of how she remembers and organizes her life, and also how she distinguishes lived experience from dream. During the catalogue of dogs, Ida remembers Basket, who comes to live with her and another dog, Never Sleeps:

> She met a white poodle he was still young and he never had a puppy life because he had not been well. His name was Basket and he looked like one. He was taken to visit Never Sleeps and they were told to be happy together. Never Sleeps was told to play with Basket and teach him how to play. Never Sleeps began, she had to teach catch if you can or tag, and she had to teach him pussy wants a corner and she taught him each one of them.
>
> She taught him tag and even after he played it and much later on when he was dead another Basket he looked just like him went on playing tag. To play tag you have to be able to run forward and back to run around things and to start one way and to go the other way and another dog who is smaller and not so quick has to know how to wait at a corner and go around the other way to make the distance shorter. And sometimes just to see how well tag can be played the bigger quicker dog can even stop to play with a stick or

bone and still get away and not be tagged. That is what it means
to play tag and Never Sleeps taught Basket how to play. Then he
taught him to play pussy wants a corner. (105–106)

Basket was the name of Stein and Toklas's white poodle, as well as
the name of the second white poodle that replaced the first when he
died. The intimacy afforded by a dog's acquaintance demonstrated,
for Stein, an exemplary method of being a relation. Being a relation
requires that one remembers and recognizes both the other and the
self. If identity is (a) play, then it is also, or more precisely, the rhythm
or equilibrium between players. In the game of tag, the one who is
"it" is "it" until the moment of transfer, through touch, with an other.
There can be no precise moment at which both or neither players are
"it": it, in itself, is a relation. To play tag successfully, you have to keep
moving: you have to run in all directions and be willing to start again
from any position.

Objects

Following her earlier novelistic texts, Stein turned her interest to portraiture, a compositional mode that occupied her for the rest of her life. Writing in this mode, Stein was concerned with the relationship between the activity of composing and the thing composed, and, more specifically, whether this relationship could describe or engage with a subject in a manner apart from representation. It can be variously figured that the subject of a portrait is the object of representation, or that the subjects of portraits are objects as perceived (and hence objectified) by the portrait maker. In the sense that the subject of any aesthetic work is necessarily objectified in order that it may even be considered a subject, the subject-object dynamic is always complicated.

Yet in the conventions of Western metaphysics and certainly in the conventions of English grammar, there is a great investment in the distinction of subject and object. The subject is active and the object is passive; the subject is the one that experiences, and the object is the thing that is experienced; the subject knows and the object is known. For Whitehead, the subject-object split is a fundamental presupposition of the "bifurcation of nature," an abstraction in which the world is imagined as the interplay of two distinct realms: one comprising matter and the other comprising qualities and attributes. In a bifurcated world, the subject is the one who grants meaning to otherwise passive matter by designating and attributing its various qualities. The subject, therefore, is necessary in order that an object may be perceived and understood as meaningful, and the object is necessary in order that the subject's life may be furnished with meaningful things. Stein, like Whitehead, rejects this schema. Alongside a number of her contemporaries, Stein's work argues against the assumptions necessary for representational models of subject-object relations. Stein's work operates according to two kinds of logic—the metaphysical and the grammatical—in order to propose and demonstrate the inextricability of subjects and objects. What this means, very basically, is that Stein's poetics is populated by a great number of subjects and objects, often in uncertain or unintelligible relations to themselves, each other, and any potential or emergent narrative.

The subjects of Stein's portraits, invariably flagged by explicit and directive titles, are immediately problematized as subjects per se in texts that refuse explicit or direct representational description, whether we understand such description in terms of naturalism, impressionism, expressionism, or surrealism. Even the ism most often equated with Stein's aesthetics—cubism—has a recognizable (deconstructive) representational principle. Stein, on the other hand, despite her tendency to proclaim compositional axioms, cannot be said to have a particular representational principle as the motor of her poetics. This is not to say that Stein's work is bereft of subjects and objects in affective relations, or of experience, meaning, or the processes of perception. Quite the opposite: Stein's work wholly comprises such things. What she fails to do is synthesize these things in constructions that describe the privileged experience of a perceiving subject negotiating a world of objects. It is on this matter that Stein is most usefully compared to Whitehead, whose philosophical system admits objects and subjects only after significant and careful redefinition.

For Whitehead, there are different kinds of objects: sense-objects, perceptual objects, physical objects, and scientific objects.[1] Using Whitehead's own example of a blue coat, the coat's blueness consti-

---

1. See the chapter "Objects" in *The Concept of Nature* for a full account of Whitehead's different categories (143–163).

tutes a sense-object, its "coatness" constitutes a perceptual object, and the particularity of a specific blue coat in a specific situation constitutes a physical object. Scientific objects refer to the smaller constituents, such as atoms, which are understood to contribute to the object in its sensed, perceived, and actualized situations. Although Whitehead carefully orders these objects (such that the perceptual object presupposes sense-objects, and the physical object presupposes sense-objects and perceptual objects), the order does not designate the way in which an object can be said to be an object per se— does not, in other words, suggest an ontological hierarchy of lower- and higher-order subjects. Rather, the order of object types simply describes the different events and the manner by which they come into relation such that a blue coat, for example, is perceived. The order denotes the degree to which the events rely on habit such that an object emerges as an object of experience via various kinds of complex responsive and suggestive processes. One perceives a certain blue and one perceives a certain coatlike object: thus one perceives a particular blue coat. Whitehead elaborates:

> Consider a blue coat, a flannel coat of Cambridge blue belonging to some athlete. The coat itself is a perceptual object and its situation is not what I am talking about. We are talking of someone's definite sense-awareness of Cambridge blue as situated in some event of nature. He may be looking at the coat directly. He then sees Cambridge blue as situated practically in the same event as the coat at that instant. It is true that the blue which he sees is due to light which left the coat some inconceivably small fraction of a second before. This difference would be important if he were looking at a star whose colour was Cambridge blue. The star might have ceased to exist days ago, or even years ago. The situation of the blue will not then be very intimately connected with the situ-

ation. . . . This disconnexion of the situation of the blue and the situation of some associated perceptual object does not require a star for its exemplification. Any looking glass will suffice. Look at the coat through a looking glass. Then blue is seen as situated behind the mirror. The event which is its situation depends upon the position of the observer.

The sense-awareness of the blue as situated in a certain event which I call the situation, is thus exhibited as the sense-awareness of a relation between the blue, the percipient event of the observer, the situation, and intervening events. All nature is in fact required, though only certain intervening events require their characters to be of certain definite sorts. (*Concept of Nature* 152–153)

Whitehead begins with the first recognizable object, Cambridge blue. Whether or not the athlete perceives the blue as he looks down at his coat or as he studies his reflection in the mirror—whether or not the athlete recognizes the blue in the coat or in an image of the coat—the object is a certain blue. It is not an abstract idea of a shade of blue, but a blue that is recognizable in the situation of its perception. For Whitehead, very simply, objects are things that can "be again." Thus one can come to recognize a color as specific as Cambridge blue by this fact of its capacity to be recognized as such—that is to say, by its capacity to be again in different contexts. James makes a similar point in *Principles of Psychology*: "What is got twice is the same OBJECT. We hear the same note over and over again; we see the same quality of green, or smell the same objective perfume, or experience the same species of pain. The realities, concrete and abstract, physical and ideal, whose permanent existence we believe in, seem to be constantly coming up again before our thought, and lead us, in our carelessness, to suppose that our 'ideas' are the same ideas" (231). Thus, he continues, "no two 'ideas' are the same" (235), which corresponds immediately to Whitehead's revision of Heraclitus's maxim: "No thinker thinks twice; and, to put it more generally, no subject experiences twice" (*Process and Reality* 29). While Whitehead's point is that a subject is always becoming, and James's is that ideas cannot be reproduced or repeated, the convergence here is on the matter of objects: objects are the things in experience which can be said *to be again*.

The athlete can recognize the blue again and again, so the blueness of his coat is an object. So too can the coatness be recognized, both as pertaining to a virtual, abstract category of coats and to an actual situation in which this one coat endures. Whitehead's point is that a blue coat is not finally located, nor is it reducible to its coordinates as a physical object: a blue coat is a confluence of object-events—each its own situation and each its own experience. Its objecthood is plastic. It is not an inert mass onto which a history of thinking-coat is projected. It is its own eventful history, and as such, it affects the one who perceives it (even from its reflected mirror image) and is affected in turn. Whitehead's object is any entity that affects, and is affected by, an experiencing subject, wherein the categories of both object and subject are unfixed and relational. In other words, any "thing" is an object when it is a factor in experience; hence any subject may be an object, and any object may be a subject. The distinction matters only insofar as it relates to a particular activity of a given situation. However, any situation will include many different events and experiences, so the objects and subjects in affective relations for any given occasion will always be multiple, and not necessarily reciprocal. Since objects can "be again," they are integral in the experience of continuity and particularity in the world: objects are the entities that ensure that the experience of a world-in-process is not mere flux and flow. The ongoingness of any object is at once an abstraction (since even at an elemental level, as Whitehead points out, atoms are always shifting around) and an actuality (since it is possible to recognize an entity by its particularity, as the athlete can recognize a certain blue coat).

Critically, Whitehead's metaphysical system de-emphasizes human consciousness. From a cosmological perspective, the fact of conscious human experience represents a tiny and rare portion of experience, and because of this, he cautions, human experience should not serve as the only model or principal exemplar of experience. When reading Whitehead, one ought not to assume that his subjects are human, or conscious. The way a nonhuman and nonconscious subject (for example, a rock or electron) perceives events and situations is, in itself, a kind of "experience." The relational affectivity of objects and subjects is "the fundamental structure of experience" ("Objects and Subjects" 130), and there is nothing that is not, in some manner, experiencing and being experienced. Therefore, all objects are also experiencing subjects, and all experiencing subjects are the objects of other experiences. From this recast notion of the subject-object relation, Whitehead builds a metaphysics that does not privilege the human subject. Considering what this de-emphasis means for language and literature and, in particular, for a kind of "poetics of objects," I will look at examples in which language refuses the ontological predicate of the human subject.

On the one hand, I am referring quite literally to grammar, since grammar in its organization of language according to conventions of signification already includes so many presumptions about the nature of experience. Also, I am talking about the broader implications of a poetics that works against the logics of representation. To doubly refuse the ontological implications of grammar as well as the ontological demands of representation is what is required in order to attempt to get at a poetics of objects, a poetics that focuses on the objects of experience rather than the construction of the lyric subject.

For Whitehead, "objectification" refers to the process through which experience becomes the stuff for future experience. A poetics of objects registers this process by attending to the various ways experience is objectified, that is, *actualized* in and through language. I argue that Stein's work is a good place to begin a discussion about a kind of poetry and a kind of language practice that designates experience (including thinking, writing, speaking, and reading) as objects as well as events. If, thinking with Whitehead, objects, subjects, and events are considered relational entities, the relation between an event, its percipient subject, and the object(s) perceived is both an event and a thing. Here we have something resembling a "radical empiricist" position, in which it is insisted that relations are things in themselves. Such a position has interesting implications for poetic language: no longer is there a definite distinction between content and form, image and text, symbol and referent, subject and object; rather, the language occasions experience.

Jan D. Kucharzewski has written on the relationship between Stein's writing and quantum physics. At the beginning of his essay "There is no 'there' there," Kucharzewski carefully situates his inquiry: "I would like to use the concepts and vocabulary of quantum mechanics as metaphors for and not as an explanation of certain aspects of Stein's writing" (500). Brian Massumi, when writing about the quantum in *Parables for the Virtual*, asserts the very opposite: "The use of the quantum outside quantum mechanics, even as applied to human psychology, is not a metaphor. For each level, it is necessary to find an operative concept for the objective indeterminacy that echoes what on the subatomic level goes by the name of quantum" (37). On this matter I am in accordance with Massumi: the relationship between, for example, Stein and Niels Bohr is not properly described as metaphorical. Their affinities and shared concerns, as well as their radically different methods and investments, point to an open field of inquiry, in which emergent theories and praxes engage with contemporary questions of thinking and existing. Despite my disagreement with the framing of Kucharzewski's metaphorical approach, his study of Stein and physics is elucidating.

While he points out that "a direct connection between Stein and quantum physics is not detectable, since large amounts of her work chronologically precede the publication of the most significant breakthroughs in this field," Kucharzewski nevertheless tracks an important link between Stein and Bohr in the philosophy of William James (500). Drawing on Gerald Holton's thesis in *Thematic Origins of Scientific Thought*, Kucharzewski suggests that Bohr was both familiar with and influenced by James's theories of consciousness, as explicated in the "Stream of Thoughts" chapter of *The Principles of Psychology*. Neither Holton nor Kucharzewski claims an explicit relationship between Bohr's apparent enthusiasm for James and his quantum theory. Nevertheless, as they both show, the correspondences are generative: "Similar to Bohr, whose quantum theory suggests a holistic universe in which the observer is as much a part of an experimental setup as the object which is supposed to be studied, James discusses the impossibility of the objectivization of thought"—or, in other words, "James points out the difficulty of objectively thinking about thinking [and] Bohr raises the issue of objective observation" (502).

Stein, by Kucharzewski's account, composed in a manner that rendered language analogous to quantum entities: Stein's constantly shifting but seemingly repetitious compositions demonstrate the impossibility of definitively locating or fixing any entity under observation. Yet through minimal movements and contradictory propositions—processes of abstraction—Stein's entities emerge. That is, Stein's writing actually produces the objects of its study. Thus, according to Kucharzewski, "a first intersection between Stein's mod-

ernism, James's *Principles of Psychology*, and Bohr's quantum interpretations emerges: the question of the relationship between subject
and object, representation and referent, human consciousness and
reality" (502). From this "first intersection," Kucharzewski considers
the three thinkers for their corresponding theories of what Bohr
called "complementarity": Bohr argued that it was impossible to "simultaneously demonstrate the wave characteristics and the particle
characteristics of an electron"; nevertheless, these characteristics are
not contradictory but complementary. James had used the same term
to describe the nonsimultaneity of experience in the different consciousness of patients with multiple-personality disorder (504). Citing an example from her lecture "Pictures," in which one sentence
presents two clauses that are almost exactly the same except for
minor punctuation and so produce two distinct meanings, Kucharzewski writes: "By shifting the emphasis of two lexically identical
[clauses], two opposing thoughts are expressed. With regard to quantum mechanics it can be argued that Stein perceives words as pure
potentials and, like James and Bohr, emphasizes the importance of
the context in which they appear" (509).[2]

Ultimately, for Kucharzewski, the reader of Stein is "confronted
with a quantum paradox: the dichotomy between Stein's emphasis
on the phonetic (and thus the physical, material, and fixed) aspects
of language and her concern with the 'continuous present,' that is,
the constant resemantization of her words and dematerializations of
meanings" (508). But this readerly experience is actually neither a

---

2. The sentence from "Pictures" that Kucharzewski refers to is the last in the following
paragraph: "There is the oil painting in its frame, a thing in itself. There it is and it has to
look like people or objects or landscapes. Besides that it must not completely only exist
in its frame. It must have its own life. And yet it may not move or imitate movement, not
really, nor must it stay still. It must not only be in its frame, but it must not, only, be in
its frame" (*LA* 87).

paradox nor a dichotomy, for in the context of complementarity, Stein's texts constitute, and are constitutive of, both "phonetic particles and semantic waves" (508). I would add that rather than imagining this complementarity as straddling an abstract distinction between materiality and immateriality, it would be efficacious to imagine that Stein's quantum language operates in virtual and actual realms. This reduces the tendency to imagine that there is an ontological difference between matter and meaning, and hence between the material of language and its emergent significations.

Karen Barad, writing in similar territories (though not to do with Stein), argues that there are two dominant conceptions of language in contemporary critical discourse: on the one hand, there is the language that adheres to a Newtonian grammar-scape, in which subject-predicate signification settles in fixed meanings; on the other hand there is the language that decenters, destabilizes, deconstructs, and delimits the fixing processes of meaning. For Barad, neither conception attends to the actual relation of matter and meaning; thus she suggests instead that a "performative" theory and practice of language is needed in order to avoid a perpetually bifurcated reality. "A *performative* understanding of discursive practices," by Barad's account, "challenges the representationalist belief in the power of words to represent preexisting things. Unlike representationalism, which positions us above or outside the world we allegedly merely reflect on, a performative account insists on the understanding thinking, observing, and theorizing as practices of engagement with, and as part of, the world in which we have our being" (*Meeting the Universe Halfway* 133). In *Touching Feeling*, Eve Sedgwick, reflecting on her own theory of performativity, corroborates Barad's account:

> I assume that the line between words and things or between linguistic and nonlinguistic phenomena is endlessly changing,

See also
Bodies
(pp. 41–44)

permeable, and entirely unsusceptible to any definitive articulation.... However I have an inclination to deprecate the assign-
ment of a very special value, mystique, or thingness to meaning
and language. Many kinds of objects and events mean, in many
heterogeneous ways and contexts, and I see some value in not
reifying or mystifying the linguistic kinds of meaning unnecessarily. (5)

If we consider Stein's poetry as "performative," we no longer need
to decide whether her work affirms or refuses meaning, or whether
it affirms or refuses material reality. The objects that occupy Stein's
work—cakes, butter, apples, dogs, roses, and so on—do not represent specific objects in an external reality, nor do they speak of a
purely linguistic realm of universal "cakeness," "butterness," "apple-
ness," "dogness," or "roseness." Similarly, as Isabelle Stengers writes,
Whiteheadian objects are "the 'respondents' of 'that which' we recog-
nise, name, judge, and compare: that is, what these operations answer to and also what can eventually answer for them. Yet although
they exhibit themselves as abstract or permanent, they cannot be iso-
lated from the concrete event, which for its part, passes without return" (79). A cake in a poem is not a cake elsewhere, nor is it, mimet-
ically speaking, a representation of cake. The metaphysical question,
for Stengers, is not whether this or that cake is general or particular,
but the fact that a cake-object can be said to be recognized as such:
in Whitehead's terms, a cake is a cake because it can *be a cake again*.
The matter and meaning that contribute to a cake's objecthood, in
different ways and as a relation, make it possible to recognize a cake
in a poem as something that is recognizable even if it has no external
reference or internal description.

The affinity between Stein's poetic interventions and the innovations in the physical sciences occurring contemporaneously were no-

ticed immediately. As Dydo reports, in 1928 poet Dorothy Dudley Harvey wrote to Stein from New York, where in the new issue of the *Saturday Review of Literature* Bertrand Russell's "Physics and Metaphysics" had just appeared. Harvey quotes from Russell and then suggests Stein as a visionary in the world of the new physics:

> "Nowadays, physicists, the most hard-headed of mankind . . . have embodied in their technique this insubstantiality which some of the metaphysicians have so long urged in vain."
>
> In connection with grammar I thought at once of you, and wondered, knowing little about them, if you have not been one of the metaphysicians as an artist, with whom the physicists have just caught up. (*ASR* 3)

The new physics had brought the hard sciences and metaphysics into a critical intimacy: considering the "insubstantiality" of phenomena, formerly considered a pursuit confined to philosophical inquiry, was suddenly a principal task of the twentieth-century scientist. What Harvey intuited in her letter to Stein is the connection between metaphysics and the description and construction of reality in language. Poetry offers a site for the study of this connection and its role in determining the nature and tendencies of lived experience and the activity of matter; poetry makes explicit the coexistence of complementary and incommensurate phenomena.

Lucretius provides an early example of the relation of language and metaphysics: his Epicurean poetics examined the atom for its capacity to account for materiality, including indeterminate or imperceptible objects and systems like language, weather, chaos, and thought. If air, dust, clouds, and mists affect material consequences (wind will ripple water, a mist will dampen grass), then their status as objects suggests that other obscure events are similarly objectlike, even if not given immediately to the senses. For Whitehead, an atom is an organism, and so too are subatomic particles and molecules. In *The Concept of Nature* he writes: "The electron is not merely where its charge is. The charge is the quantitative character of certain events due to the ingression of the electron into nature. The electron is its whole field of force. Namely the electron is the systematic way in which all events are modified as the expression of its ingression" (158–159). An electron is an organism because it refers to the "whole field of force" that is both affected by, and affects, its environment. Similarly, atoms and molecules are organisms in which the event-field is the object. Recasting the notion of the atom from an indivisible minimal unit of matter to an organism, further shifts the discourse of atomism such that material reality is composed of events and fields rather than small, solid bits. For Lucretius, units of language correspond to units of matter: letters are atoms, and meaning emerges from the assemblage of smaller units into comprehensive complexes (*On the Nature of the Universe* 54–55). Reading Lucretius via Whitehead and in the context of the new physics, an atomistic conception of language posits the units of language as organisms and, thus, posits the meaningfulness of language as emerging from the correspondences of organisms in dynamic and unfixed relations.

If, as I have argued, the early twentieth century was a crucial moment in the reimagining of science in relation to well-worn metaphysical questions, then the exact opposite is also true: the early twentieth century also resulted in a fissure between the hard sciences and metaphysical inquiry. The entanglement of physics and metaphysics has tended to privilege the hard sciences, working on the assumption that philosophy needs science in order to validate its claims to an external reality. And while science today is thoroughly invested in radical notions of indeterminacy and multiplicity, normative discourses around language and the grammar of signification remain rooted in the logics of a (Newtonian) world in which objects and sub-jects, time and space, matter and meaning, are distinct. Assumptions about how language is used and to what effect have not yet caught up with physics, which in turn has not yet reconciled its efforts with metaphysical questions and propositions: there is a kind of triply dis-sonant temporal lag between discourses of physical, metaphysical, and linguistic reality.

I propose that the objects in Stein's poems argue for the dy-namism of matter; in this respect, Stein is close to the "posthumanist performativity" that mobilizes Barad's theory of "agential realism." Barad characterizes performativity as an alternative to representa-tionalism: instead of focusing on the veracity of the correspondence between description and reality, performativity focuses on the "prac-tices, doings, and actions" that are co-constitutive of reality and its many descriptions (*Meeting the Universe Halfway* 135). Moving away from representationalist theories of the human subject as the central and uniquely meaningful agent of experience and conscious reality, Barad's call for a *posthumanist realism* requires that the category of the subject of experience is broadened to include both human and nonhuman agents (while acknowledging that agential experience is necessarily radically varied and variable). Barad's construction not only seeks to move away from representationalism as a metaphysics; it also attempts to rejoin critical accounts of physical and metaphys-ical reality. In this way, Barad's inquiry converges with Whitehead's, since both refuse the bifurcation of nature and the countless reso-nant binaries that are produced in its wake. For example, as Barad points out, the distinction between animate and inanimate objects has persisted even in non-normative configurations of materiality and agency: "It takes a radical rethinking of agency to appreciate how lively even 'dead matter' can be" (*Meeting the Universe Halfway* 419 n. 27). In developing her theory of posthumanist and performative agential realism, Barad leans heavily on Bohr's philosophical-physical propositions. According to Barad, Bohr necessarily revised Democritean atomism: whereas the Democritean (and so the Epicurean and Lucretian) doctrine figured the world as comprising compounds and admixtures of tiny, indivisible units of matter, Bohr's model of the atom refuses the fixity and certainty of boundaries and properties. For Bohr, therefore, atoms and the things they constitute are *phenomena*. "Things" have no inherent and determinate coordinates, properties, or meanings; location and identity are always approximate because phenomena are eventful.

See also
Identity
(pp. 119–121)

At this point, it is necessary to mention the considerable body of work that has emerged in the last few decades, more or less under the rubric of "thing theory." Bill Brown's editorial introduction for *Critical Inquiry*'s 2001 special issue titled "Things" includes a comprehensive intellectual history. Brown traces the various distinctions made between things and objects: whereas objects remain (perhaps unfortunately) tethered to the realm of the human subject, who perceives and so objectifies phenomena so as to "use" them in the service of meaningful experience, things are never able to be fully perceived but rather are what elude objectification and problematize their own use-value in the construction of meaning. Thus, for Brown, "we look through objects because there are codes by which our interpretive attention makes them meaningful, because there is a discourse of objectivity that allows us to use them as facts" ("Thing Theory" 4). Things, then, can be understood as

> what is excessive in objects, as what exceeds their mere materialization as objects or their mere utilization as objects—their force as a sensuous presence or as a metaphysical presence, the magic by which objects become values, fetishes, idols, and totems. Temporalized as the before and after of the object, thingness amounts

to a latency (the not yet formed or the not yet formable) and to an excess (what remains physically or metaphysically irreducible to objects). But this temporality obscures the all-at-onceness, the si- multaneity, of the object/thing dialectic and the fact that, all at once, the thing seems to name the object just as it is even as it names some thing else. (5, emphasis in original)

Brown's distinction calls to mind Heidegger's own attempt in "The Thing" to differentiate things and objects (*Poetry, Language, Thought*). Thinking specifically of an earthenware jug, Heidegger perceives the jug's thingness as its capacity for containment, that is, its capacity to be a container (literally, to hold and to facilitate pouring) as well as its capacity to be self-contained (to hold on, to keep holding, to be inde- pendently holding even when not in use for pouring) (164). The jug is a thing when it is a vessel, and it becomes an object only if and when it is present alongside a subject who takes it up in use. For Heidegger, there seems a strict, if vague, ontological organization of things and objects via vessels, tools, and equipment. An object is a thing with a determinate and determined function. In the case of *dysfunction*, an object's relation remains a meaningful one, for only insofar as it can be "taken up" can it be designated as an object, even if it ultimately fails to function in its designation (164–167).

In basic terms, Brown seems to agree with Heidegger: things are in excess of objects, which exist only when they have been objectified. But ultimately Brown's account is far less concerned with the human subject who perceives, names, uses, and is failed by objects: Brown's "thing theory" approaches the subject-object relation from the other side, by considering the process by which the subject emerges from a world of objects and things. Brown tracks the trend, in much West- ern philosophy, of situating the subject as prior to the object: that which decides on the object. He then tracks the oppositional strain of contemporary thought which argues that subjects and objects are co-constitutive of each other. Brown appeals to Latour, whose adoption of Serres's terms "quasi-subject" and "quasi-object" represents a recent and major revision of object theory ("Thing Theory" 12).

For Serres (*The Parasite*) and Latour (*We Have Never Been Modern*), quasi-objects are the objectlike relations that mediate experience, and quasi-subjects are the subjectlike objects that experience the relation and its mediation. The quasi-subject is redolent of Whitehead's superject—the subject that becomes via experience of a phenomenal world—and includes but is not restricted to humans. In *The Parasite*, Serres introduces the concept of the quasi-object and - subject by way of an analogy with games like Button, Button, Who's Got the Button, or Hunt the Slipper, in which a small object is passed between players or else hidden, and the aim, very simply, is to locate the object and to commit it again to circulation. In these kinds of games, the player wants to simultaneously possess the object and keep it in motion, keep it as a relation in play. Serres writes of Hunt the Slipper, in which the object is known as a *furet* (ferret):

> This quasi-object is not an object, but it is one nevertheless, since it is not a subject, since it is in the world; it is also a quasi-subject, since it marks or designates a subject who, without it, would not be a subject. He who is not discovered with the furet in his hand is anonymous, part of a monotonous chain where he remains undistinguished. He is not an individual; he is not recognized, discovered, cut; he is of the chain and in the chain. He runs, like the furet, in the collective. The thread in his hands is our simple relation, the absence of the furet; its path makes our indivision. Who are we? Those who pass the furet; those who don't have it. This quasi-object, when being passed, makes the collective, if it stops,

it makes the individual. If he is discovered, he is "it" [*mort*]. Who is the subject, who is an "I," or who am I? The moving furet weaves the "we," the collective; if it stops, it marks the "I." (225)

Steven Connor, tracing similar territory to Brown in his essay "Thinking Things," cites this same passage from Serres and adds: "The most important thing about quasi-objects is that they travel" (5). The quasi-object is a thing that moves between, divides, yokes, mediates, hyphenates, appears alongside, and brings together subjects. Quasi-objects "stabilise or instantiate social forms and processes that, without them, would be too fleeting to endure" (5). Objects and subjects are not only relational, but are also relations in themselves. Their status as objects or subjects emerges from their traveling and circulating. Brown concludes his essay by appealing to Theodor Adorno's "argument against epistemology's and phenomenology's subordination of the object and the somatic moment to a fact of consciousness" (12). By Brown's account, Adorno "understood the alterity of things as an essentially ethical fact. Most simply put, his point is that accepting the otherness of things is the condition for accepting otherness as such" (12).

Thus a thing's otherness is never fully or finally disclosed. Properly speaking, the objects that occupy Stein's language are *things*, for they are always in excess of their own representability and assimilability. Stein's poetics is interested in the becoming of things and not in the representation of worldly objects. Her portraits are portraits of things in their habitual vagueness and obscurity—things that contribute to, circulate within, and problematize experience and its relation to language. Stein's portraits are portraits not only because they are "studies" in objects, subjects, scenes, and events, but also because the compositional process was an object for study. Stein made a careful distinction between the material sources and conscious preparation that implicitly affect the act of writing, which is always something other than the expression of one's own experience or intentions.

By her own account, Stein's portraits were unanticipated studies: she composed alongside, with, and toward otherness. As Meyer notes, there is something Romantic about Stein's assertion that writing occurs in a moment of "sudden creative recognition" (*Irresistible Dictation* xv). And yet, again following Meyer, Stein's concept of this "sudden creative recognition" differed critically from Romantic tropes of poetry as "overflow" (xv). For the Romantics, the poet is positioned centrally; it is the poet who overflows and who synthesizes the excess and ecstasy of a world that fills the poet and impels her to expression. For Stein, the composition is positioned centrally; the poet's "sudden recognition" is not recognition of the self, but recognition of the situation of finding oneself in the activity of writing. Such recognition is sudden because it is unanticipated, and not because it happens in a flash: one might suddenly recognize that one is writing, even if one never quite recognizes *what* one is writing. To orient oneself in relation to the composition and to write from this orientation seems to be the task of Stein's model poet. The recognition is "creative" in that it generates thinking, in and of the text.

Meyer aligns Stein's shifting of the poet from the center to the periphery of writing with William James's "philosophical attitude" of radical empiricism (Meyer, *Irresistible Dictation* 11). James asserts that in its radical mode "an empiricism must neither admit into its constructions any element that is not directly experienced, nor exclude from them any element that is directly experienced" (*Radical Empiricism* 20). For the radical empiricists (among whom Meyer counts Stein as a member) *"the relations that connect experiences must themselves be experienced relations, and any kind of relation experienced must be accounted as 'real' as anything else in the system"* (20, emphasis in original). Stein's sense of how writing emerges from and produces new, real relations was in the manner of a radical empiricist: she was continually and emphatically invested in making truth claims, which she was always willing to modify or abandon, and she was confident that such a methodology was necessary for registering the experiences of a world in process.

Stein's writing doesn't attempt to describe the world in a way that seeks to explain away disjunctive experiences. Indeed, for Stein, as well as for Whitehead and James, these disjunctive experiences are what constitute a world. As long as the notion of experience is not tethered to (human) consciousness, the world can be described in terms of the experiences of subjects. Stein's portraiture is therefore a study of writing around a set of relations. For example, in "A Box," from the "Objects" section of *Tender Buttons*, Stein writes:

> Out of kindness comes redness and out of rudeness comes rapid same question, out of an eye comes research, out of selection comes painful cattle. So then the order is that a white way of being round is something suggesting a pin and it is disappointing, it is not, it is so rudimentary to be analysed and see a fine substance strangely, it is so earnest to have a green point not to red but to point again. (*TB* 4)

This "A Box" precedes a second poem of the same name. The second "A Box," which appears two pages later, reads, in part:

> A large box is handily made of what is necessary to replace any substance. Suppose an example is necessary, the plainer it is made the more reason there is for some outward recognition that there is a result.
>
> A box is made sometimes and them to see to see to it neatly and to have the holes stopped up makes it necessary to use paper.

A custom which is necessary when a box is used and taken is
that a large part of the time there are three which have different
connections. The one is on the table. The two are on the table. The
three are on the table. The one, one is the same length as it is
shown by the cover being longer. The other is different there is
more cover that shows it. The other is different and that makes the
corners have the same shade the eight are in singular arrangement
to make four necessary. (6–7)

It is unclear whether the "A Box" poems are two parts of one poem,
translations or alternate versions of each other, or two distinct poems
with the same name. Since Stein has an enduring interest in twinning, or doubling, we might imagine that naming two poems with
one title, such that the question of sameness is raised even despite
obvious difference, would have appealed to Stein as a vague kind of
riddle. In fact, all the poems in *Tender Buttons* might be read as riddles, in which the "answer" is given first in the title and the clues are
distributed ambiguously throughout the text, pointing like evidence
in all directions. But I must be careful here. To suggest that the title-
poem relation is analogous to the answer-clue relation of a riddle is
also to suggest that Stein's poems are cryptograms. While they may
very well invite cryptographic readings, and may yield many instances of laudable cryptogrammatic readings, it is always the case
that such readings will be hypothetical. Therefore, if each portrait
can be said to be riddlelike, it is because the poem impels a reader to
read riddles in every sentence, and not because a total system of riddles at the end of the poem will point back to the title. If a reader is
convinced by a conclusion it is because the labor of generating a
framework that accounts for every variable and relation is in itself a
pleasurable achievement. But the pleasure is in the effort, surely, and
not in the application of that framework to the poem in order to fix

its meaning, for that would foreclose the enduring promise of the poem: that it will continue to be riddlelike.

If the riddles of *Tender Buttons* are open-ended and proliferating, the question is, what do they do other than elude any impulse for closure? There is something else at play in the relation of the objects in the poems. In "A Box" and "A Box" there seem to be two very different experimentations in writing a box. The first portrait is utterly vague, suggesting, in run-on syntax, the inexplicit facticity of things coming from other things, things contradicting and coexisting, things admitting affect. If Stein was writing of or beside a box, she is taking the box as a broad virtual category: a box is a container as well as its states of fullness or emptiness; a box is a shape as well as a design; a box is a binary machine that is either open or closed; a box is a constructed object or an improvised interior; a box is a bounded concept or an organizing logic. In this portrait, Stein engages with the box as phenomena (again, the plural is intended). Thinking of the poem in terms of the phenomena of a box does not demand that the portrait choose whether it is describing the ideal box or an actual box. In fact, it problematizes this distinction as a distinction per se. "A Box" is a composition that takes the phenomena of a box as its prompt, and considers the activity of the composition as a network of relations concerning this phenomena. In the second "A Box," a different tact is evident: this portrait comprises multiple propositions concerning a box—it is both a list poem and a thought experiment. The poem asks in what way, and to what end, the phenomena of the box can be catalogued by a string of positional descriptions. If it is possible to list a variety of ways in which a box can be found functioning as a box per se, is it then possible to abstract a shortlist of probable situations for a box? And if so, would this shortlist then describe a virtual field that includes within it the local instances of actual boxes?

In the first portrait, the box is considered a phenomenal complex,

See also
Queering
(pp. 183–187)

and in the second a virtual box is constructed in order to hold and or-
ganize box-related concepts (for example, a graphic box, a cardboard
box, a rhetorical box, and a generic four-sided geometrical type).
Stein's task is not to exhaust the realm of boxes but to demonstrate
the breadth of phenomena and concepts that constitute objects. The
portraits defy an easy corroboration of title and text, but, at the same
time, the title-poem relation is not arbitrary. It is not the case that the
poems of Tender Buttons could be named otherwise, or substituted
for each other. "A Box" concerns a box, and "Roastbeef" concerns
roastbeef. This is categorically true because the relation between a
poem and its title is particular and eventful. Stein, in her convergences with the methods and orientations of radical empiricism,
wants to explore the facticity of her thinking and writing around objects, while also admitting that these facts are mutable and liable to
need modification.

Play

In its many variations "play" is a word close to Stein's poetics. She wrote, and wrote about, plays. Her work is often noted for its "word-play," and critics have regularly suggested an affinity with childhood games and children's literature. It has been read as an imperative to play with, or in, language, and as a result has been understood as a kind of exploration of language's sensual and ludic qualities.[1] In contrast, her apparent invocation to play has elsewhere been read as a disingenuous provocation; some critics have argued that her work fails to meet the expectations established by their claims to generic forms and styles and thus that her play is meaningless and self-defeating.[2] Other critics, most notably Perloff, have read Stein alongside the Wittgensteinian notion of the "language game"—in this context, Stein is perceived as a writer committed to the exploration of the infinite potentials of/for meaning of language-in-use ("'Grammar in Use'"). Wittgenstein proposes "language games" as ways of thinking philosophically about language without recourse to theories of language as external to language-in-use. For Wittgenstein, language is participatory, contextual, emergent, and negotiated—its meanings are situated. Perloff demonstrates that context can always be imagined or reconstructed; I argue that Stein's interest in language-play is

See also

Grammar

(pp. 101–103)

---

1. See, for example, Elizabeth Fifer's "Is Flesh Advisable? The Interior Theater of Gertrude Stein"; Shari Benstock's "Beyond the Reaches of Feminist Criticism: A Letter from Paris"; and Lisa Ruddick's *Body, Text, Gnosis: Reading Gertrude Stein*.

2. Sylva Norman, for example, wrote of *Useful Knowledge*: "If Miss Stein's useful knowledge points out anything, it is that the loafing mind, equipped with language, can read a triumph of chaotic imbecility" (qtd. in Reid, *Art by Subtraction* 10).

more locally invested in the intracontextual relations of language in a particular poem, portrait, novel, play, or essay. In this study, Stein's playfulness is not merely a "playing with" language but something like *playing-as-writing*.

In her lecture "Plays" Stein describes how she came to write plays and operas. While she had enjoyed the theater in her youth, she recalls that by the time she began to write plays herself, she was no longer in the habit of going to see them. Her interest had shifted to writing plays, and, more specifically, to how writing plays differed from other kinds of writing. By her own account, her switch from writing portraits to writing plays was not permanent: when she felt that she had done all she could in composing plays, she returned to composing portraits. Her plays signify a temporary, albeit productive, excursion into dramatic composition with the explicit aim of investigating the relationship between drama and composition, action and writing. The lecture opens with a thesis: in a play, "the thing seen and the emotion did not go on together" (*LA* 94). That is, with "the thing seen and the thing felt about the thing seen not going on at the same tempo," one's "emotion" as a member of the audience is "never going on at the same time as the action of the play," and this asynchrony "makes anybody nervous" (93–95). Nervousness generates and is generated by the attempt to slow down or speed up in order to come into the same time as the action of a play: "Nervousness consists in needing to go faster or to go slower so as to get together. It is that that makes anybody feel nervous" (95). A play differs from other texts for this reason, since a play, as Stein notes, can be "read or heard or seen" there are a number of ways that one might experience the disjunctive temporalities of language, gesture, and "emotion" in action (94). In *Irresistible Dictation*, Steven Meyer proposes the term "neuroaesthetics" to refer to "the general condition of sensitivity to the physiological operations of one's own nervous system" (58).

Meyer reads Stein's work as being informed by her university studies on the brain's neural functions and nerve cells and, as such, engaged with language's neuroaesthetic affect: literally, the way language is registered in the body and excites the nervous system.[3] Read in this way, Stein's interest in the nervousness of the theater's disjunctive temporality can be understood as an interest in the neuroaesthetics of performativity.

Stein acknowledges that the experience of reading a play is entirely different to that of watching a play—even though each form gestures toward the other in its realization. Thus, for Stein, the *writing* of a play must engage with its own action; the one who writes a play must write with reading, hearing, and seeing in mind, and, further, must write according to the syncopated rhythms of its different potential iterations. The question of "emotion" is a difficult one to parse here, since Stein does not define what she means by such a term. Elsewhere she employs "emotion" to signify the affective dynamics of daily life—a broad term for the range of experience engaged in and through perception and cognition. The language in a text framed "as" a play always suggests the possibility of its actualization in performance—a performance that might, in any way, depart from the text in its scripted form. Thus a play, in its triple modality of a written, spoken, and performed text suggests for Stein an exemplary form for the investigation of emotional multiplicity. It is for this reason that Stein declares the language of a play "more lively"

See also
Grammar
(pp. 104–110)

3. Meyer notes that Stein's experiments in neuroscience at Harvard were contemporary with the development of the neuron doctrine. "The nervous system as characterized by the neuron doctrine is anatomically discontinuous and physiologically or functionally continuous, and as such it offers a model for an organicism that combines discontinuity and coherence. The sense of a whole, the overarching sense of acquaintance displayed in Stein's dissociative practices, may not correspond to any particular anatomical, or subanatomical, structure, yet it itself is a function of a properly functioning nervous system" (*Irresistible Dictation* 111).

than in other textual forms (*LA* 111). But her comparison is complex: a play written "in" poetry is more lively than other kinds of poetry; a play written in poetry is more lively than a play written "in" prose; and a play written "in" prose is less lively than other kinds of prose. From this we can deduce that the liveliest words are the words written *in* poetry *for* plays. Their liveliness is what makes them nerve-racking: lively words are unpredictable players. Liveliness thus marks an important difference between a story and a play in Stein's compositional theory: by her own account, a story attempts to explain what is happening or has already happened, whereas a play engages with action one does not know is happening—that is, action still in the process of happening.

Stein conceived the play as kind of *landscape*—a spatiotemporal context for drama. I take Stein's use of the word "landscape" here as referring to a kind of framing, an approach to contextualizing occasions of contemporary events in a particular duration. According to Stein, a landscape always remains a landscape, despite what occurs or changes; in this way, a landscape is "indifferent" to its own action. Thus while a landscape frames a set of coexisting durations, it is not reducible to any one of its constitutive objects or events. A landscape is an abstraction that flattens, to use another word from Stein, its contingent durations such that they may be perceived as an arrangement of coalescent instances. Hejinian, writing on Stein, suggests that "no condition, or set or array of conditions, achieves a finalized form of landscape—which makes landscape an exemplary case, a spread of examples" (*Language of Inquiry* 105). "Landscape" suggests the virtual and actual range of activities copresent locationally and durationally: drawing a frame around a landscape, like naming a text a play, is a moment of performative definition, from which a particular kind of attention emerges: an attention to the relation of objects and events in a space of time.

In the introduction to *Last Operas and Plays*, Bonnie Marranca writes of Stein's plays that the "pictorial composition replaces dramatic action, emphasizing frontality and the frame, flatness and absence of perspective" (*LOP* xi). Marranca's analysis figures Stein's plays in their relation to landscape as attentive to the artifice of framing and designating a "scene": just as a landscape painting (perhaps despite its efforts) is a study in the artifice of representation. Stein's equation of plays and landscapes is a way of framing her playwriting efforts as conscious of the construction of, to cite a title of one of her plays, "Scenes. Actions and Disposition of Relations and Positions" (*GP* 97–121). The collection *Geography and Plays*, selected by Stein and containing works written between 1908 and 1921, suggests in its title Stein's notion of the affinity between plays and landscapes. Geography is the study of formations, patterns, layerings, and interactions of human and nonhuman phenomena; geography is one way to describe the study of landscape. *Geography and Plays* can be read as a study of the relation between two distinct but affiliated modalities: the landscape, which frames the rhythms of the relation of space and time; and the play, which frames the rhythms of language in space and time. The works of *Geography and Plays*, like those in the later collections *Operas and Plays* and *Last Operas and Plays*, are variously and aberrantly "plays." Each problematizes the category of the play by way of variations on the typical cues of a script: characters are sometimes listed and sometimes not; directions are explicit, vague, or missing; large tracts of text are unattributed to a speaker; scenes and acts are numbered out of order or change illogically; dogs appear and sing. Marranca writes: "Within her frame, Stein played constantly with the idea of the authorial voice, the author's intention, and authority. Her plays demolish arguments about the correct way to do a play, because the relations among author, text, reader, and spectator are confounded by the structures of the works" (*LOP* xiii).

"Scenes. Actions and Disposition of Relations and Positions" was written in 1913 shortly after *Tender Buttons*, with which it shares many formal correspondences. It is composed in prose and arranged in paragraphs and employs a similar syntactical and logical structure as *Tender Buttons*: each sentence is more or less a proposition (*x* is *y*; *x* makes *y*; if *x*, then *y*). Unlike *Tender Buttons*, however (which is categorically not a play), "Scenes" comprises an excessive number of negative constructions, such that one can parse the logical proposition of each statement only by counting back through the negations in order to find what remains. These constructions are often complexly made: "Not a time when there is occupation not such a time is the time that is not used and a knock that has no intention has some hope. It is not open to stay" and "It is not the same that which is not sad with that which is repeated. It is not the same and the sight is so different that there is that hope and no more excitement. Then the change is there and there is all the comparison. The rising of the wedding is not the same as one child if there are no children but one child has that to use and there is enough to give it a cold. This is not seasonable. This is not the way to despair" (*GP* 97, 101).

In this play, there is "no mending, no mining, no motto, no mine, no pine, no purchase no salad no oyster, no practice, no more, no thought, no happy day and the best is there and there is everywhere" (113). This is a bit of a joke, though, because those things are in fact "there," even if by way of invoked absence. "Scenes" seems to investigate the ways in which a landscape can be framed in vague terms—through the process of elimination in a riddlelike description that needs to be read backward. Much of the language references temporal and locational "types": farms, tables, breakfasts, weather, birthdays, seasons, months, and so on. At one point, a single character called Thomas is seen (or, rather, the reader is invited to "see Thomas") to bring grain—this micropastoral moment lasts a tiny paragraph (108). The iterative negation seems to be a game: what is left at the end of this landscape or play?

In conceiving plays as landscapes, Stein argued that a play is, by nature, indifferent to its own action, including the emotional experiences of the audience:

> I felt that if a play was exactly like a landscape then there would be no difficulty about the emotion of the person looking on at the play being behind or ahead of the play because the landscape does not have to make acquaintance. You may have to make acquaintance with it, but it does not with you, it is there and so the play being written the relation between you at any time is so exactly that that it is of no importance unless you look at it. (*LA* 122)

Stein's reconfiguration of the relation between audience and text as a kind of uneven investment leads to a nervous audience, since the one who engages with the action of a play is never made certain of her role: her investments are unreturned by an apparently indifferent scene of action. Thinking of the play as a landscape, Stein perceived a way of redesigning the nervousness of engaging with a play so that it was less a nervous reaction to the action itself, and more a nervous affect generated by the event of being implicated in, but also excluded by, a scene of eventful relation. It seems, for Stein, that this nervous relation between an audience and a text was ideal for a compositional practice that worked against the assumption that emotional synchronicity is required for the comprehension of textual meaning. The play is a form that emphasizes the difference between the audience and the action, and thus problematizes the aim of synchronizing the two in the service of the transmission of narrative. A play is a landscape because its textuality, its being-play, is to be found in its abstraction "as" play. Because a play is a play, its activities are flattened so as to appear as a set of related actions coalescing as dramatic narrative. The simple act of framing a play as a play changes its language and activity, because a play is an entire site of a set of related actions and, further, because the outcomes of actions in relations cannot be predetermined, since the enactment of a script is never a mere reproduction of action. Thus the theater is a nervous place to be: one might never be sure what will happen. An actor or audience member might act out or act up; a line might be forgotten; a voice might falter; a thunderclap might intrude on the action; a scene might descend into disaster, hilarity, or farce.

Stein adds dances and battles, alongside plays, to her category of the landscape (cited in Hejinian, *Language of Inquiry* 110). Both dances and battles depend on bodies entering, departing, moving, and converging in space; yet neither a dance nor a battle is reducible to its bodies or its site—rather, dances and battles refer to the relation of bodies and sites. Stein's ongoing investigation into the nature of part-whole interplay accounts for her attraction to industrial and mechanical objects, such as cars and kitchen appliances, as well as her commitment to perceiving action as a landscape. Stein's fascination with automobiles is ultimately an appreciation of the cooperation of discrete components—including the one who drives—cohering as mobility. Her theory of the landscape as a mode of framing large-scale sequences or assemblages of potential relations and mobilities was ultimately an attempt to develop a compositional practice that generated its own energies and activities. Like dances and battles, plays occupy the very landscape that they become in their happening: a dance opens the field, a battle claims the ground, and a play sets the scene for the space of time.

See also
Bodies
(pp. 51–54)

In "Plays," Stein recalls how she came to compose her first play:

> I had just come home from a pleasant dinner party and I realized
> then as anybody can know that something is always happening.

Something is always happening, anybody knows a quantity of stories of people's lives that are always happening, there are always plenty for the newspapers and there are always plenty in private life. Everybody knows so many stories and what is the use of telling another story. What is the use of telling a story since there are so many and everybody knows so many and tells so many. So naturally what I wanted to do in my play was what everybody did not always know nor always tell.

I had before I began writing plays written many portraits. I had been enormously interested all my life in finding out what made each one that one and so I had written a great many portraits. I came to think that since each one is that one and that there are a number of them each one being that one, the only way to express this thing each one being that one and there being a number of them knowing each other was in a play. And so I began to write these plays. And the idea in What Happened, A Play, was to express this without telling what happened, in short to make a play the essence of what happened. (*LA* 119)

Essence is a difficult word to reconcile with Stein's poetics, which is often (including here in this study) read as being at odds with conceits of the essential. Dana Cairns Watson, whose critical survey is titled *Gertrude Stein and the Essence of What Happens*, suggests that essence in this instance can be read alongside its meanings in French, which include *petrol* and *gasoline* (66). The "essence" of "what happens" is that which makes the happening happen—the energy, fuel, or guts—of an eventful *something*. Whether Stein was consciously referring to French or not, her "essence" is a happening, not a substance—or perhaps, more properly, a substance in a state of perpetual happening, just like petrol burnt as fuel is in a perpetual state of peak activity. Watson cites critics who have read Stein's essence in the opposite direction, that is, as pertaining to quality and not activity. Betsy Alayne Ryan, for example, claims, "Gertrude Stein found that life was indeed a quality and not an action," and Kenneth Burke writes, "The essence of a thing would not be revealed in something that it does. It would be something that a thing is" (qtd. in Watson, *Gertrude Stein* 67). "In spite of these opinions," Watson writes, "I keep hearing 'what happens' as action, which reflects back on 'essence' and changes it into something more dynamic than an inherent truth about something" (67). Importantly, for Stein, the *essence of what happened* was a vague notion: it is not an essence that can be located, concentrated, extracted, or mined, but the broadest possible context for action to occur.

What Happened's five acts are split further into irregular sections, numbered nonchronologically in parenthetical subtitles. Section (one) of act 1 begins: "Loud and no cataract. Not any nuisance is depressing" (*GP* 205). From this opening, the play progresses through similar kinds of constructions: apparently descriptive but persistently nonspecific, definitional but often via negation. In her introduction to the play in *A Stein Reader*, Ulla Dydo suggests that, as Stein herself recollects, this piece was written as a kind of response to a dinner party, in which the rhythms of conversation and social interactions were tuned into, rather than represented by, language. Dydo writes: "Boundaries of phrases and sentences blur, and idiom falls apart so that one sentence or phrase wipes out the next, or superimposes itself on the preceding one to make new combinations, often apparent but never complete nonsense" (*ASR* 268). The play seems at once a kind of accurate analogue to, as well as abstraction from, actual conversation. Anyone who has transcribed a recorded discussion will know that language is very difficult to track and map across a number of speakers contributing at once to an emergent discourse. But Stein's play is not discernable as a back-and-forth or collective conversation—it appears as a concentrated or selected arrangement of transformations. The language, which in its rhythms and phrasal stylistics is also very similar to *Tender Buttons*, is therefore indicative—as opposed to descriptive—of the peculiar metonymic relay of concepts and objects in speech. Consider, for example, sections (two) and (four) of act 3:

(Two.)

A cut, a cut is not a slice, what is the occasion for representing a cut and a slice. What is the occasion for all that.

A cut is a slice, a cut is the same slice. The reason that a cut is a slice is that if there is no hurry any time is just as useful.

(Four.)

A cut and a slice is there any question when a cut and a slice are just the same.

A cut and a slice has no particular exchange it has such a strange exception to all that which is different.

A cut and only a slice, only a cut and only a slice, the remains of a taste may remain and tasting is accurate.

A cut and an occasion, a slice and a substitute a single hurry and a circumstance that shows that, all this is so reasonable when every thing is clear. (*GP* 207)

Here, as in *Tender Buttons*, the operative logic is one of transformative definition: something is what it is not, or perhaps something is by becoming other. Often these constructions are proposed and shifted by grammatical negations ("a cut is not a slice"), other times by radical transformations at the level of equivalence ("A cut is a slice"). Cuts and slices suggest photographic or filmic editing: speech and logic are being cut and sliced into occasions. Stein was aware of, and interested in, the relationship between her work and early cinema, though she was careful not to overstate the resonance. In "Portraits and Repetition" Stein writes of her experiments in shifting meanings through the almost repetitions of the sentences in *The Making of Americans*: "I was doing what the cinema was doing, I was making a continuous succession of the statement of what that person was until I had not many things but one thing" (*LA* 176–177). She goes on to say:

> what one repeats is the scene in which one is acting, the days in which one is living, the coming and going which one is doing, anything one is remembering is a repetition, but existing as a human being, that is being listening and hearing is never repetition. It is not repetition if it is that which you are actually doing because naturally each time the emphasis is different just as the cinema has each time a slightly different thing to make it all be moving. (179)

Stein was aware of the affinities between her compositions and new filmic sequences; however, she never claimed that she was affecting a kind of "cinematic" poetry. Nevertheless, cuts and slices speak to a new technology of conceiving part-whole relations in an aesthetic work. If Stein's plays are cinematic, it is precisely in this way: their "scenes" are cut and layered in heavy contrasts and with virtual, conceptual, and temporal spaces between. Plays are plays when the actual text—the script, or score—index an indefinite scope for action. In other words, plays *play*.

In *The Poethical Wager*, Joan Retallack draws on D. W. Winnicott's foundational theory of play to describe a mode of attentive engagement with experience that she posits as the critical context for poetics. Retallack defines play as the "imaginative activity that constructs a meaningful reality in conversation with the world as one finds it" (*Poethical Wager* 6). For Retallack, play is an essential part of experimental composition, and, more broadly, necessary for social, political, and cultural engagement. Retallack positions "play" seriously as a mode of being in the world and being a relation. Retallack takes Winnicott's distinction between fantasy (a passive, self-enclosed, and internalized activity) and play (a constructive and active reaching-out) to recommend play as *the* mode by which one participates in the world and, thus, *the* critical apparatus of experimentalism. Far from advocating a kind of "play for play's sake" position, Retallack argues that experimentalism is the process by which interesting things happen: not only in science and the arts, but in the complex and dynamic systems that make a complex and dynamic world.

Retallack suggests (with an echo of Whitehead) that the endemic problem of Western modernity is the "chronic bifurcation" that can somehow imagine a subject as distinct from the complexity of perception (91). The bifurcations of mind/matter, subject/object, theory/practice, nature/culture, substance/quality, and so on (the list is endless) suggest an irreconcilable split between aesthetic and scientific experimentation, or to put it differently, between innovation of form and innovation of fact. By this construction, experimental art is "merely" an interrogation of affect. Thus aesthetic experimentalism is imagined as separate from other kinds of interrogations, investigations, interventions, and constructions of intellectual and material inquiry. Retallack writes:

Experiment—with its carefully structured invitation to surprise— is the paradigmatic interrogative conversation between the insistent intelligible and the silent unintelligible, intention and chance, structure and process. In an aesthetic context the question is always a tripartite composition—of material, form, and meaning

(what has been made of possibility). What twentieth-century innovative artists came to see is that the form that the experiment
takes is not preliminary to the answer, not preliminary to the creation of the art object. It is the answer. It is the art. Just as the essay
is not the result of the investigation, it is the investigation going
on in writing that, at any given point, knows entirely where it's going. This means that its openness to its inability to conclude, its
refusal to know, rather than to sense, suspect, consider, theorize,
contemplate, hypothesize, conjecture, wager . . . forms it as an experience of being in the world where uncertain and unpredictable
life principles (in contrast to prescriptive rules) always exceed the
scope of logical inference or imagination. (97–98)

Here Retallack makes explicit the relation between the essay (literally,
a trial) and the experiment—the essay is a particular kind of long-
form experiment in rhetorical/conceptual/critical thinking. Poems
and essays are closely affiliated in this way, and certainly in the case
of Stein, poems and essays are in constant conversation. The relation
between Stein's essays (which are often originally composed "as" lectures) and her poems do not sit comfortably in a theory-practice relation. The essay's propositions can rarely be applied, as it were, to
exemplary passages of her work, even if she herself does so or suggests an explicit link. The essays do not explain the poems, and the
poems do not prove the essays; they can be read alongside each other
but will only generate more questions and problems from their relation. And this is where play, and the play as form, are particularly
vital to Stein's poetics: the play literally dramatizes—that is to say,
stages—the generative dissonances between materials, forms, and
meanings, between the space of time in a landscape, and between
language and gesture in social relations. The play is the necessary
context for Stein's poetics, which includes a significant body of the-

oretical essays and aesthetic axiom; play is the necessary mode for reading Stein's body of work.

Throughout *The Poethical Wager*, Retallack figures Stein as principally engaged with modes of play. By Retallack's account Stein's work, in its "purposeful play," stays true to the "spirit of inquiry" through which meaning is made and interrogated (159). In its tendency to construct, deconstruct, and reconstruct habits and associations of signification, Stein's language is "playful" because it never ceases to play. And since play often includes a kind of cruelty, especially in the form of ceaselessness, Stein's playfulness is not always pleasurable. The nervousness one feels when watching a play is analogous to the nervousness one feels when playing: at any moment, the rules of the game may change; and often the stakes of a game are so high that one must risk much in order to play. Games can be devised for the specific aim of excluding, alienating, ridiculing, confusing, disorienting, or shaming the one who is the object of play.

Stein works in and with two different modes of play: in the first case, an expectation is purposefully unfulfilled; in the second, a slight difference amplifies a greater distance. In this second mode, play is made through shifty repetition, or else, the proximity of words whose textual point of difference is inversely proportionate to its semantic or contextual point of difference. In both cases, the play depends on expectation: one is either failed by expectation (and therefore surprised), or else one's expectations are exceeded by the amplification of meaning through repetition and/or difference. By both failing to deliver, and delivering too much at once, Stein is humorous in contradictory ways. And both of these modes of play are tinged with the cruelty that privileges the one who makes and changes the rules of the game. Any reader might be delighted, pleasured, angered, or put off by wordplay, but in a sense, these reactions are far from being the most interesting outcome. It is not a pun in itself that is interesting, but the fact that a pun can be made at all, drawing as it does on a complex of related and doubling meanings across various planes of literal and nonliteral signification. A pun, in its slightest vibration, points to the processes that cohere as meaning, where meaning is an event and not an essence. In *The Language of Inquiry*, Hejinian writes: "It is precisely differences that are the foundation and the point of devices such as rhyming, punning, pairing, parallelisms, and running strings of changes within either vowel or consonant frames. It is the difference between rod and red and rid that makes them mean. Wordplay, in this sense, foregrounds the relationship between words" (102).

By foregrounding relationships and differences between words, this kind of play also admits that there are relationships in language other than the ones made by a subject in full command of meaningful utterance. That relationships occur between words independent of a speaking subject and independent of intended meaning—by accident, circumstance, or some shared root now representing an abstract affinity—is in itself a challenge to dominant assumptions about the function of signification. Rather than positing meaning as something applied, meaning can be understood as something generated. Despite all of this—or perhaps precisely because of this—some critics want to take Stein's work as a meditation on the affect of wordplay.[4] There is a risk, in this critical position, of overemphasizing language as somehow independently and abstractly playful, such that the frictions and distances of puns, rhymes, repetitions, and metonyms are figured as merely symptomatic of language at play with itself.

4. Neil Schmitz, for example, writes of *Tender Buttons* that it "serves no end but itself, necessarily denies the factor of its being read, and yet because the field of its play is language, not graphic abstraction, this writing does not seal itself off from meaning" (qtd. in Hoffman 120).

Wordplay can be a problematic description when it implies that play can be reduced to the local level of discrete words in a discrete text. Wordplay is easily dismissed as "merely" so, or else it is used in defense of a much larger claim as to the actual effects of textual play. DeKoven, for example, as Perloff notes, claims Stein's wordplay as evidence of her "pre-Oedipal" interventions against patriarchal language (*Different Language* 21). DeKoven's thesis outlines several exemplary modes of intervention, such as dissonance, surprise, and play, that function as strategies of dislocation or disruption, thus critiquing dominant language and its power relations, heteronormative privileges, subjective hierarchies, and essentializing agendas ("'Grammar in Use'" 51). Perloff, reading DeKoven, argues that not all "dislocations" are of equal value, and to assume that Stein merely plays (which she perceives as meaning composing randomly) is to deny the very careful decisions apparent in Stein's language (51). While Perloff perhaps unnecessarily makes the assumption that "play" is involuntary, or unthinking, her criticism of DeKoven's disproportionate emphasis on play as a key move in Stein's demolition of patriarchal signification is productive in that it problematizes the signal paradox of "play": one must play knowingly, with awareness and a strategy; and yet one can never predict the results of play.

Stein claims that the method for "finding out how you know what you know" is by way of asking questions: "And in asking a question one is not answering but one is as one may say deciding about knowledge" (*LA* 114, 102). By coming to consciously know what one might already know by way of *other* kinds of perceptive and/or nonconscious experience, one is engaging in a mode of inquiry that could either be called play or experimentation. One way to reclaim "experimental" from its current role as an aesthetic category would be to figure experimentation as a compositional method that is explicitly concerned with the processes of knowing and unknowing across multiple modes of conscious, nonconscious, and perceptive experience. This includes, but is not limited to, language use, and it considers the one who composes and the composition constructed as distinct, even though each must be understood as suggesting the other. Correspondences between types of experimental process surely account for the affinities between science and art. It is important, however, to describe this affinity *as an affinity*, rather than to insist on one thing as a metaphor for another. To speak of composition in terms of experimentation neither claims art and science synonymous, nor does it borrow experimentation from science by way of a metaphor.

There remains the relation of play and humor—for it is doubtless that playing is often funny, or at the very least remains open to the possibility of being funny. Stein's humor is a curiously under-theorized and certainly under-appreciated aspect of her work. Often the charge of difficulty or repetitiveness overshadows the acknowledgment of wit, irony, wryness, cleverness, and parody, all of which operate in subtle economies throughout her writing. But the fact that Stein's work is funny—often inscrutably—is of critical importance to the way her work can be read and engaged. Steven Connor writes on the relationship between comedy and cognition, which, as he puts it, "are not only fully and affluently compatible but also closely, even definitionally affiliated," so much so, in fact, that Connor asserts that "thinking is essentially comic" ("Writing, Playing, Thinking, Laughing" 1). Drawing on W. B. Bion's theory of thinking as a kind of negativity, Connor suggests that comedy functions according to the same principle: that is, *something* emerges from a "sense of the null, the negative, the nihilate, the not-there" (3). Connor tracks Freud's argument in *Jokes and Their Relation to the Unconscious*, which ultimately posits comedy in terms of an "economy of effort," to use Connor's phrase, in which a certain amount of energy is invested, or accumulated in advance, and when the need for the energy is suddenly removed (via a punchline) or made void (by a sudden reversal or inversion of expectation), the excess energy is released in the form of laughter (or perhaps bewilderment). Though this basic economic process appears simple enough, Connor points to its complexity: "The positive profit of the laugh is derived from the fictional capital of the virtual effort, that is never made and so can paradoxically both be dispensed with and dispended in the sense of being paid out, or cashed in, in the form of laughter" (4–5). In other words, the calculation is never balanced: something always comes from nothing. Connor asks: "What does this stuff consist of? What precisely is being accumulated, invested, expended and squandered?" (5)

Freud, as Connor points out, habitually theorizes according to the concept of economy. In the case of his writings on jokes, the economic model is "based around various forms of expenditure, saving and profit but is never really able to identify what the substance of this currency . . . actually is" (5). Where comedy is concerned, Connor wonders whether perhaps the substance is literally *nothing*. If so, where does the surplus come from? "One answer might be," suggests Connor, "from itself, the tensive structure of which makes it impossible ever to get one's books in balance" (5). "Another answer," he continues, "is that the surplus is generated from the play of friction of thought against itself " (5). Here Connor invokes "play" as the mode that brings joking and thinking into relation—jokes are "a kind of playing on thought itself, here in the sense of playing the market, or playing the tables" (6).

From Freud, Connor moves to Kant. When laughing, Connor summarizes, Kant argues that one is "responding to the sudden replacement of a sensible idea by a nonsensical one" (7). This response is a "minor mental shell-shock or internal vibration," in other words, not quite a thought (since Kant insists that laughter is a physical sensation and not a judgment), but not quite not-a-thought since it is a sensation of mental negativity or nonsense. Connor reads this paradox in Kant as a question: "Is thinking nothing, or does it involve the thought of (thinking of) nothing? Is this a thought that can be thought through to the end, or is one not noosed in a feedback loop?" (9–10). By way of an answer, Connor suggests that the concept of the "not-quite nothing" is fundamental to both comedy and thinking. Jokes and thoughts are similarly occasioned between abstraction and emergence; joking and thinking are both deconstructive and constructive processes. It is in this sense, and for this reason, that it is impossible to say precisely what goes on in a joke or thought. Toward the end of his essay, Connor concludes:

> Thinking is comic in the sense that it enables us to cleave together in our dividedness. . . . But comedy is itself divided, between the tendency to simplify things complexly by dividing something from nothing, which we can see in the expulsive action of laughter, and the tendency to allow things and no-things to coexist and even to propagate. Perhaps the relation between comedy and thought is itself just such a complex coaction of things and no-things. Comedy is a kind of play-thinking, a thinking that is not quite itself. In this sense, it may be possible to read comedy as a straining against laughter, as well as aiming to induce it. This would make comedy, or one side of it, a kind of immune-suppressant. (14)

In this study, I am not particularly concerned with the notion of nothingness, so much as I am with the notion of no-thing-ness, as Connor describes, or perhaps to go even further, *no-one-thing-ness.* This construction comes close to fitting the obscure humor of Stein's work, which is camp (but seemingly not self-consciously), ironic (but not in the sense of wanting to undo or overexpose), witty (but not exactly satirical or cynical), playful (but often also grave, macabre, or deadpan), and funny (but never whimsical). Contra Kant, even if one is not certain why one laughs at Stein, one is certainly engaging in a kind of thinking while doing so—a thinking that appeals and contributes to a vague and indeterminate knowledge, something like William James's *knowledge of acquaintance,* emerging from the experience of a world that far exceeds the capacity for capture and critique. In *Principles of Psychology,* James writes:

> There are two kinds of knowledge, broadly and practically distinguishable: we may call them respectively knowledge of acquaintance and knowledge-about. . . . I am acquainted with many people and things, which I know very little about, except their presence in the places where I have met them. I know the colour blue when I see it, and the flavour of a pear when I taste it; I know an inch when I move my finger through it; a second of time, when I feel it pass; an effort of attention when I make it; a difference between two things when I notice it; but about the inner nature of these facts or what makes them what they are, I can say nothing at all. I cannot impart acquaintance with them to any one who has not already made it himself. I cannot describe them, make a blind man guess what blue is like, define to a child a syllogism, or tell a philosopher in just what respect distance is just what it is, and differs from other forms of relation. At most, I can say to my friends,
>
> Go to certain places and act in certain ways, and these objects will probably come. All the elementary natures of the world, its highest genera, the simple qualities of matter and mind, together with the kinds of relation that subsist between them, must either not be known at all, or known in this dumb way of acquaintance without knowledge-about. (221)

James's notion of *knowledge of acquaintance* speaks to a more common variety of thinking than *knowledge-about,* which requires that thinking pass through a series of tests and processes in order to end up a concept, fact, or proposition. In this sense, Stein's appeal to knowledge is one that moves slyly between the vagueness of acquaintance and the rhetorics of "about"—at least in part to demonstrate the apprehension of the world that, though vague, is no less real nor less demanding of exact designations. In her lecture, Stein commends the play as a form that emphasizes the movements between knowing and not-knowing, and between different kinds of knowing. A play is a play of the unknown and the known, the knowing what one doesn't know, and the unknowing of what is anticipated. A play plays with one's *knowledge of acquaintance*—with what one finds oneself alongside in the presentness of perception. This is what makes a play a nerve-racking thing to deal with: one never knows what one might come to know.

That Stein is a queer writer and that Stein's texts are queer are claims that underpin my reading and this study. But questions of the relation between this queerness and sexuality in the construction of Stein as a social, cultural, and political subject makes complex territory for criticism. Looking to Eve Sedgwick, Lee Edelman, Daniel Tiffany, Deleuze and Guattari, and Sara Ahmed, I argue that Stein's sexuality—often rendered "illegible" by heteronormative criticism—becomes legible to such criticism only when it is interpreted as encoded lesbian desire; and, further, that the binary of illegibility/legibility serves to affirm normative strictures regarding what constitutes a queer sexuality and a queer textuality. Working against both this "decoding" reading approach and the binary on which it depends, I suggest that Stein's work is queer precisely because it queers the category of queerness that is legislated by the logics of a hetero/homo axis.

In *Epistemology of the Closet,* Sedgwick theorizes the closet as the signifier of queerness in a heterosexist context, that is to say, queerness as an "open secret" (22). Citing D. A. Miller, who writes that "the phenomenon of the 'open secret' does not, as one might think, bring about the collapse of those binarisms and their ideological effects, but rather attests to their fantasmatic recovery," Sedgwick argues that it is both the openness and the secrecy of queerness that enables the paradoxical condition of being marginalized while also being the focus of intense scrutiny (67). Sedgwick argues that on the one hand, queer sexuality is figured as illegitimate; on the other hand, it is a public concern (in both senses of the word: something the public needs to fear, as well as something for which the public assumes a kind of responsibility). The closet is the site of the emergence of a queer subject—voluntarily or involuntarily—in a public context: literally, the closet is the site of the private disclosure and/as public scrutiny. Furthermore, it is a space from which the queer subject is required to emerge over and over again—such is the "deadly plasticity" of heterosexist presumption (68).

Sedgwick argues that the in/out binary—represented by the closet and signifying the hetero/homosexual divide—corresponds to a "whole cluster of the most crucial sites for the contestation of meaning in twentieth-century Western culture," not merely as one example but as *the* foundational split. Some of the derivative binaries include "secrecy/disclosure," "private/public," "masculine/feminine," "majority/minority," "natural/artificial," "health/illness," and "same/different" (72). Sedgwick describes her work in *Epistemology of the Closet* as "propos[ing] that many of the major nodes of thought and knowledge in twentieth-century Western culture as a whole are structured—indeed, fractured—by a chronic, now endemic crisis of homo/heterosexual definition, indicatively male, dating from the end of the nineteenth century" (1). That this definition is concerned with male sexuality testifies to the enduring hiddenness of female sexuality and especially of female queerness. Since female sexuality is so often imagined exclusively in relation to heterosexual coupling and male desire, a queer woman's sexuality perpetually risks being absorbed into normative structures, or else ignored entirely.[1] This study considers Stein's interpellation as a queer writer as one that reads her work according to the contradictory expectations and assumptions of heteronormative logics.

---

1. Adrienne Rich's essay "Compulsory Heterosexuality and Lesbian Experience" is a key text dealing with this issue.

In *Infidel Poetics*, Daniel Tiffany theorizes the "poetic and cultural ethos of obscurity" in which obscurity is taken not as a quality intrinsic to poetry, but as a matter disclosed on reception, that is, a matter encountered in the reading experience (1–2). Obscurity, proposes Tiffany, is "native to the ontology of poetry": it is "perhaps the only fact a poem yields to its readers" (3). Whether it is read as a problem or a virtue of poetry (in the case of the former, accessibility and transparency are demanded; in the case of the latter, obscurity is revered for its proliferation of meanings), obscurity has emerged as a critical concern of contemporary aesthetics, philosophy, and literary studies. Tiffany traces a history of lyric obscurity back to the riddle, that odd little construction that contains, as Tiffany writes (citing Georg Simmel), "the formal attractiveness of secrecy" (4). For Simmel the secret is "a primary sociological fact," and every social relation possesses a "quantum of secrecy" (qtd. in Tiffany, *Infidel Poetics* 5). "Because of its sociological properties," writes Tiffany, "secrecy implies exposure, yet one could go further, following Simmel's argument, and say that *every secret is an open secret*" (5, my emphasis).

See also
Identity
(pp. 128–131)

Poetry in its obscurity presents a dilemma to the reader as to whether the riddlelike cues of a text can be—and, if so, ought to be—disclosed. For those who seek to extract meaning from obscurity, reading is a matter of devising an effective hermeneutical approach. For those who take obscurity as resistant to interpretation, reading is a matter of devising a discourse that attends to the experience of incomprehension and unknowingness (6). In the first instance, meaning is central to the text; in the second instance, it is not. And it is in this second instance that Tiffany aligns poetry and philosophy: "A theory of metaphysics seeks to explain relations between domains which appear to be incommensurable: Being and beings, substance and phenomenon" (9). In addition, "the most powerful and enduring theories of metaphysical substance posit the existence of discontinuous elements," and from this perspective metaphysics offers "critical insights into the relational powers of hermetic forms" (9). Obscurity is not an affect of poetry, open to interpretation by the canny decoder; rather, it is one example of a "foundational obscurity replicated in our understanding of the phenomenal world, in forms of sociability, and (of course) in language itself " (11). For a reading practice invested in poetic obscurity, the distinction between expressive and communicative correspondences is key: one reads according to a method that aims to perceive the relations of a text's discontinuous elements (disjunctions, temporal shifts, semantic leaps) alongside the relations of discontinuous elements inhering in the reading experience (disjunctions, temporal shifts, distractions, interferences), rather than to interpret the communications of a text's implied meaning. Tiffany suggests that a model of such a reading practice can be found in the "queer negativity" of Lee Edelman's *No Future: Queer Theory and the Death Drive*. In *No Future*, as Tiffany summarizes, Edelman argues for the "interdependence" between queer negativity and linguistic obscurity: "Queer theory must always insist on its connection to the vicissitudes of the sign, to the tension of the signifier's collapse into the letter's cadaverous materiality and its participation in a system of reference wherein it generates meaning itself" (13).

Tiffany then turns to Sedgwick and adds the closet to his set of exemplary obscure things. The closet—an open secret—"presents itself as a *spectacle* to be consumed, deciphered, judged" (15). Tiffany writes: "The secrecy of the closet, which Sedgwick describes as a 'riddle,' can be reduced to a purely formal operation" (15). The rhetoric of the closet and the spectacle it presents to a culture consumed and divided by the question of sexuality extends beyond the context of the individual and her sexuality, pointing to the root binary of a bifurcated cultural ideology. If the rhetoric of the closet makes a riddle, one way to challenge the primacy of this rhetoric is to study the affects and tricks of riddles—as Tiffany argues, "The riddle reminds us of the abysmal nature of words by displaying its obscurity, by turning secrecy into an event and making a spectacle of incomprehension" (16). The privacy of the closet "is only its most obvious—and misleading—feature; its permeability and expressiveness remain concealed, unacknowledged" (16–17). Rather than obscuring hidden meaning, riddles display the obscurity of meaning: the trick of a riddle is to be found in the realization that the riddle reveals nothing new. A riddle cannot be decoded, only solved by virtue of its own formal operation, and the solution is not an answer but a perception of the operations of obscurity. While many critics read Stein's work as cryptographic, I argue that her writing is riddlelike rather than encoded. This is not to say that Stein composed a discrete series of riddle texts, or that she composed a continuous riddle corpus. Rather, the obscurity of her language proliferates little riddlelike constructions that confound any attempt to get underneath the obscurity. Stein's poetics is riddled with riddles, but the riddles rarely yield revelation.

See also
Objects
(pp. 156–158)

Perhaps the key example of Stein's penchant for the riddle is *Tender Buttons*, whose portrait-poems are riddles in the extended sense considered here. The relationship between any one poem and its title capitalizes on the expectations of both title and poem as formal signifiers: to the extent that a title is expected to suggest or indicate the subject of a poem, a poem is similarly expected to represent or describe the subject of the title. With this two-way expectation in mind, it seems, Stein composed a suite of exceedingly obscure little portraits: obscure not least because they literally obscure the relationship between their title-subjects and poem-objects. There is very little evidence to support any claims of a direct or literal representational link between, for example, "Sugar" as a title, "Sugar" as a text, "sugar" as a particular substance in the world, and "sugar" as a unit of an abstract category of the substance known as sugar. Thus "Sugar" is a riddle for which there is never a moment of revelation.

Stein writes in open-ended and solutionless riddles, and one of the great achievements of her work is the labor it demands of the reader: the reader must work hard to engage the riddles that roam ambiguously through topoi, and they must work not for closure but for practice: what one ultimately learns, from reading Stein, is that one must always learn to read. Some of Stein's riddles, like "A Box" in *Tender Buttons*, turn on the disjunction between subject and object. Others work from an unspecified subject-object, or collection of subject-objects, whose identity or identities is/are never revealed. In these riddles, one of the first uncertainties is whether the "it" is constant or variable. For example, "What Is This" from *Useful Knowledge* reads:

> You can't say it's war.
> I love conversation.
> Do you like it printed.
> I like it descriptive.
> Not very descriptive.
> Not very descriptive.
> I like it to come easily.
> Naturally.
> And then.
> Crystal and cross.
> Does not lie on moss.
> The three ships.
> You mean washing the ships.
> One was a lady.
> A nun.

She begged meat.

Two were husband and wife.

They had a rich father-in-law to the husband.

He did the dry cleaning.

And the third one.

A woman.

She washed.

Clothes.

Then this is the way we were helped.

Not interested.

We are very much interested. (*GSS* 165)

This poem, which could suggest a dialogue, a conversation, or perhaps a collection of unrelated sentences, responds to its interrogative title "What Is This" with a set of indefinite subjects and objects. First, it seems, whatever *it* is is defined negatively as not-war, but from this fairly tenuous relation, the likelihood of "it" remaining steady—that is, not-war—seems quite low. Thus "it" mutates, finally seemingly describing a group of people: a nun, a couple (with a father-in-law), and a woman. The poem ends with a "we" being helped and being interested. This kind of multiply occupied narrative-set is typical of Stein's work, even when there is a more explicit subject indicated by a title. Whether writing an indefinite or definite subject, Stein consistently works against any presumption of the subject's definiteness.

Stein's work can be understood as an interrogation of the potentialities and limits of "homographesis," the term that Edelman gives to the inscriptive and textual multiplicity of queerness—in other words, the capacity for queerness to signify incommensurate meanings simultaneously. Edelman introduces the term to describe the inscription of "the homosexual" as a cultural subject: "I want to call attention to the formation of a category of homosexual person whose very condition of possibility is his relation to writing or textuality, his articulation, in particular, of a 'sexual' difference as visibly homosexual. This inscription of 'the homosexual' within a tropology that produces him in a determining relation to inscription itself is the first of the things that I intend the term 'homographesis' to denote" (*Homographesis* 9).

The masculine pronoun here is pertinent: historically, the category of the homosexual is a male subject whose emergence *as* a subject is tied up with moral panic, legal definitions, and judicial rulings to do with sexual relationships between men. The question of how a queer woman is imagined, homographically or otherwise, is even more indistinct. The countless ways a queer woman's sexuality have been dismissed, or else pathologized, contribute to the exceptionally marginal status, historically speaking, of the nonstraight and non-male subject.[2] Thus while the gay male subject becomes a text to be scrutinized for signifiers of essential difference, the queer female subject is understood as signifying a lack of signification. Considering its already-plural status, the obscure (un)writtenness of the queer woman can be added to Edelman's account of homographesis.

Continuing his introduction, Edelman writes:

Like writing . . . homographesis would name a double operation: one serving the ideological purposes of a conservative social order intent on codifying identities in its labor of disciplinary inscription, and the other resistant to that categorization, intent on describing the identities that order has so oppressively inscribed. That these two operations, pointing as they do in opposite direc-

2. It is crucial to note here that race is part of this equation, irrevocably so. The *non-white*, nonstraight, and non-male-identifying experience is radically different from (that is to say, exponentially more marginalized) the white, nonstraight, and non-male-identifying experience.

tions, should inhabit a single signifier, must make for a degree of confusion, but the confusion that results when difference collapses into identity and identity unfolds into différance is . . . central to the problematic of homographesis. (*Homographesis* 10)

The double occupation of a signifier—the homograph—is what produces the ambiguity, and therefore mobility, for queerness to *queer* the terms of its designation. "Queer" functions homographically as both noun and verb: the noun identifies and the verb disidentifies. Their double occupation of a single signifier calls to mind the adoption by nonheterosexual communities of "queer," a word that had earlier been used as a homophobic slur and that had originally been used as a term variously signifying peculiarity or irregularity.[3] In a sense, *all* words have homographic tendencies: evident in their habit of indexing, if not retaining, previous meanings and usages. Repetition, punning, and irony, are all versions of homography. In many ways, homography better describes the multiplicity of language than a term such as "polysemy"—"polysemy" speaks to the multiple meanings of a single sign, which operates in its variations as a kind of root meaning, and, as such, the different meanings of the word are not only related, but are networked in such a way that the root meaning always determines the meaning of the derivative. Homography, by contrast, does not assume a root meaning. The sameness of a hom-

---

3. In Heather Love's *Feeling Backwards: Loss and the Politics of Queer History*, she gives some historical background to the word "queer" and its permutations throughout the century: "As in Foucault's discussion of the 'invention of homosexuality,' the invention of queer studies depends on the strategy of reverse discourse. [Judith] Butler's emphasis on the need for constant turning and constant reclamation is striking. Those who would risk taking on the name queer are subject to a double imperative: they must face backward toward a difficult past, and simultaneously forward, toward an 'urgent and expanding political purposes.' According to this vision, the work of 'queering' is never done" (18; Love is quoting Butler's essay "Critically Queer").

ograph is apart from familial structures and inheritances: its relations are lateral and independent. Where polysemy implies different
locations and mutations of a sign, homography refers to the event of
different signs operating under the same name. A homograph is susceptible to error, ambiguity, confusion, or surprise.

A homograph highlights "the necessity of reading difference
within graphemes that appear to be the same," where the sameness
that contains this difference is a "metonymic accident" (Edelman,
Homographesis 12–13). Homographs "insist upon the multiple histories informing graphic 'identities,' insist upon their implications in
various chains of contingent mutations [. . .] that lead . . . to situations in which the quality of sameness, once subjected to the 'graphesis' that signifies writing as de-scription or as designation through
differentiation, reveals the impossibility of any 'identity' that could
be present in itself " (13). It is in the second sense of the term "homographesis," its deidentifying tendency—the "strategic or analytic
resistance to the logic of regulatory identity"—that Edelman emphasizes the relation between homographs and homographesis, thus
pointing out "the extent to which the homograph exemplifies something central to the writing or graphesis with which homosexuality
is linked by the institutionalization of homographesis as a discipline
of social control" (13). Homographesis contains two metonymic logics: one specific to writing, and one specific to the "writing" of subjects. Edelman goes on:

> Bearing no singular identity, the homograph (elaborating, in this,
> a property of writing—and therefore of language—in general)
> precipitates into meaning by virtue of its linear, its metonymic, re-
> lation to a context that seems to validate, which is to say "natural-
> ize," one denotation over another. Invoking, in this way, the alea-
> tory collocations of metonyms to call into question metaphor's
> claim for the correspondences of essences or positive qualities

present in themselves, homographesis (as it articulates the logic of the homograph) works to deconstruct homographesis (as it designates the marking of a distinct and legible homosexual identity). By exposing the non-coincidence of what appears to be the same, the homograph, like writing, confounds the security of the distinction between sameness and difference, gesturing in the process toward the fictional status of logic's foundational gesture. (14–15)

Thus homographesis is a two-part process. The queer body is inscribed *as such*, is demanded to be read *as such*, and it is *as such* that the queer body challenges the interpellation of queerness. Since a heterosexist ideology assumes that sexuality is a question of one-or-the-other, and since this distinction is of utmost importance, it is demanded that sexuality be able to be "read" on the body. The insistence on the readability of queerness is evidence that the "textual significance . . . attributed to homosexuality is massively overdetermined" (Edelman, *Homographesis* 6). This would account for the trend in critical accounts of Stein's work of reading explicit sex acts in ambiguous language. Also, it would account for the critical trend of "outing" Stein's queerness by reading queerness in every word, as if every word homographically meant "queer."[4]

See also
Bodies
(pp. 47–51)

Critics have imagined a good deal of self-loathing, shame, anger,

4. On this point, Edelman writes: "As soon as homosexuality is localized, and consequently can be read within the social landscape, it becomes subject to a metonymic dispersal that allows it to be read into almost anything. The field of sexuality—which is always, under patriarchy, implicated in, and productive of, though by no means identical with, the field of power relations—is not, then, merely bifurcated awareness of homosexual possibilities; it is not simply divided into the separate but unequal arenas of hetero- and homosexual relations. Instead, homosexuality comes to signify the potential permeability of every sexual signifier—and by extension, of every signifier as such—by an 'alien' signification. Once sexuality may be read and interpreted in light of homosexuality, all sexuality is subject to a hermeneutics of suspicion" (*Homographesis* 7).

and despair as the foundational experiences of Stein's sexual development, a narrative which is then understood as the reason for particular works or styles.[5] The self-loathing, shame, anger, and despair—among many other things—that a queer person, no matter what age, might experience as she negotiates heterosexist ideology and homophobic culture are entirely real. But the narratives that are built to explain the life and work of a queer writer in these terms can sometimes, even when the intention is quite opposite, serve to reinforce queer difference as essential: an internal struggle of the queer subject "coming to terms" with herself. I argue for a queer reading of Stein's queerness that queers the terms on which queerness is predicated by heteronormativity. This would mean, in part, reading Stein's work as an extension, rather than representation, of queerness; further, reading queer writing as a modality through which the binary of homo- and heterosexuality is not merely challenged but rendered inoperable by exposing its repressive and paranoid speciousness.

"Miss Furr and Miss Skeene" was published in the 1922 collection *Geography and Plays*, though Ulla Dydo dates it as being composed in 1911. Significantly, the *Oxford English Dictionary* lists this text, with its 1922 publication date, as the first "official" instance of the word "gay" meaning homosexual (s.v. "gay," *Oxford English Dictionary*). Dydo, on the other hand, argues in *A Stein Reader* that "gay" was not yet a signifier of homosexuality at the time that Stein composed the portrait and therefore should be read "literally" as meaning pleasant,

---

5. Margaret Dickie, for example, argues that Stein's "deep anxiety about her sexual identity" was the reason for her "coded" language. She goes further and claims that "Stein struggled nonetheless even within the code to come to terms with her sexual identity and experience even as she worked to find a means of writing it" (*Stein, Bishop and Rich* 19). DeKoven writes of Stein that her "sexual identity had been a terrible problem for her early in life. Essentially, she connected her self-hatred, insecurity, fearful dependency, passivity and inertia, to her female gender" (*Different Language* 134).

cheerful, bright, or gaudy (*ASR* 254). At the very least, this disagreement proves that gay was emerging, precisely during this period, as a marker of queerness. Whether Stein had this in mind while composing the text is not clear.

The piece begins:

> Helen Furr had quite a pleasant home. Mrs. Furr was quite a pleasant woman. Mr. Furr was quite a pleasant man. Helen Furr had quite a pleasant voice a voice quite worth cultivating. She did not mind working. She worked to cultivate her voice. She did not find it gay living in the same place where she had always been living. She went to a place where some were cultivating something, voices and other things needing cultivating. She met Georgine Skeene there who was cultivating her voice which some thought was quite a pleasant one. Helen Furr and Georgine Skeene lived together then. (*ASR* 255)

Helen Furr, the "Miss Furr" of the title, is distinct from her mother, "Mrs. Furr." While Mrs. Furr and Mr. Furr are both "quite . . . pleasant," Helen Furr "did not find it gay living in the same place where she had always been living," that is to say, at home with her parents, whose perpetual and settled pleasantness seems only to reaffirm in Helen her desire for something else. She "did not mind working," and "worked to cultivate her voice," even though she recognized such middle-class practices as the enabling activities of a life she was not interested in living. In these opening lines, there is already a kind of queering of heteronormative coupling and the naturalness of marriage (which, here described, is a permanent settlement or dwelling). This queering is achieved in part through a theory of the labor of "cultivation" as the central practice of identity formation, which could also be described as a theory of becoming: Mrs. Furr is becoming-wife, while Helen Furr is becoming-other.

This theory of cultivation-as-becoming proposes that identity is made, and therefore requires labor. Rather than Helen's queerness replacing heterosexuality (and its flagship institution of marriage) as the more natural mode of being—that is, rather than making an ontological argument for Helen's queer turn—Stein suggests that Helen's queerness is to be found in her recognition of the *making* of becoming. Once Helen recognizes this, she moves to "a place where some were cultivating something, voices and other things needing cultivating" (255). In this ambiguous place, cultivation occurs in unspecified circumstances and for unspecified reasons: here one might cultivate *anything*. Having moved, Miss Furr meets Miss Georgia Skeene, and the two quickly come to be living together. Subsequently, both are "regularly working" and "regular in being gay" (255): "To be regularly gay was to do every day the gay thing that they did every day. To be regularly gay was to end every day at the same time after they had been regularly gay. They were regularly gay. They were gay every day. They ended every day in the same way, at the same time, and they had been every day regularly gay" (256).

From this point, and for the rest of the text, the notion of regulation replaces cultivation as the primary activity of becoming. Or, perhaps more accurately, regulation joins cultivation in order to form a dialectics of becoming: one *cultivates* (tends to, by way of digging and loosening) and *regulates* (organizes according to rhythm) one's living and being. The regularity of being-gay—achieved via the insistence of becoming-gay—for Miss Furr and Miss Skeene inaugurates a rhythmic principle for the activities of living: traveling, learning, visiting, remembering, and telling. At the end of the poem, when they are no longer living together, Helen is "living very well": "She was gay then, she went on living then, she was regular in being gay, she always was living very well and was telling about little ways one could be learning to use in being gay, and later was telling them quite often, telling them again and again" (259). In the final sentence, Helen is recalled as having told "them" "again and again" the "little ways one could be learning" to be gay. Implicit in the repetition of Helen's telling is a queer resistance: the refusal to be oriented according to predetermined norms. In its insistent yet differential repetitions of the becomings of being gay, "Miss Furr and Miss Skeene," a becoming that is regular but always shifting and resignifying, Stein inaugurates a prototype of a queer text: one that moves apart from dominant signification.

See also
Identity
(pp. 119–131)

"Miss Furr and Miss Skeene" does not name a sexual relationship, nor is it a love story in any typical sense. Yet again, the ambiguity of Stein's work makes a designation of queerness impossible: this is what is thoroughly queer about Stein. As Wayne Koestenbaum puts it: "Stein's writing is at once luminously clear about lesbian sexual pleasure, and bafflingly nonspecific" (*Cleavage* 319). I would perhaps more broadly suggest *queer relations* rather than "lesbian sexual pleasure" as being "luminously clear" in Stein's writing and would go further to suggest that it is precisely the space of this clear/obscure contradiction (which is not in fact a contradiction at all) that queerness occupies: queerness is absolutely clear about the right to obscurity. Koestenbaum, who claims that "queer" is the "single best adjective to describe Stein's sensibility and style," writes: "Words experience the gravitational pull of nonmeaning, or of fluctuating significance: this, Stein suggests, is a queer tug. A word or category is queered when it slips away from past definitional fixity" (318).

Joseph Conte, looking for examples of "smooth" and "striated" writing to match Deleuze and Guattari's oppositional spatial/textural tropes set out in *A Thousand Plateaus*, describes "Miss Furr and Miss Skeene" as "smooth" in the manner of *felt*: "Felt can be cut in any direction and still produce a patch indistinguishable from the others," and in the poem, "Long passages of closely reiterated phrases produces a felt-like smoothness, or a nomadic space of shifting sand in which the reader may soon become disoriented" ("The Smooth and the Striated" 60). For Deleuze and Guattari, felt, although "smooth," is far from homogenous: as an "aggregation of intrication" it "contrasts point by point with the space of the fabric" (*A Thousand Plateaus* 475). Conte, responding to the suggestion of fur and skein in the poem's titular characters, invokes Deleuze and Guattari's smooth felt model to describe the aesthetic and grammatical space of Stein's language. He suggests that the reader must read *nomadically*, or "across the weft," in order to engage the smoothness of Stein's language (60). This smoothness, however—as in the case of a slice of felt—may admit perforations or topological shifts: it is not a gloss or slick. The question of how to move in a smooth space is a question of how one "distributes oneself in an open space, according to frequencies and in the course of one's crossings" (Deleuze and Guattari, *A Thousand Plateaus* 481). Smoothness corresponds with queerness in its dissolution of the "determinate intervals" and "assigned breaks" of striation; the nonspecificity of sex in Stein's poetics that Koestenbaum is happily baffled by speaks to this smooth and queer language.

Reading "cow" as code for "orgasm" is the norm for Stein scholars, and conflating orgasm with literary achievement is a popular carry-on.[6] Dydo, in fact, claims that the sexual/literary "cow" is "the key to the life and work" of Stein, who by her account was only ever interested in pleasuring and fulfilling Toklas (*ASR* 451). "As making love

6. Fifer has perhaps the most imaginative reconstruction of the alleged signification of "cow": "While expressing the idea of sexual pleasure in this privately pastoral mode, she never attempts to suppress her 'barnyard' meanings. She also varies her meaning of the word 'cow' itself, so that it alternately bears the feeling of sexuality, the organ itself, food, protection, or the mythical idea of lesbian birth. It is both a derogatory female symbol (in the beast's placidity, stupidity) and a positive symbol of mothering and unselfishness, of pure animal sensuality and nurture in an Edenic world of simplicity and warmth" ("Is Flesh Advisable?" 481).

concludes with the cow," writes Dydo, "so writing concludes with a book. Sexuality and writing become one" (*ASR* 451). Elsewhere Dydo makes this assertion in even more specific terms: Stein is understood to be the one who administers orgasms, literally and metaphorically (by way of poetic offerings), and Toklas is the one who receives the pleasure. Toklas's passivity and receptiveness to pleasure is therefore the single motivation for Stein, whose labor becomes an indistinct blur of writing and lovemaking. In other words, by this account, Stein's writing is bound to the act of giving sexual pleasure, and her sexuality is bound to the act of composition. The implication is that Stein's sexuality is exclusively a textual practice; Dydo seems convinced by this logic when she suggests that Stein did not experience sexual pleasure in her body, but only ever by way of "writing" to, for, and onto Toklas's body, thus managing to both hypersexualize and desexualize Stein. Not only that: it also makes for a one-way channel between biography and text, for here textuality means only one thing. Her writing is all sex; she herself is asexual. This paradox repeats itself in descriptions of Stein and Toklas as role-playing heterosexuality: Stein evidently (and privately) referred to herself as "Mister" and "Hubby" and referred to Toklas as "Wifey," and in some instances, interpretation of these nicknames has argued that Stein's performance of masculinity removes her from, or substitutes for, her relationship. Others have argued that Stein and Toklas are radical in their take-up of pseudo-hetero domesticity, proving, as it were, the theatricality of the categories of husband and wife (Turner, *Baby Precious Always Shines* 18–19). But even in this figuration, the emphasis is on the external and abstract effects of sexuality and desire as they function allegorically or parodically, and not as they function in and as relations. Stein's being-husband will always be read as an ironic gesture, not a serious claim. And since Stein also refers to herself as "Baby," she is read as triply asexual in her queerness: Stein, a baby, dressed up as a husband, manifests pleasure only in the act of writing. Her writing in turn registers these non-normative erotics as an explicit admission of queer desire. I am making a complex argument that connects the different ways that Stein's sexuality is written in order to be read. The fact that Stein can be infantilized, masculinized, and desexualized in order to be understood as queer clearly points to an impulse to explain the perceived unknowability of queerness by any means. That "cow" so perfectly represents an ultimate meaning and aim for Stein's writing makes it an attractive explanation for Stein's abstract-yet-explicit poetics. If we follow the trend of reading cow as orgasm, we find a life's work directed tirelessly and devotedly to the fulfillment of a spouse and the fulfillment of a literary career—a queerness abstracted from Stein and made legible as textuality. All the "cows" that populate Stein's work here signify an orgasmic conclusiveness that Stein herself is denied. That the wife should have a cow is the imperative of the poetics—a thoroughly normative reading, indeed.

Kay Turner, in her introduction to an edited collection of love letters between Stein and Toklas, problematizes the discussion of Steinian cows by claiming that they refer, if not exclusively then certainly additionally, to scatological matters. Turner suggests that Toklas suffered from digestive problems and Stein was invested in making sure that everything was done to alleviate the discomforts of irregularity. Stein's particular dedication to Toklas's digestive rhythms, demonstrative of no small amount of pleasure and delight, may have had something to do with the so-called "cult of regularity" of the early twentieth century, in which bowel movements were a point of discussion and an index of bodily health (*Baby Precious Always Shines* 29). Certainly, it is a record of intimate exchange between lovers, whose concern for and enjoyment of each other is extensive and inclusive. And perhaps it is demonstrative of a particular inflection of Stein's libidinal interests: certainly, she may have been erotically attached to scatology. If and how the scatalogical cows of her love notes relate to other cows elsewhere in her work is unclear. Whether Stein intended plural meanings for "cow"—including feces and orgasm—is also unclear. Whether Stein figured "cows" as a signifier capable of containing a collection of distinct, related objects, is quite possible. As Turner points out, some critics have already hinted at this conclusion: Bridgman, for example, says "The 'cow' is associated with food, with wetness, and with an emergence, which on one occasion is not unlike birth" (qtd. in Fifer, "Is Flesh Advisable?" 480). Turner's intervention into the dominant interpretation of cow-as-orgasm is at the very least a useful reminder that the likelihood of a one-to-one transmission between word and meaning is negligible. More likely, a cow is a network of meanings, an index for a set of relations.

Responding in part to the scatological interest, Lisa Ruddick considers Stein's work for its implicit anality. She declares *The Making of Americans* a "spectacularly anal text"—knowingly so, but "just subliminally enough to have escaped commentary" (*Reading Gertrude Stein* 77). Ruddick's reading, relying as it does on this balance of conscious/unconscious erotic fixation, gives way to a psychoanalytical diagnosis of Stein. Ruddick theorizes Stein's anal eroticism in strict accordance with Freud's designation of anality as an infantile libidinal fixation. There is scant consideration of anal eroticism outside the Freudian context—which figures anal fixation as regressive, aiming back to infancy: either voluntarily and so a form of resistance against phallic symbolism, or involuntarily and so the demonstration of pathology—let alone a female anal eroticism, let alone a *queer* female anal eroticism.

For Ruddick, Stein's anal fixation is decidedly pre-Oedipal in its attempt to write against the symbolic order by emphasizing the undifferentiated anus as the locus of meaning. She goes on to suggest that Stein's anal fixation—manifest in repetitive language that is inflected with a dialectics of filling and emptying, accumulating and evacuating—betrayed a desire to construct a characterology predicated on *undifferentiation*, in which subjects are subsumed and then released by the dialectical process driving narrative (77). This, claims Ruddick, was a desire to quite literally eat, digest, and excrete characters in order to become an "omnipotent narrator" of a narrative that aggressively abolishes difference (81). In *The Making of Americans*, according to Ruddick, Stein writes her vision of anality through a narrative composed from repetitive language that both signifies and enacts the pleasures of filling and emptying—pleasures that can be said to work against delineating rules of Oedipal arrangements and patriarchal rule (81).

The problem with this designation of anality is that it discounts eroticism beyond that associated with infantile fixation. Early childhood learning, relearning, mastering, controlling, and manipulating of bodily function and control, by way of repetition, is read as resonant in Stein's repetitive prose, thus representing an anal fixation rooted in the most basic and early experiences of development. It is no doubt true that the rhythms and constraints of learning to control the body are connected to a certain kind of pleasure—specifically, an autoerotic pleasure. But that this pleasure persists in Stein's work, and in *The Making of Americans* in particular, as *the* signifier of anal eroticism, would seem to miss an opportunity to discuss Stein's anal eroticism in broader terms. In its various scatological, romantic, domestic, erotic, and critical manifestations, Stein's anal eroticism serves as a reminder of the current situation in which, as Sedgwick writes, there is *"no important and sustained Western discourse in which women's anal eroticism means. Means anything"* ("A Poem Is Being Written" 129, emphasis in original). For this reason, it is nearly impossible to locate Stein's anality without recourse to Freud and the relevance granted, however limited, to anal eroticism that is not immediately male. As such, Ruddick's reading of Stein offers a rare and necessary effort to further the discussion of anality in a woman's writing explicitly.

To be sure, Stein's work is pleasurable and is concerned with pleasure. The question is: what kind of pleasure is it? Pleasure theories abound in critical reviews of Stein; mostly these argue that Stein's pleasure is a general and linguistic pleasure, in which pleasures of experience cohere as and through pleasures of language use. According to Roland Barthes's distinction of the "text of pleasure" and the "text of bliss," Stein writes something like the bliss text: "the text that imposes a state of loss, the text that discomforts (perhaps to the point of a certain boredom), unsettles the reader's historical, cultural, psychological assumptions, the consistency of his tastes, values, memories, brings to a crisis his relation with language" (*Pleasure of the Text* 14). As Deleuze points out, the pleasure/bliss distinction that Barthes theorizes proliferates a series of subsequent divisions thoroughly caught up in the Cartesianism of twentieth-century psychoanalysis ("Dualism, Monism and Multiplicities"). Such divisional proliferations affirm the split subject, the one who, to quote Barthes, "simultaneously enjoys, throughout the text, the consistency of his selfhood in its collapse and fall" (*Pleasure of the Text* 21). Deleuze argues that pleasure and bliss, desire and *jouissance*—imagined as they are in an impossible relation of incommensurability and transcendence —never escape the split between the subject of statement and the subject of enunciation ("Dualism, Monism and Multiplicities" 97). Barthes's readers, when attempting to reconcile or engage simultaneously the text of pleasure and the text of bliss, find themselves "split twice over, doubly perverse" by participating in a culture while also enjoying the threat of its destruction, and by enjoying the rhetorical unity of subjectivity while also seeking *its* destruction (97). The way out, by Deleuze's account, is to rethink the very terms of pleasure.

In the first place, this would mean disturbing the assumed relation between desire and pleasure: that desire seeks pleasure; that pleasure is desire's "discharge" or its "unit of measure"; and, finally, that pleasure-discharge will in turn seek *jouissance* (96). What if, asks Deleuze, we think of desire as a process within which pleasure and *jouissance* are "suspensions or interruptions" and which actually brings things into being, rather than merely urging to fill a lack (98). Desire then would be conceived as constructive, and pleasure would be conceived as a variable of desire. From this shifted position, we can rethink the "pleasure of the text" as the specific construction of a textual experience. That is to say, the pleasures of writing and the pleasures of reading coexist, sometimes uncomfortably or erratically, in a complex that includes, but is by no means limited to, the production of texts. What is needed is a term that can describe the contradiction of pleasure (its investment in futurity *and* in destruction) without getting snagged in a loop of perpetually splitting subject-models. Edelman's "homographesis," precisely *because* of its intimacy with psychoanalysis, achieves this critical adjustment by describing the writtenness of legible subjectivity as a question of ideology and not only as a designation of language. To put it another way, homographesis always points to the grammar that makes language functional. Since Edelman's term refers specifically to the designation of the queer subject, the queerness inherent in his intervention can be seen as a major interference with the rhetorical operations that legislate heteronormative ideology. Following Sedgwick's assertion that the crisis of homo/heterosexual definition is the crisis of modern Western logic, predicated as it is on an impossible binary compelled by the notion of coherent "identity," it figures that Edelman's queering of identity is the critical move in his study:

> That the interrogation of identity proceeds in the name of the identity it sets out to interrogate testifies, as I see it, to the importance, on the one hand, of resisting the temptation to set aside any pre-defined space for a fantasmatically coherent and recognizable, because totalized and prematurely closed off, "gay" identity, while

continuing, on the other hand, to affirm the energies—always potentially *resistant energies*—that can be mobilized by acts of gay
self-nomination that maintain their disruptive capacity by refus-
ing to offer any determinate truth about the nature or manage-
ment of "gay" sexuality. Indeed, as I would inflect it, the signifier
"gay" comes to name the unknowability of sexuality as such, the
unknowability that is sexuality as such: its always displaced and
displacing relations to categories that include, but also exceed,
those of sex, gender, class, nationality, ethnicity, and race. (*Homographesis* xv)

The pleasures of this interrogation, replete with resistant energies,
come to be known alongside, indeed *as*, a process of becoming-plea-
sure. As is the case with Stein, whose work is endlessly suggestive of
emergent pleasures, the coming-to-be-known of pleasure lends itself
to being under suspicion of conspiracy with libidinal desire. A queer
erotics, smooth in the sense of "felt," registers pleasure as intensity,
frequency, variation, suspension, and interruption. There can be
pleasure in anything; pleasure roams.

Thus Stein's pleasures are risky. The particular unknowability of
a queer woman's pleasure risks dismissal, abjection, or fetishization.
First, Stein is at risk of being dismissed as a writer of "mere" personal
pleasures.[7] Second, Stein is at risk of the violence and/or anxiety of
homophobia.[8] Third, Stein is at risk of being overdetermined as a

---

7. Michael Gold writes: "In Gertrude Stein, art became a personal pleasure, a private
hobby, a vice. She did not care to communicate because essentially there was nothing to
communicate. She had no responsibility except to her own inordinate cravings. She became the priestess of a cult with strange literary rites, with mystical secrets" (qtd. in Hoffman 77).

8. Patricia Meyerowitz, who edited and introduced collections of Stein's work, responded to a series of articles and letters published in the *New York Review of Books*
on the topic of Stein's sexuality and its representation in her work. Quite spectacularly,

writer of lesbian erotic code.[9] In all three cases, the pleasures of Stein's texts are read as intrinsic to sexual identity, even when this identity is acknowledged via denial or repression. Stein never "came out" by way of a public declarative speech act. This is not surprising, considering the social contexts of her public life. It is also not surprising considering her tendency to elude definite identifications. Stein's queerness thus is a mode of thought, a way of being a relation, and a compositional ethos. It succeeds in clouding attempts to pin her down, this way or that; for her writing is apt to roam quickly, even under examination.

At the end of *Queer Phenomenology: Orientations, Objects, Others,* Sara Ahmed considers the closet:

> While the closet may seem a betrayal of queer (by containing what is queer at home) it is just as possible to be queer at home, or even to queer the closet. . . . To queer homes is to also expose how "homes," as spaces of apparent intimacy and desire, are full of rather mixed and oblique objects. It is also to suggest that the intimacy of the home is what connects the home to other, more public spaces. . . . Within homes, objects gather: such objects arrive and they have their own horizons, which "point" toward different worlds—even if this "point" does not make such worlds within reach. (175–176)

For Stein, the home and its objects were undoubtedly queer and queered—a space in which the diverse material of life and thought

---

Meyerowitz denies Stein's queerness: "Just before [Stein] died, she was operated on and found to have carcinoma of the stomach as well as a calcified uterus. . . . The following may be speculation but I would very much doubt if any woman who had experienced any kind of pleasurable genital activity in her adult life, even masturbatory, would develop calcification of the uterus" ("Lesbianism Never?" n.p.).

9. See, for example, Fifer's "Is Flesh Advisable?"

collected, if temporarily, in knots and affiliations. Readers of Stein have long labored to get inside her home, as if the space of her domesticity could answer the questions that arise from her work, as if her private life was the index to her public inscrutability. It assumes that to read Stein as queer, one must have access to her private life in order to witness and so make public her queerness. As Ahmed suggests, the designation of queerness as a private life made public by heteronormative scrutiny need not be the terms by which queerness is lived. Queerness, she argues, is an approach—an orientation toward, a becoming. Such an approach always occurs at an oblique angle, thus it does not presume a central or neutral position from which one becomes or moves or deviates.

Repetition

Stein's thoughts on repetition can be summarized by a neat contradiction: there is no such thing as repetition; nevertheless, one repeats oneself, and one's habit of repeating (that is, the way that one repeats) is what constitutes one *as* one, and recognizable as such to the other: "Every one in continuous repeating, to their minutest variation, comes to be clear to some one" (*MA* 284). A distinction can be made here between repetition (a noun) and repeating (an adjective or verb). For Stein, pure repetition does not exist, for in the act of repeating, the thing repeated is never the same—its "emphasis" will always and necessarily be different (*MA* 167). Thus "repetition" is a kind of *insistence* and continuous repeating is the minimal modality of differentiation. Stein's logic is not contradictory but axiomatic: there cannot be true repetition, but existence is repeating.

Stein's work is repetitive in a very basic sense—her compositions include the repetition of words, phrases, sentence formations, and grammatical constructions. *The Making of Americans* is her exemplary work of/on repetition. At once a history of national mythology, familial relations, psychological character, social taxonomy, and the novel, *Americans* commits to the enormously athletic task of showing, through quasi-repetitive and verb-heavy prose, the differences and nuances that emerge from "minutest variation." *Americans* is an epic, as well as an ironic commentary on the genre of the epic, in which the constant interruptions of the reflexive narrator unsettle and challenge the fiction. The long excursions into metaconceptualism in *The Making of Americans* correspond closely to the theories explicated in Stein's later lectures and essays, and for this reason, they

signal long-term preoccupations as well as provide a kind of immanent critique of the category of the novel. Stein's long-term study of
repetition-as-difference aligns her philosophically with Deleuze, who
likewise figures repetition as the principal agent of change. For Stein
and Deleuze, repetition is never repetition of the same and is always
repetition with a difference. Repetition speaks to the alterity and temporality of becoming; it describes the process through which variations (in form, intensity, volume, mood, and so on) are registered and
the process by which things become other.

In "Portraits and Repetition," from *Lectures in America*, Stein gives
a history of the development of her theory of repetition by way of
three memories from her childhood. Each indexes a moment of the
awareness of being or becoming decentered, disoriented, or dislocated. In the first memory, Stein recalls the feeling of learning that
"stars are worlds and everything is moving" (*LA* 168). In the second,
Stein describes the feeling of coming to realize that the history of the
world contains the histories of countless different civilizations. The
concept of multiple histories of the present world—histories of living
and dying, networks and empires, human and nonhuman cosmolo-
gies—"makes one realize repetition and at the same time the difference of insistence," because "each civilization insisted on its own way
before it went away" (*LA* 168). Finally, in the third memory, Stein recalls that her aunts, who lived together in Baltimore and with whom
she lived as a teenager after the death of her parents, tended to repeat
themselves incessantly, since each needed to know exactly what was
being said at all times. In remembering her aunts' habit of repeating
over the din of each other's repetitions, Stein invokes William James
and posits a social theory of difference-through-repetition:

See also
Contemporaneity
(pp. 64–69)

> If they had to know anything and anybody does they naturally had
> to say and hear it often, anybody does, and as there were ten and

eleven of them they did have to say and hear said whatever was said and any one not hearing what it was they said had to come in and hear what had been said. That inevitably made everything said often. I began then to consciously listen to what anybody was saying and what they did say while they were saying what they were saying. This was not yet the beginning of writing but it was the beginning of knowing what there was that made there be no repetition. No matter how often what happened had happened any time any one told anything there was no repetition. This is what William James calls the Will to Live. If not nobody would live. (*LA* 169)

Stein conceives what she calls "human expression" as a kind of performativity: one becomes through the insistence of a shifting singularity; and one insists in order to be heard and understood. Her reference to James and the "Will to Live" situates her theory of singularity and multiplicity, repetition and difference (from cosmological, historical, and social perspectives) in the context of *liveliness*. As Steven Meyer points out, the closest James comes to the phrase "will to live" is his essay "The Will to Believe," in which he investigates faith in terms of choice (*Irresistible Dictation* 213). For James, "liveness" describes the condition of a choice made "irrevocably," that is, a choice that occasions a definite change (*The Will to Believe* 3). The will to live, here imagined through the optic of Stein's reading of James, becomes something like the will to engage with the liveness of experience. Stein's philosophical attitude is not especially concerned with questions of choice, faith, or decision making. She is more interested in what Steven Shaviro calls the "aesthetics of existence"—the rhythms of intensity that constitute liveliness (*Without Criteria* 156). Lyn Hejinian notes Stein's fondness for the concept of liveliness: "For Stein vitality—liveliness—is a supreme good; the first and highest value of anyone (or anything) lies in their 'becoming completely living'" (*Language of Inquiry* 112). For Whitehead, an entity is alive insomuch as it experiences inheritance (continuity, or, in Stein's terminology, repetition) and novelty (irrevocable change, difference). Novelty is occasioned in the entity's becoming and is produced immanently. In other words, an entity changes because it responds to its own becoming. In doing so, Whitehead writes, "emphasis, valuation and purpose" are introduced in the entity; thus the entity's composition is always in the process of self-alteration (*Process and Reality* 108). Whitehead calls his metaphysics a "philosophy of organism," and Stein's refutations of pure repetition are similarly organismic: "It is like a frog hopping he cannot ever hop exactly the same distance or the same way of hopping at every hop. A bird's singing is perhaps the nearest thing to repetition but if you listen they too vary their insistence" (*LA* 168). Stein's theory of repetition-as-difference is also a theory of vitality, which in its description of liveliness is resonant with both James and Whitehead.

Stein defines "genius" as the ability to talk and listen at the same time, a quality that she equates with "being most intensely alive" (*LA* 170). A genius can talk and listen with mobility and ease—the category of genius serves as the limit case for the maximal mobility of experience. The genius can talk and listen simultaneously and in constant motion; thus the genius has no need to remember, for even though the remembering subject never remembers the same thing twice, the activity of remembering is a step back from the contemporary demands of talking and listening. Anxiety about remembering is a critical aspect of Stein's poetics. Her work variously asks: What is the relationship between memory and identity, and how can it be radicalized? Stein considers remembering and identifying as connected and regressive activities, equally uninteresting for their reliance on a false sense of unity. Repetition occurs only when one falsely attests to the unity of their identity and repetitiously asserts

See also
Contemporaneity
(pp. 69–72)

this unity via identifying and memorializing claims. In other words, it is only in the form of faith in the efficacy of repetition that repetition exists. Stein's preoccupation with "bottom natures" might seem similarly attached to a theory of a unified self, but in fact *The Making of Americans* proposes a theory of bottom natures as composite and unfixed assemblages of divergent habits, emphases, insistences, and aberrances. A subject emerges from the constituent interactions of their bottom nature: their bottom nature is a complex. The emergent singularity of becoming must be imagined quite apart from the essential singularity of being.

In *Difference and Repetition*, Deleuze proposes a metaphysics in which difference is conceived as difference-in-itself rather than the difference between two essences or identities. Such a proposition is explicitly opposed to metaphysical systems rooted in the primary and original fixity of identity and its representation, for which difference is figured as contradiction or otherness (that is, difference as "not-this"). If, as Deleuze argues, difference is *in-itself*—that which is made and which makes itself, that which distinguishes by distinguishing itself—then pure difference drives the process by which an entity becomes. Pure difference refers to the immanent potential for difference in an entity, and repetition—differential process—is what changes an entity that nevertheless also remains itself. Put simply, an entity changes by the way it repeats its difference. In her lecture "The Gradual Making of *The Making of Americans*" Stein writes: "Everybody said the same thing over and over again with infinite variations but over and over again until finally if you listened with great intensity you could hear it rise and fall and tell all that that there was inside them, not so much by the actual words they said or the thoughts they had but the movement of their thoughts and words endlessly the same and endlessly different" (*LA* 138).

In *The Making of Americans*, the narrator (in one of many meta-compositional intrusions) asserts that the infinitely variable repetitions are not only what make one *one*, but also what make one available to the other. In other words, repetition has a social function —relations are made through correspondences of repetitions. Stein names this correspondence "resemblance":

> Everyone is one is one inside them, every one reminds some one of some other one who is or was or will be living. Every one has it to say of each one he is like such a one I see it in him, every one has it to say of each one she is like some one else I can tell by remembering. So it goes on always in living, every one is always remembering some one who is resembling to the one at whom they are then looking. So they go on repeating, every one is themselves inside them and every one is resembling to others, and that is always interesting. There are many ways of making kinds of men and women. In each way of making kinds of them there is a different system of finding them resembling. Sometime there will be then a complete history of each one. Every one always is repeating the whole of them and so sometime some one who sees them will have a complete history of every one. Sometime some one will know all the ways there are for people to be resembling, some one sometime then will have a completed history of every one. (*MA* 290)

For "some one" to know "all the ways there are for people to be resembling" there must be a finite set of correspondences between types of people. One would have to first identify the elemental character types and all their possible relations. The "completed history of every one" is thus the potential (that is to say virtual) goal of a total characterological system. *The Making of Americans* is a durational experiment, attempting to account for all the possible types and trends of repeating, resembling, and relating.

As Leon Katz has argued ("Weininger and the Making of Americans"), Otto Weininger's *Sex and Character* influenced Stein's *Americans* project. While Weininger's infamously hateful tract was explicitly homophobic, misogynistic, and anti-Semitic, Katz suggests that its commitment to the construction of an elaborate pseudological system impressed Stein, who at the time was trying to develop a compositional method that could account for the diversity and autonomy of experience as well as the complexity of relations.[1] Katz proposes that Stein's attraction to Weininger was not merely *despite* its disastrousness but precisely *because* of the "blunt, dogmatic, unshaved, and unqualified clarity of his reasoning" (10). The central proposition of *Sex and Character* is that maleness and femaleness are "factors" and that the figures of the absolute man and absolute woman exist only as abstract ideals. Actual human subjects are always a mixture of sexed characterological factors—every individual comprises maleness and femaleness in varying proportions. Collectively, everyone in his or her mixed state contributes to the "permanently bisexual condition" of humanity (7). It's important to note that Weininger's notion of "bisexuality" has little to do with sexuality and simply refers to the mixed presence of male and female factors in all subjects. While Weininger's theory of bisexuality may have been seen to be progressive in principle, there is nothing radical about it in terms of a theory of nonheteronormative relations. In fact, he only ever affirms the ideal of heterosexuality by insisting on complementary, oppositional pairings of maleness and femaleness as the model couple form.

For Weininger, character is a permanent morphological form that underpins all physiological experience: "Just as every cell bears

1. Weininger was a very unusual figure. He wrote *Sex and Character* in his early twenties and committed suicide shortly thereafter. Though he was both Jewish and gay, his polemic was foundationally anti-Semitic and homophobic.

within it the characters of the whole individual, so every psychical manifestation of a man involves not merely a few little characteristic traits, but his whole being, of which at one moment one quality, at another moment another quality, comes into prominence" (83). Weininger calls for a new psychology, a "doctrine of the whole" that works against "two great enemies": on the one hand, the idea that character is ultimate, soul-like, and has no relation to science; and on the other hand, the idea that character is nonexistent and that sensational experience is the only reality (83–84). His characterology posits a part-whole dialectics—factors comprise the individual, individuals comprise humanity, and humanity participates in cosmic harmony. Weininger believed that his system would trump late-nineteenth-century psychology because his concerns were metaphysical and epistemological and not merely based on empirical theories of sensation and perception. Sensation and perception were of little interest to him, and he argues that it is possible to obtain information "as to all the differences in the nature of men" by way of typology (81). His typological system was organized according to the capacity for a subject to approach ultimate consciousness. Leon Katz writes:

> [Weininger's] psychology of "character" moves unswervingly toward the definition of "ultimate" human being, which is defined in terms of consciousness. Ultimate self-consciousness embraces absolute memory, absolute self-comprehension, and truth; and ultimate cosmic consciousness embraces absolute identification and unqualified relation of the self with the universal and the eternal. For Weininger, therefore, the completed individual is one whose consciousness—and therefore whose true existence—has moved outside of time and has thereby conquered it. (15)

Ultimately, Weininger presents an ontology of transcendence, achievable only to the Christian male subject. His single concern regarding women is to find a way to effectively exclude them from his philosophical system. By the end of the book, women are nothing more than the negative complement of men. The most common line among scholars on the topic of Weininger suggests that Stein identified as a sexually intermediate individual with a well-developed masculine side.[2] Weininger classifies intelligence, creativity, talent, and self-awareness as masculine factors, present at least in traces in so-called "masculine women." But even if Stein saw herself as a "manlike woman," it seems unlikely that she felt moved by Weininger's scant concessions. Stein may come out on top of Weininger's list of women—as long as her Jewishness is ignored—but the crucial point of his system is that *no* woman, no matter how "manly," ever comes close to the most feminine man. No matter how widely mixtures of maleness and femaleness vary, Weininger's "spectrum" affirms an irreducible difference between men and women.

I argue that Stein was interested in Weininger not because she figured she passed his character test, but because he offered a model for her own typological inquiry. Weininger provides the framework for a typology with a simple, modular infrastructure that could be reproduced in other contexts. It's not hard to imagine Stein being attracted to a version of his characterological system that used language as its marker of difference in place of sexual factors. *The Making of Americans* attempts to trace character through repeated language patterns, and its composition required a method for diagramming language as it is used in time—how it changes its emphasis, how it reproduces itself in patterns. "I was sure that in a kind of a way," says Stein in "The Gradual Making," "the enigma of the universe could in this way be solved. That after all description is explanation, and if I went on

2. See, for example, Barbara Will's *Gertrude Stein: Modernism and the Problem of Genius.*

and on and on enough I could describe every individual human being that could possibly exist. I did proceed to do as much as I could" (*LA* 142). Whereas Weininger wanted to devise a system for the description of all humanity based on sexually distinctive constituents, Stein wanted to devise a system for the description of all possible kinds of people by listening to the talking and repeating of everyone around her. To know someone is to become intimate with how they repeat themselves: if Stein could come to know enough people, she could map the repetitions and variances in language in order to determine different characterological types. Like Weininger, Stein's central focus was the play between one and many, self and relation, part and whole, repetition and difference. According to Katz, what Stein most importantly inherited from Weininger was an answer to the "twin problem"—the problem of becoming dissociated from one's self via self-consciousness (15). Weininger solves this existential question by way of a transcendent theory of ultimate character, in which an ideal complete individual transcends time and identity and assumes eternality. Stein, however, had no such theory of transcendence. For her, the "twin problem" was to be solved by conceiving of consciousness as something apart from self-identification. Being conscious of one's consciousness leads to a paradoxically inextricable and dissociated perception of the self with and from itself, the world, and the cosmos. This crisis was of central importance to Stein and can be seen in her three-part story of coming-to-know repetition: the realization of the self in one world of many; the realization of the world as a history of worlds; and the realization of otherness as a primary social fact. Stein's interest is in how an individual is depersonalized through double consciousness; consciousness of the self as a conscious subject is not a totalizing experience, but an affective encounter through which one is faced with one's own multiplicities and intensities.

See also
Identity
(pp. 132–135)

In *The Making of Americans*, Stein's narrator makes a critical distinction between the human being as a noun and the human being as verbal process (having human being, having being human, human having being): "Always more and more I love repeating, it may be irritating to hear from them but always more and more I love it of them. More and more I love it of them, the being in them, the mixing in them, the repeating in them, the deciding the kind of them every one is who has human being" (*MA* 289). That one little word "has" turns the category of the human being from a definite and discrete group into a group of entities bound by the shared fact of having human being. In other words, a human subject is one who "has" human being, and a human being is a process of becoming through which one becomes by repeating: every one comes to be one by repeating their singularity. For both Stein and Deleuze, all existence is processual, and being is affirmed by becoming. In Halewood's comparative study of Deleuze and Whitehead, Whitehead's philosophy of organism and its emphasis on the materiality of process and becoming are considered alongside Deleuze's ontology of difference and repetition ("On Whitehead and Deleuze" 68). Deleuzian becoming is not mere flux and flow: there is a quiddity to becoming that accounts for the materiality of processes and events. Halewood summarizes Whitehead's ontological position as being "focused upon process and becoming as the ultimate characterization of being and materiality" (*A. N. Whitehead and Social Theory* 63). Halewood cites Whitehead, who writes in *Process and Reality*: "*Experience* involves a *becoming*, that *becoming* means that *something becomes*, and *what becomes* involves *repetition* transformed into *novel immediacy*" (136–137, emphasis in original). The key to Whitehead's concept of becoming, according to Halewood, "is that each becoming occurs in a specific environment and in a specific fashion" (63). And so becomings (including the becomings of human subjects, but by no means restricted to them) are always becoming-singularities. "Prehension" is the term designated by Whitehead to refer to the relationality of becomings: prehension describes the capacity for an entity to "grasp" its environment and to admit other entities into its becoming. Becoming is never becoming in isolation, nor is it becoming as a correlation. In Halewood's terms, prehensions "enable the description of the complexity of the process whereby subjects are both created and create themselves through the assimilation of previous diverse elements" (64). In *The Making of Americans*, "making" is key: as the narrator emphatically insists, every one comes to be one by repeating their singularity (their difference) *and* in relation to otherness (by prehending the context of their individuation).

Stein's early work—*Q.E.D.*, *Three Lives*, and *The Making of Americans*—can be contrasted with her later portraiture (to which I include her biographical and autobiographical writings, plays, and novels such as *Ida*). In these later texts, Stein is interested in finding a way of composing according to the rhythms and intensities of becoming rather than in cataloguing the narrative possibilities of becoming-characters. We can see, for example in her portrait of Picasso ("If I Told Him: A Completed Portrait of Picasso"), a particular kind of repetition: the repetition that registers, rather than represents, the intensities and multiplicities of Picasso's becoming-singular:

See also
Contemporaneity
(pp. 62–64)

If I told him would he like it. Would he like it if I told him.
Would he like it would Napoleon would Napoleon would would
he like it.

If Napoleon if I told him if I told him if Napoleon. Would he
like it if I told him if I told him if Napoleon. Would he like it if
Napoleon if Napoleon if I told him. If I told him would he like it
would he like it if I told him.
Now.
Not now.
And now.
Now.

[. . .]

Exact resemblance. To exact resemblance the exact resemblance
as exact as a resemblance, exactly as resembling, exactly
resembling, exactly in resemblance exactly a resemblance,
exactly and resemblance. For this is so.
Because.
Now actively repeat at all, now actively repeat at all, now actively
repeat at all.
Have hold and hear, actively repeat at all.
I judge judge.
As a resemblance to him. (*GSS* 190)

The repetition occurs in the perception of Picasso; Stein is interested
not in Picasso's psychological patternings, but in his affective
rhythms. "Exact resemblance" can be read as a transitive verb—"to
exact resemblance"—suggesting the process of coming-to-write a
subject as a subject-in-writing. The question of the affinity between
Stein and Picasso in their approaches to alternatives to representationalism, perspective, and plan, and the obvious correspondences
between them in terms of part-whole and rhythmic dynamics,
makes this dedicational piece particularly dialogical and ekphrastic.
The exact relations between Stein, Picasso, and the portrait remain
undisclosed, however, for this is not a portrait of Picasso's painting,
but a portrait of a painter: it is not intended to simulate cubism, but
instead seeks to compose alongside the rhythm of Picasso's affective
repeatings.

In Brian Reed's analysis of a recording of Stein reading "If I Told
Him," he describes the way that Stein intones difference in the repetitive language. In the following excerpt, he is initially referring to the
refrain "If I told him would he like it / would he like it if I told him":

The delivery suggests that the repetitions and chiasmatic mirror-
ings could continue ad infinitum. Stein then, without transition,

launches into a second segment: "now / not now / and now / now."
The tone is emphatic, as if she were issuing orders. "Now" take
action! But this "now" appears in isolation, decontextualized, so it
is not exactly clear how it is to function as a command—unless,
perhaps, Stein is directing listeners to attend to "now" itself, that
is, the moment of utterance. Of course, strictly speaking, once
such a present-tense "now" is pointed out, it ceases to be "now."
That is, once singled out for attention, it inevitably becomes a
"then," a moment receding even further into the past. Thus, paradoxically, every "now" is, at one and the same time, "not now."
One cannot hold onto the present moment. The most one can do
is register the series of nows as they tick by ("and now / now")....
As performed orally, "If I Told Him" provides a listener with discrete, well-demarcated segments of time that resist being inte-
grated into a larger governing scheme such as the prose versus
verse binary suggested by the print version. . . . Stein's recording
resembles . . . cell-based musical compositions such as Steve Reich's *Music for Eighteen Musicians* and John Adams's *Phrygian
Gates*, works in which each segment of time is characterized by a
repetitive pattern sustained long enough for a listener to perceive
and appreciate in isolation its distinctive rhythm, melody, and mix
of timbres. ("Now Not Now" 108)

Reed argues that the written and spoken versions of "If I Told Him"
differ from each other in ways that are perhaps quite obvious. The
text version plays with the dynamic between prose blocks and versi-
fied lines, and neither its repetitive language nor its transitions between sections are marked by any tonal or temporal cues. The spoken
text, read by Stein, obscures the prose/poetry distinction and instead
performs the language according to its tonal and temporal cues. In
addition, Reed challenges the assumption that Stein wrote consciously in the manner of the cubist painters by aligning her instead

with contemporary composers. Specifically, Reed suggests that Stein's interest in repetition has a stronger affinity with later-twentieth-century musical composers than with her painter contemporaries.

Sianne Ngai suggests a similar thing in *Ugly Feelings*, in which she theorizes an aesthetic category she calls "stuplimity"—a kind of stupefying or tedious sublime. Citing Stein in *The Making of Americans* ("Listening to repeating is often irritating, listening to repeating can be dulling"), Ngai goes on to say:

> In that book, which presents a taxonomy or system for the making of human "kinds," repeating is also the dynamic force by which new beginnings, histories, and genres are produced and organized. As [Jacques] Lacan similarly suggests, "repetition demands the new," including new ways of understanding its dulling and irritating effects. It thus comes as no surprise that many of the most "shocking," innovative, and transformative cultural productions in history have also been deliberately tedious ones. In the twentieth century, systematically recursive works by Andy Warhol, Robert Ryman, Jasper Johns, John Cage, and Philip Glass bear witness to the prominence of tedium as an aesthetic strategy in avant-garde practices; one also thinks of . . . the permutative logics at work in the writings of Beckett, Raymond Roussel, Georges Perec, Alain Robbet-Grillet, Jackson Mac Low, and of course Stein. (262)

To this list we could add Kenneth Goldsmith, whose practice of "uncreative writing" is dedicated to repurposing text by way of copying, rewriting, sampling, and deforming. By his account, the uncreative writer engages with "the wonderful rhythms of repetition, the spectacle of the mundane reframed as literature, the reorientation to the poetics of time, and fresh perspectives on readerliness" (*Uncreative Writing* 4). In Goldsmith's work, so-called uncreativeness engenders different kinds of reading experiences, away from the guided revelations of narrative and drama and toward the consideration of minor affects that are felt when enduring long, repetitive, or bureaucratic language. Stein figures for Goldsmith as a precursor to the uncreative impulse—in *The Autobiography of Alice B. Toklas* Stein writes that she was not interested in the trend of "fabrication": her métier, she asserted, was the English language itself, not its capacity to produce or reproduce "imitative emotionalism" (Stein qtd. in Goldsmith, *Uncreative Writing* 4). Like Goldsmith, Stein was interested not in literatures that fabricate worlds but in literary practices that engage with the events and experiences cohering as and occasioning the world. A similar compositional focus can be read in the musical avant-gardes of the twentieth century, as Ngai suggests. In the work of composers like John Cage or Steve Reich, melody and rhythm are emergent and not essential qualities, and the dynamics of the composition focus on the relation between sound and nonsound. In "Portraits and Repetition" Stein writes of her own compositional ethos: "Melody should be a byproduct it should never be an end in itself it should not be a thing by which you live if you really and truly are one who is to anything" (*LA* 201). For Stein, melody is a kind of aesthetics of meaning of representational language: it's something that happens, but not something to be simulated.

To the list of contemporary works interested in the "stuplime" we can also add those by poet, critic, and artist Tan Lin. In an interview with *BOMB Magazine*, Lin responded to a question about his interest in boredom and its relationship to the ambient novel—a text-assemblage with multiple formats and versions that resist being organized into (and fetishized as) a discrete book object. Referring to one such ambient novel, *Seven Controlled Vocabularies*, Lin writes that his work

emulates the ambient textuality or generalized medium . . . of reading as it is structurally coupled to other things. I'm interested in the formats and micro-formats of reading, and their coupling to other things in the world, like restaurants, yoga mats, poems, former boyfriends or girlfriends, wives and husbands (and their photographs), and of course other books (and their photographs they contain within them). So I would say boredom is a very loose medium in which the heterogeneity of the world can be gathered without coalescing into something meaningful—like a book. (Saunders, "Tan Lin" n.p.)

Lin posits boredom as a kind of multiple and distracted attention that focuses on many things at once. In this way, boredom is both creative, in the sense that it makes thing happen and brings them into quasi-focus, and "uncreative" in the Goldsmithian sense, because it is interested not in the representation of attention but in its continuation, extension, and dilation. Lin and Goldsmith, in different ways, are constructively read alongside Ngai's notion of stuplimity, a term that describes an aesthetics of "repetition, permutation, and seriality" which results in a compositional "agglutination"—that is, "the mass adhesion or coagulation of data particles" (*Ugly Feelings* 263). While it might be a stretch to call Lin's ambient novels agglutinative, since they require the relations between the "data particles" to be spacious, contingent, movable, and abstract, Goldsmith's large-scale repetitive projects seem aptly so, since their affect is variable only in intensity. Stein's work sits somewhere between the two: not quite as ambient as Lin's and not as gluggy as Goldsmith's. Stein's work sits exactly where the contingency and banality of everyday life and activities— like dogs, meals, gossip, and arguments—are organized by the compositional logics of rhythm, temporality, and repetition, from which patterns and tendencies are mapped and inventoried. The result, for a work like *The Making of Americans*, is a text that is at once boring (almost impossibly so), compelling, scandalous, and suspenseful.

Stein's relationship to her "home" country, and her sense of being American, were complex and contradictory. She saw herself as a key figure of a new century invented by America. At the same time, she perceived herself as being somewhat outside the American cultural context. The difficulty of Stein's Americanness persists as a theme in critical accounts of her work: Stein's theory of Americanness and her sense of her own Americanness are equally (but differently) difficult. As we begin to examine some of these difficulties, a brief summary of her ideas of linguistic, national, and cultural affiliation will be useful.

Stein was born in the United States but spent part of her childhood and the whole of her adult life in Europe. The German and French she spoke as a child were discouraged when she was a teenager back in the United States with her family; as a writer, she considered the subject and object of her work to be, at all times, the English language. This tension between an idealized, autonomous English and the multilingualism of her daily life figures importantly in her theories about language and identity. In many ways, Stein was a nationalist—she supported the American soldiers sent to France during World War I; she admired American history, technology, and literature; and she venerated the modern democratic ideals of individuality and mobility, which she regarded as American inventions. In other ways, she was uncertain about her national belonging: most infamously, she has been accused of collaborating with the Vichy government during World War II, and she sometimes expressed an uneasiness to do with her relationship with American culture. She seemed at once excited by and anxious about her status as an outsider, both in the United States and in France. Her desire for recognition and celebrity sometimes manifested as ambition, even hubris, and at other times betrayed frustration with being overlooked, underpublished, misrepresented, dismissed, and belittled. After the success of *The Autobiography of Alice B. Toklas*, she became more confident about her place in literary history and culture, but her confidence was never without a certain kind of defensiveness. She was most nervous about her American audience; she was writing because of and into the new century, an invention of the new American industrial sublime, and Americans would be the inheritors and arbiters of her work. It is important to explain my use of the word "America" in the following section. I do not mean to use it as synonymous with the United States. I use it to correspond to the particular kind of abstracted fantasy of Stein's historiographical concepts, while keeping in mind that there is no one America but, rather, many heterogeneous *Americas*.

In 1928, *Transition*, a Paris-based literary journal of experimental writing, invited a number of American expatriates to respond to the question *Why do Americans live in Europe?* Respondents were encouraged to respond with "stories of themselves . . . conceived from the standpoint of deracination," while also answering a set of specific queries, including

Why do you prefer to live outside America?

How do you envisage the spiritual future of America in the dying face of Europe and in the face of a Russia that is adopting the American economic vision?

What is your feeling about the revolutionary spirit of your age as expressed, for instance, in such movements as communism, surrealism, anarchism?

What particular vision do you have of yourself in relation to twentieth century reality? (*HWW* 51)

Stein's response, comprising two short paragraphs, does not answer the questions directly. Despite its briefness, she gave her response a title ("Why I Do Not Live in America") and used it to articulate her theories of an American national and aesthetic character and the benefits of elective exile. It begins: "The United States is just now the oldest country in the world, there always is an oldest country and she is it, it is she who is the mother of the twentieth century civilisation. She began to feel herself as it just after the Civil War" (*HWW* 51). That the United States was the oldest country, having "created" the twentieth century during the Civil War, was a claim that Stein made a number of times. In *The Autobiography of Alice B. Toklas*, she explains further: "Gertrude Stein always speaks of America as being now the oldest country in the world because by the methods of the civil war and the commercial conceptions that followed it America created the twentieth century" (*ABT* 86–87). The twentieth century began with the innovative notion of "assembling the whole thing out of its parts" (*HWW* 152). Since civil war is a crisis that deals explicitly with part-whole relations, for Stein the American Civil War reconceptualized the notion of industrial assemblage and advanced mechanistic technology, serving as the catalyst for innovations in methods of mass production, machinery, communications, and transport. Such advancements, she argues, were foundational for the construction of the contemporary American nation: an assemblage of individual but unified states. The United States made the new century when it succeeded in making itself an assemblage in the manner of the automobile—an emblem of the new American industrial-capitalist future.

If the twentieth century was created by America, then the nineteenth century was created by England. Stein theorizes the decline of the British empire and its impact on literature and philosophy in the lecture "What Is English Literature." Stein describes a period of about "six centuries" prior to the nineteenth in which English literature enjoyed a stable period of "completeness" by "describing the daily living" of "island life." This changed in the nineteenth century, when the British empire expanded such that "they came to own everything" that was "outside" the "island life":

> They owned everything inside of course but that they had always done, but now they owned everything outside and that reinforced their owning everything inside, and that was as it was only more so but as they owned everything outside, outside and inside had to be told something about all this owning, otherwise they might not remember all this owning and so there was invented explaining and that made nineteenth century English literature what it is.
>
> (LA 40)

The English invented "explaining" in order to defend the legitimacy of empire; English literature of the nineteenth century was invested in an aesthetics of explanation. "Explaining" is done in phrases rather than whole sentences—phrases, for Stein, are "soothing," incomplete, sentimental, and predetermined, and, as such, the ideal rhetorical unit for the valorization of empire: the precarious naturalizing and moralizing of possession such that the inside-outside dialectics of occupation reinforce, rather than destabilize, the central cultural identity of the imperial state required a careful and convincing literary discourse. Phrases lend themselves to canny arrangements and strategic deformation and reformation, through which anything can be explained. This, according to Stein, cultivated a literature of phrasal inference and nondisclosure that was, above all, "soothing" and placating:

> Think really think about any big piece or any little piece of nineteenth century writing and you will see that it is true that it exists by phrases. Compare Jane Austen with Anthony Trollope and you will see what I mean and how the volume of the phrasing gradually grew and when you read Dickens, compare it with and they are both sentimental with Clarissa Harlowe and you will see what I mean. One lives by its whole the eighteenth century and the nineteenth century thing lives by its parts. You can see what I mean that this connects itself with explaining. The same thing is true with nineteenth century poetry. The lake poets had other ideas, they felt that it was wrong to live by parts of a whole and they tried and they tried they wanted to serve god and not mammon, but they too inevitably as they wrote longer and longer live by parts of the whole, because god and mammon were interchangeable since in the nineteenth century England lived its daily island life and owned everything outside. Oh yes you do see this. (LA 44–45)

What Stein essentializes about English cultural politics and its effect on literature, as well as what she essentializes about nascent Americanism and its independence from cultural imperialism, can be criticized variously for sweeping assertions and arbitrary distinctions. What interests me is not the veracity of her comparison, however; rather, it is her argument's implications for twentieth-century form, particularly the restructuring and hybridizing of genres such as the epic, novel, poem, play, autobiography, and so on.[1] What Stein

1. In "Gertrude Stein for Anyone" Jennifer Ashton writes: "Stein's argument that American writing supersedes English writing on the basis of its wholeness and completion begins to look like a political critique. But while it does engage politics at some level, Stein's

perceives as "being" American—the space and time of the twentieth century and a space and time for new experiments and new methods of composition and criticism—corresponds with other discourses of Americanness similarly interested in moving away from the histories and conventions of the English literature tradition. This emergent Americanness was as much a theory of what it means to be American as it was a theory of American form—in other words, it was an aesthetic philosophy.

Joan Richardson tracks the mythos of Americanness in *A Natural History of Pragmatism*: a history both preceding and succeeding the texts most directly associated with American Pragmatism, and including the poetics of Stein and the transplanted metaphysics of Whitehead. Richardson argues that the signal motive of Pragmatism is the realization of thinking as a life-form (1), dependent on and defined by its susceptibility to evolution and transformation. In fact, she argues, theories of evolution and development first took language as a guiding example: language is not merely resilient to the events of permutation, revision, inversion, and restructuration; it also depends on such things in order to continue to be language (2). Richardson's study considers the New World context in which the inadequacy of established discourses to describe the contemporary moment betrayed an incommensurable difference between the colonialist paradigm and the experience of being elsewhere. Such incom-

See also

Food

(pp. 77–81)

---

critique of imperialism is above all an effort to anatomize a problem in literary representation, a problem that is central to her own literary project. This problem revolves around the philosophical questions pertaining to the ontological and epistemological status of wholes: what makes a thing whole; how one knows it is whole; and what counts as an adequate representation of the whole, especially when the whole is made up of an infinite number of parts. As a practice of endless acquisition, imperialism poses the same difficulties for national self-definition that the idea of a whole with an infinite number of parts poses for literary representation" (292–293).

mensurability occasioned a particular kind of philosophical attitude in which one's experience and thinking-about experience appeared alien to one's sense of self. Alienation of self from self, according to Richardson, impels one to consider what kinds of processes and events actually contribute to one's subjectivity—a consideration that constructs an aesthetics of experience and requires a new form of language: "Left with the feeling of what happens, thrown into the paradoxical situation of being both inside and outside their language at once, forced to live in a world but outside of existing conceptions of it, the most attentive and concerned seventeenth-century doers of the word were to devise solutions that were in the purest sense 'aesthetic,' before the term itself had become established as a category of experience" (3). These early revisions to conventional metaphysical formulations of self, world, word, and so on, were quickly rerouted into a discourse of individualism; after all, the foundational imperative of the colonialist is self-naturalization.

Aesthetic solutions to metaphysical problems, Richardson continues, were to be found in the evolution of and desire for language forms "where questions and questing reflexively undermined predication: for forms of paradox; for a preponderance of analogy; for repetitions imitating ritual and prayer; for paratactic listings of phenomena not encountered before" (10). Richardson reads Stein's work as a concentrated effort to catalogue the history of these new forms and the psychological types they created—in and through formal innovations. The principal text of Stein's effort, for Richardson, is *The Making of Americans*, which in its attempt to document the varieties of the "bottom nature" of being American reflected her vision of the Pragmatist project—the study of language as a life-form in process, and the study of experience as it registers, and is registered by, language. In contrast to the dilemma facing England—that is, how it could maintain rhetorical claims to empire—America, by Stein's ac-

See also

Repetition

(pp. 209–217)

count, was enjoying the achievement of having created the "space of time" of the twentieth century. Stein's America was a perfect assemblage, with its states' boundaries drawn exactly and each state's capital tucked away carefully in a safe place, and with "only air" instead of a proper sky, which meant that one could walk around or stand still freely, with "no lid on top" (*EA* 202). The image of a lidless nation, supporting mobility and restlessness, is evidence of Stein's investment in individualism, imagined as the right to roam and dwell as one pleases.

Throughout Stein's constructions of "America," there are scant mentions of indigenous history or culture apart from occasional mentions of "Indianness" that serve to emphasize abstract distinctions between premodern and modern experience. *Everybody's Autobiography*, which recalls Stein's lecture tour of the United States, mentions indigenous culture in three instances, each equally revealing in their interpellation of indigenous identity. In one case, she draws an analogy between the movements of American football and "Indian dance" (both said to be "angular"). She then claims the reason for this connection: "Art is inevitable everybody is as their air and land is everybody is as their food and weather is and the Americans and the Red Indians had the same how could they not be the same how could they not, the country is large but somehow it is the same if it were not the same it would not remain our country and that would be a shame. I like it as it is" (*EA* 197–198). This passage is initially assured in its theory of environmental influence on "art": a connection between indigenous and nonindigenous people is assumed through the simple fact of sharing land, food, air, and weather, all of which determines how anyone anywhere "is." But then the argument becomes anxious, with Stein suddenly becoming paranoid that the land, food, air, and weather might someday change. This reveals the foundational paradox of Stein's new and oldest America: as soon as

America is imagined with a history, the history is unsettling. It is difficult to romanticize a shared space in which landscape—history
manifest—impresses a site-specific ontology, since any claim that
colonial occupation is a kind of "sharing" is immediately specious.
But more than that, it is difficult to reconcile what Stein considers the
determining ontological "is"-ness of being rooted to one's geography
and landscape and the more radical claim of the self-invention of the
modern nation in, by, and for the twentieth century. Stein's contradiction requires America to have always been what it is in order that
the one who roams its lidless surface can move and be freely; also, it
requires America to be the sum of its own paroxysmal debut, a rup-
ture from Anglo humdrummery and antiquated modes of being.

In the second case, in a passage from *Everybody's Autobiography*,
Stein briefly mentions the "Indian collection" of a museum in Indianapolis. The event is described as follows:

> Indiana Indianapolis and Indians. He [the curator] showed us how
> they were slicing in thin slices the Indian mounds I suppose they
> have to slice them if they want to know what is inside in them and
> of course they do want to know what is inside in them and of
> course they do want to know what is in them and each one might
> be different from the one they had had open. Well anyway Indi-
> anapolis had not been in any way a disappointment. (220)

The installation of indigenous objects in museums is one method
through which indigeneity is dislocated and objectified as anthropo-
logical capital. In Stein's account, this is rendered particularly vio-
lently in the "slicing" of mounds in order to see whether one mound
might contain something different from another. Indianapolis had
not been a disappointment, presumably at least in part because it had
delivered on the promise of its name by providing access to a historicized Indianness. "Well anyway" is suggestive of genuine interest as

well as genuine indifference. Stein's America can never deny its history, but it can never engage with it fully either.

In the third case, Stein cites a childhood meme while professing her love of counting: "I always liked counting but I liked counting one two three four five six seven, or one little Indian two little Indians three little Indian boys counting more than ten was not interesting at least not to me" (*EA* 120). Stein claims that "counting" is the single activity separating humans and nonhumans and, furthermore, that there has never been so much "counting" going on as in the twentieth century. "Counting is the religion of this generation," she continues, "it is its hope and its salvation" (120). Elsewhere Stein elucidates further: "The natural way to count is not that one and one make two but to go on counting by one and one. . . . One and one and one and one and one" (*LA* 227). By Stein's account, counting by accumulation (one and one make two) loses the qualitative "oneness" of that which is being counted, whereas counting as process (one and one and one) retains, even emphasizes, "oneness." When Stein writes that she enjoys counting along with the proverbial "little Indians," she is assigning special relevance to a style of counting that she perceives as being contemporary. Using a counter to ritualize and perform counting, one must imagine the ontological and qualitative difference between the counters and the entities that they stand for. That the counter she uses in her example is the *little Indian boy* reveals a common rhetorical gesture of colonialist cultural discourse: the indigenous subject exists, but only as citation.

Stein's construction of post–Civil War America corresponds to an interest in vernacular; in a number of her early prose fiction works, Stein explicitly appropriates African American idiom, and elsewhere she theorizes typologies of racial characteristics, in part derived from speculative speech analysis. Critics have suggested that her preoccupation with nonstandard and diverse dialects was connected to her own experience as the child of immigrants who spent time overseas and in many different language contexts and who was no doubt accustomed to a "broken English" that offered her a working model for an alternative national language (Bernstein, *A Poetics* 149). Charles Bernstein suggests that the prevalence of localized and nonstandard Englishes was for Stein a "linguistic utopia," "a domain not colonized by England, not Island English's sovereign subject" (149). Juliana Spahr similarly argues that Stein's work is, in part, an exploration of "what it means to get off a boat and enter into a completely different language system that is most likely learned through a terrifying immersion, not through orderly classrooms" (*Everybody's Autonomy* 31). This, in turn, "points to a polylingual American literature rooted in the localities of dialect and idiolect" (31). Spahr suggests that Stein's poetics opposes "segregated and ethnically representational models" of language via works that "refuse to mark their linguistic engagements as the property of a specific ethnicity" (26). Stein's appropriation, as well as her fascination with describing race in terms of highly problematic psychological and biological profiling, must not be imagined as distinct from her concept of racial and linguistic difference. In the best case, Stein's appropriative gestures are a kind of naive fetishism. In the worst case, her writing contributes to efforts to claim scientific reasons for racial difference. Stein's language is undoubtedly racist at times, stereotyping and fetishizing blackness from a position of casual, careless entitlement. Her commitment to the varied and various linguistic landscapes that co-constituted Americanness—indeed, that exemplified its unity in heterogeneity—was no doubt genuine. Like so many writers, not only of her time but also long before and since, her engagement with race was uncritical of its own reproductions of the rhetoric of racial violence. Writers like Bernstein and Spahr are careful to carve out the uneasy space of Stein's engagement with intersections of language, ethnic-

See also
Grammar
(pp. 103–104)

ity, race, and nationhood. Harryette Mullen, whose prose poetry responds in part to *Tender Buttons*, reimagines Stein's formal experimentations alongside an immanent critique of Stein's essentializations of race.[2]

Central to the Stein's America was the question of the relationship between the individual and the collective (how one becomes in a network of becomings). Stein's image of a lidless landscape filled with the movements of unencumbered and interrelated subjects is in many ways a typical description of the fantasy of liberal democracy. In "What Are Masterpieces and Why Are There So Few of Them?" Stein outlines her compositional ethos (which she claims comes from Gustave Flaubert and Paul Cézanne) in which any one part is of equal importance to another. This, Stein claims, was an ethos that corresponded directly to her ideal of equality: "After all to me one human being is as important as another human being and you might say that the landscape has the same values, a blade of grass has the same value as a tree" (*WAM* 98). Grass-blades and trees ought to exist on equal terms in a landscape, and so too should every unit of language in a composition (words, spaces, punctuation [or the absence thereof] and line breaks), and every citizen in a republic. Stein argues for total participation: "Just as everybody has the vote including women, I think children should, because as a child is conscious of itself then it has to me an existence and has a stake in what happens. Everybody who has that stake has the quality of interest and in the *Making of Americans* that is what I tried to show" (99). In the same passage, though, she acknowledges that "there are of course people who are more important than others in that they have more importance in the world but this is not essential and it ceases to be. I have

2. In a 1997 interview with Farah Griffin, Michael Magee, and Kristen Gallagher, Mullen discusses her engagement with Stein in (Griffin et al., "A Conversation with Harryette Mullen").

no sense of difference in this respect because every human being comprises the combination form" (99). She therefore argues that inequality is produced in the world; it is not preexistent. That is, "importance" is a value applied and not innate. Stein's republic admits to the unequal distribution of value at the level of social and political organization. She claims that she practiced her republican ideals in the ethics of her composition by stripping back punctuation, which by her account imposed a hierarchy of language: "I was trying to get ... this evenness of everybody having the vote and that is the reason I am impatient with punctuation" (99–100). Stein's republic appears to be a kind of imagined interface of Emersonian self-reliance, manifest equally in a society of equal subjects whose differences are of type and mood, and the sublime functionality of the automobile.

See also Grammar *(pp. 100–101)*

In response to the questions posed by *Transition*, Stein suggests that since the United States had already created the twentieth century, it was essential that someone like her—someone dedicated to the study and practice of composition—live in an environment that was in the process of *becoming* twentieth century. "And so," she explains, "America is a country the right age to have been born in and the wrong age to live in" (*HWW* 51). She preferred to be American and to compose in Paris, since Europe provided the exciting context of "attaining" the twentieth century. America "naturally produces the creators," and Stein wanted to create outside the already-established innovations of her nation. Also, in Paris Stein found a particular kind of linguistic solitude that allowed her the room to experiment with the English language. English was the language of her most intimate activities: her relationship, her composition, and her reading. Although she had grown up in a multilingual environment, Stein was firmly attached to English as the lingua franca of her poetics, which she could enjoy more fully in an otherwise non-English life. This enjoyment, Stein suggests, accounted for the number of

American writers in Paris—a city in which "they are free not to be connected with anything happening" (*WAM* 68). An American living in England has a sense of shared history, a sense of a historical going-together, and thus a sense of an interrelated, if divergent, present and future. An American in France has no such sense of going-together and is thus relieved of the burdens of historical narratives on the activities of thinking and writing. The expatriate experience allows for manual adjustments to the manner in which one participates in multiple and coexistent realities: geography, language, culture, and aesthetics. By having "two civilizations," as Stein puts it, one can compose in an ideal manner:

> There is no possibility of mixing up the other civilization with yourself you are you and if you are you in your own civilization you are apt to mix yourself up too much with your own civilization but when it is another civilization a complete other a romantic other another that stays there where it is you in it have freedom inside yourself which if you are to do what is inside yourself and nothing else is a very useful thing to have happen to you and so America is my country and Paris is my home town. (*WAM* 62–63)

Transition's prompt to frame her memoir in terms of "deracination" was no doubt irrelevant to Stein's own experience as an expatriate. Living in Paris did not leave her rootless. On the contrary, living in Paris seemed only ever to amplify her sense of being American and her ability to "use" her Americanness to its full capacity: by setting up elsewhere, Stein had the privilege of distance. This distance was an excellent vantage to look back (or, rather, forward) to America, and it offered the space to work autonomously and industriously on her experiments in English composition. Finally, it was a distance that provoked a set of metaphysical questions that Stein understood as being critical to composition—questions to do with the origin of thinking and writing: what is *inside* thinking and writing, and what is *outside*, and how does the outside affect the inside, and the inside articulate itself so as to become outside?

From her Parisian perspective—indeed, probably because of it—Stein wrote much about America. In 1934, after three decades away from the United States, she finally returned for a six-month lecture tour across the country. The talks themselves, collected as *Lectures in America*, are some of the most accomplished texts in her oeuvre. Though they can be read as direct, retrospective commentaries on her work, they are more constructively read as works in their own right. Their critical axioms, as well as their considered explication of Steinian poetics, aesthetics, and compositional process, cohere as statement and example, but they also always function to problematize their claims. Stein's work is never as American as in her lectures—in their assertions and self-readings as much as in their address and demands. Stein said that she didn't want to return to the United States until she was a celebrity, and by her own account, she was one by 1934.[3] The tour, therefore, was more than a homecoming. It was her debut as an American celebrity in America.

Her first time traveling in an airplane, which occurred during the American tour, greatly impressed her and confirmed many of her intuitions about the correlation of landscape and language. Her first impression of the airplane was the tremendous sound it made, which excited her because it precluded conversation and so focused all attention on the fact of flying. Flying, as she quickly discovered, was a "natural and pleasant thing much more simple and natural than anything even than walking, perhaps as natural as talking but certainly more natural than doing any other thing" (*EA* 190). And

3. In *Everybody's Autobiography* Stein writes: "I used to say that I would not go to America until I was a real lion a real celebrity at that time of course I did not really think I was going to be one. But now we were coming and I was going to be one" (168).

even though Stein was "not really surprised that being high was not frightening"—it being such a natural thing—she was bothered as to "why being up so high nothing happened" (*EA* 190, 191). When one is up in the mountains, she speculates, "everything happens," that is, one feels "funny" being up at that height, so the experience is eventful (191). By contrast, up in the air, nothing happens, so it is not frightening. That flying was not frightening was tremendously exciting for Stein; elsewhere she theorizes that the reason it feels natural to fly is that there is no historical-experiential precedent for being in the sky. Flying was a truly new invention that bore no relation to previous human experience, so it could not be frightening. Being in the air and looking down at the land was a triumph of the contemporary imagination.

Excited by her first experiences with air travel, Stein theorizes the geography of America: "In the United States there is more space where nobody is than where anybody is. This is what makes America what it is" (*W* 367). Such space suggests itself endlessly as the site for movement and activity, two modes of being that Stein posited as thoroughly American—the tendency to find a space and to fill it with things: "An American can fill up a space in having his movement of time by adding unexpectedly anything and yet getting within the included space everything he had intended getting" (*LA* 224). This "movement of time" in space was foundational to Stein's notion of geography, as well to her notion of Americanness. "Geography" was a mode of thought that problematized a landscape's relation to its history and identities. Since *landscape* can refer to the location or orientation of an event or duration, as well as to the event or duration itself, the American way of being in a landscape and of producing a meaningful geography was ultimately a way of being in time and space.

See also

Play

(pp. 162–167)

In "Gradual Making of the Making of Americans," Stein writes:

> I am always trying to tell this thing that a space of time is a natural
> thing for an American to always have inside them as something in
> which they are continuously moving. Think of anything, of cow-
> boys, of movies, of detective stories, of anybody who goes any-
> where or stays at home and is an American and you will realize that
> it is something strictly American to conceive a space that is filled
> with moving, a space of time that is filled always filled with moving
> and my first real effort to express this thing which is an American
> thing began in writing The Making of Americans. (*LA* 160–161)

A sense of the "space of time" affords the American a special affinity
for "abstraction and action," which Stein emphatically describes as a
"disembodied" characteristic. "Disembodied" here does not refer to
an alienation of/from the body; rather, it marks a shift from conceiving identity as something "inside" the body to something that one participates in, or is complicit with. Americanness, therefore, is not a
quality "inside" a subject, but a way of moving and perceiving movement (in the "space of time"); Americanness is a mode of being, of
and for the twentieth century.

See also
Bodies
(pp. 49–51)

In *The Autobiography of Alice B. Toklas*, Toklas recalls Stein's argument with Bertrand Russell (which occurred when Stein and Toklas
were in England being entertained by the Whiteheads) about whether
Americans had suffered or not in their neglect of the Greek classics.
Russell insisted that they had and that the educational system ought
to correct the error. Stein, of course, disagreed and declared that the
Greeks are irrelevant to Americans. Her reasoning—never fully explained—is based on the logic that Greek classicism corresponds to
English psychology, which is incompatible with American psychology. Toklas narrates: "She grew very eloquent on the disembodied abstract quality of the american character and cited examples, mingling
automobiles with Emerson, and all proving that they did not need

greek" (*ABT* 165). Somewhere in the mingling of automobiles and Emerson is Stein's ideal mode of abstraction per the American method: an abstracted individualism that relies on the self in process, a becoming-self. What makes an American an American is the same as what makes an automobile an automobile: the ability to move around. In the same way that a car makes abstract the more embodied experiences of travel, an American abstracts the embodiedness of experience by emphasizing the connectedness of time and space.

Stein's ideas about an American national character make critical adjustments to common assumptions underpinning nationalist arguments—to do with history, identity, body, language, and land—and challenge the notion that national identity is located "in" the citizen. By dissociating Americanness from the body, Stein aligns herself with alternative discussions of national literatures. Bernstein and Spahr, for example, see in Stein's America a transnational and polyglot reality, a reality that Stein herself experienced as both the child of immigrants and as an adult expatriate. "[Stein's] goal," writes Retallack, "perhaps more than that of any other American modernist, was to create the first great American literature not at all parasitic on British and European cultural inflections." Her attempts at this literature were made via experimentations with "simple, functional vocabulary and dynamically innovative grammars," emblematic of an ideal of American democratic principles and the notion of the functional assemblage ("Introduction," *GSS* 32). But clearly, the notion of a national literature is a tremendously problematic one. As Bernstein argues, the aim of writing a new American poetics apart from British influence always ends up erasing the very differences that it tries to emphasize. The difficulty of Stein's sense of Americanness is in the impossibility of her goal—to both totalize and radicalize what such Americanness might mean.

Nature is not natural and that is natural enough. —I 141

During the course of this project, I kept a file on my computer called "violent and hygienic metaphors." In it I collected excerpts from critical responses to Stein's work. I had been struck, while researching, by the tendency for critics to describe Stein's writing by way of tropes of destruction, extraction, and purification. In different ways, these tropes all seem to strive for the same thing: either a claim that Stein's language was somehow purer than, or prior to, communicative modes, or a claim that her work inaugurated a return to a pure or prior state of language.

Consider, for example, Mina Loy's "Gertrude Stein":

Curie

of the laboratory

of vocabulary

she crushed

the tonnage

of consciousness

congealed to phrases

to extract

a radium of the word. (*Lost Lunar Baedeker* 94)

or William Carlos Williams, who wrote that Stein was "smashing every connotation that words have ever had, in order to get them back clean" (qtd. in Mellow, *Charmed Circle* 369), or Bravig Imbs, who claimed that she "stopped at nothing in order to get to the essential naked language" (qtd. in Dydo, *Language That Rises* 17), or Ulla Dydo, who argued (with militaristic rhetoric) that Stein "attacked" language in order to make it "free" (*Language That Rises* 15, 16):

One way to free words was to remove them from habitual association and treat them as things rather than as signs. Repeating a
word over and over gradually breaks the bond of word and reference. A form of punning, repetition gives body to the word and as-
saults meaning. . . . She did not use made-up or nonsense words,
but she broke the vocabulary down into syllables until they became
new words. . . . Such reductions create a double jolt, removing the
meaning and destroying the anticipated grammatical behavior of
a word. (16)

Common to all these descriptions is the unconscious revelation
of a reader's desire—a desire for a language experience unattached
to the residues and sediments of meaning. This desire is quite apart
from, I think, Stein's work itself, for her work is no less free of meaning than it is singularly comprehensive. What is interesting is not the
question of whether Stein can possibly grant access to the "radium
of the word" but the question of why reading Stein elicits the desire
for such a thing in the first place. For her part, Stein aimed for exactness, regularity, and ordinariness in her writing. She maintained
that it was far more difficult, and more complex, to think about how
an object or event—such as a written text or an occasion of writing—
comes to be normal (that is, comes to be regular to and in itself) than
to point to its abnormalities. Stein and Toklas founded their own
small press, Plain Editions, whose title was surely both ironic and
genuine: until the success of *The Autobiography of Alice B. Toklas,*
Stein had difficulty gaining publisher support; nevertheless, her literary ambitions were indeed "plain." In *The Making of Americans,*
Stein's narrator, whose presence is significant throughout the novel,
early on makes an unembarrassed but self-conscious pledge to be
committed to the monotony of the middle class. Here again, Stein is
both ironic and genuine: the middle class is not a remarkable subject

of literary representation; nevertheless, her own aesthetic commitment to "monotony" was a serious one. Stein was interested in the complexities and rhythms of phenomena—including (one might even say especially) the entities that are so often passed off as being ordinary and mundane, like families, bureaucracies, or snacks. Stein's interest in the monotony of the middle class was also an interest in the repeated actions that bring about monotony: the very practices by which the middle-class family becomes a kind of naturalized and thus ordinary fact. In John Ashbery's review of *Stanzas and Meditation*, he describes the "monotony" of Stein's language as a "fertile" kind, which "generates excitement as water monotonously flowing over a dam generates electrical power" ("The Impossible" 254).

There are a number of ways to read Stein's interest in normality, regularity, exactness, ordinariness, and monotony: as an anxiety or projection; as an ironic gesture; or as a reaction against the pathologizing habits of nineteenth-century scientism. Or—and this is what I argue—Stein's emphasis on normality as a condition more complex than abnormality is an important rhetorical inversion of the normal/abnormal axis. Every entity is abnormal in the sense that it is other; every entity is normal in the sense that is particular to itself. When I began this project, I set out to make a case for Stein as an exceptional writer and thinker. I wanted to argue that Stein, *because* she was exceptional, effectively radicalized any discourse that her work was read alongside. At the end of the project, I realize that what Stein's work has taught me, perhaps most crucially of all, is that the kind of binary that produces the category of the exceptional is an inadequate system for thinking about experience and literature. That which is exceptional—that which is an exception—necessarily presumes that there is a rule from which to wander. Conversely, the notion of the exception is necessary in order to affirm and maintain rules: a rule can be a rule only when its exceptions are known. Stein's interest in teasing out the categories of normal and abnormal, conventional and exceptional, was an attempt not only to deconstruct their logic but also to demonstrate the eccentricities and inefficacies of their distinctions. In a very basic sense, the investigation into the ways in which entities can be said to be normal was more interesting to Stein than pathologizing aberrance.

In the tropologies of destruction, extraction, and purification, I read critical accounts of Stein as implying her exceptionalism by appointing her the task of "returning" language to poetry in a renewed state. In this study I have tried to do something else—to read Stein not as an exception but as an example. Stein's work is exemplary of a mode of thinking and writing that attends to the broad and often incommensurate phenomena that constitute experience. Such a mode might be called *suggestive*, for it aims not to exclude any aspect of perception, despite how vague or contradictory it may seem. Stein's work is an example of a long and diverse strand of writings and thinkings concerned with mobility, relationality, process, and transformation.

One of the first books I read at the outset of my study was *Against Method* by Paul Feyerabend. Largely without my realizing it, this book, which I have come back to in these final weeks, has left its trace in this project. In *Against Method*, Feyerabend theorizes "epistemological anarchism," which he proposes as an alternative to rationalism. Feyerabend's subject is science—its history and philosophy—and the odd habit of conceiving scientific progress as a neat succession of falsifications and innovations. Things change, he argues, not because science gets better at applying its own methods, but because rules are violated, hypotheses contradicted, and methodological strictures broken (however unwittingly). Feyerabend calls for a shift from the concept of the scientific method to a model of thinking alongside different, contradictory, and ad hoc methodologies. Interestingly, Feyerabend emphasizes that his "anarchism" is quite different from its political relative, and he expresses regret that he didn't choose the term "Dada" instead. The critical difference, for him, is the issue of play: "A Dadaist is prepared to initiate joyful experiments even in those domains where change and experimentation seem to be out of question (example: the basic function of language)" (*Against Method* 21 n. 12).

In the end, this study has been one conducted in the spirit of epistemological anarchism: not seeking to find the one or essential key to Stein, but reading Stein for her exhausting and itinerant suggestions and finding a way to put their generous energies into writing.

Agamben, Giorgio. *Nudities*. Translated by David Kishik and Stefan Pedatella. Stanford, CA: Stanford University Press, 2011.

Ahmed, Sara. "Open Forum Imaginary Prohibitions: Some Preliminary Remarks on the Founding Gestures of the 'New Materialism.'" *European Journal of Women's Studies* 15.1 (2008): 23–29.

———. *Queer Phenomenology: Orientations, Objects, Others*. Durham, NC: Duke University Press, 2006.

Antin, David. *Radical Coherency*. Chicago: University of Chicago Press, 2011.

Ardam, Jacquelyn. "'Too Old for Children and Too Young for Grown-ups': Gertrude Stein's To Do: A Book of Alphabets and Birthdays." *Modernism/Modernity* 18.3 (2011): 575–595.

Ashbery, John. "The Impossible." *Poetry* (1957): 250–254.

Ashton, Jennifer. "Gertrude Stein for Anyone." *ELH* 64.1 (1997): 289–331.

Austin, J. L. *How to Do Things with Words*. Oxford: Clarendon, 1975.

Barad, Karen. *Meeting the Universe Halfway: Quantum Physics and the Entanglement of Matter and Meaning*. Durham, NC: Duke University Press, 2007.

———. "Posthumanist Performativity: Toward an Understanding of How Matter Comes to Matter." *Signs: Journal of Women in Culture and Society* 28.3 (2003): 801–831.

Barthes, Roland. *The Pleasure of the Text*. Translated by Richard Miller. New York: Farrar, Straus and Giroux, 1975.

Benstock, Shari. "Beyond the Reaches of Feminist Criticism: A Letter from Paris." *Tulsa Studies in Women's Literature* 3.1/2 (1984): 5–27.

Bernstein, Charles. *Content's Dream: Essays, 1975–1984*. Evanston, IL: Northwestern University Press, 2001.

———, ed. "Gertrude Stein's War Years: Setting the Record Straight." *Jacket2*. May 9, 2012. https://jacket2.org/feature/gertrude-steins-war-years-setting-record-straight.

———. *A Poetics*. Cambridge, MA: Harvard University Press, 1992.

———. "Stein's Identity." *Modern Fiction Studies* 42.3 (1996): 485–488.

Bernstein, Charles, and Bruce Andrews, eds. "Reading Stein," special issue, *L=A=N=G=U=A=G=E* 6 (1978).

Brown, Bill. "Thing Theory." *Critical Inquiry* 28.1 (2001): 1–22.

Brown, Steven D. "Michel Serres: Science, Translation and the Logic of the Parasite." *Theory, Culture and Society* 19.3 (2002): 1–27.

Butler, Judith. *Bodies That Matter: On the Discursive Limits of Sex.* 1993. Reprint, New York: Routledge, 2011.

———. *Gender Trouble.* 10th anniv. ed. New York: Routledge, 1999.

Cage, John. *Silence.* Middletown, CT: Wesleyan University Press, 1973.

Cavell, Stanley. *This New Yet Unapproachable America: Lectures after Emerson and Wittgenstein.* Albuquerque: Living Batch, 1989.

Connor, Steven. "The Impossibility of the Present: or, From the Contemporary to the Contemporal." *Literature and the Contemporary.* Edited by Roger Luckhurst and Peter Marks. New York: Longman, 1999.

———. "Thinking Things." 2008. stevenconnor.com/thinkingthings/ (accessed April 1, 2010).

———. "Topologies: Michel Serres and the Shapes of Thought." 2004. stevenconnor.com/topologies/ (accessed April 1, 2010).

———. "Writing, Playing, Thinking, Laughing." 2008. stevenconnor.com/wptl/ (accessed April 1, 2010).

Conte, Joseph. "The Smooth and the Striated: Compositional Texture in the Modern Long Poem." *Modern Language Studies* 27 (1997): 57–71.

Crenshaw, Kimberlé. "Mapping the Margins: Intersectionality, Identity Politics, and Violence against Women of Color." *Stanford Law Review* 6 (1991): 1241–1299.

Damon, Maria. *The Dark End of the Street: Margins in American Vanguard Poetry.* Minneapolis: University of Minnesota Press, 1993.

———. "Gertrude Stein's Jewishness, Jewish Social Scientists, and the 'Jewish Question.'" *Modern Fiction Studies* 42.3 (1996): 489–506.

DeKoven, Marianne. *Different Language: Gertrude Stein's Experimental Writing.* Madison: University of Wisconsin Press, 1983.

DeLanda, Manuel. *Intensive Science and Virtual Philosophy.* London: Continuum, 2002.

Deleuze, Gilles. *Bergsonism.* Translated by Hugh Tomlinson and Barbara Habberjam. Brooklyn: Zone Books, 1990.

———. *Difference and Repetition.* Translated by Paul Patton. New York: Columbia University Press, 1994.

———. "Dualism, Monism and Multiplicities (Desire-Pleasure-Jouissance)." Translated by Daniel W. Smith. *Contretemps* 2 (2001): 92–108.

———. *The Fold: Leibniz and the Baroque.* Translated by Tom Conley. London: Continuum, 2006.

————. *Negotiations*. Translated by Martin Joughin. New York: Columbia University Press, 1995.

Deleuze, Gilles, and Félix Guattari. *Anti-Oedipus: Capitalism and Schizophrenia*. Translated by Robert Hurley, Mark Seem, and Helen R. Lane. Minneapolis: University of Minnesota Press, 1983.

————. *A Thousand Plateaus: Capitalism and Schizophrenia*. Translated by Brian Massumi. Minneapolis: University of Minnesota Press, 1987.

————. *What Is Philosophy?* Translated by Hugh Tomlinson and Graham Burchell. New York: Columbia University Press, 1994.

Dershowitz, Alan. "Suppressing Ugly Truth for Beautiful Art." *Huffington Post*. May 5, 2012. www.huffingtonpost.com/alan-dershowitz/met-gertrude-stein-collaborator_b_1467174.html.

Dickie, Margaret. *Stein, Bishop, and Rich: Lyrics of Love, War, and Place*. Chapel Hill: University of North Carolina Press, 1997.

Doane, Mary Anne. "Indexicality: Trace and Sign: Introduction." *differences: A Journal of Feminist Cultural Studies* 18.1 (2007): 1–6.

Dworkin, Craig. "Penelope Reworking the Twill: Patchwork, Writing, and Lyn Hejinian's 'My Life.'" *Contemporary Literature* 36.1 (1995): 58–81.

Dydo, Ulla E. *Gertrude Stein: The Language That Rises: 1923–1934*. Evanston, IL: Northwestern University Press, 2008.

Edelman, Lee. *Homographesis: Essays in Gay Literary and Cultural Theory*. New York: Routledge, 1994.

————. *No Future: Queer Theory and the Death Drive*. Durham, NC: Duke University Press, 2004.

Emerson, Ralph Waldo. *The Essays of Ralph Waldo Emerson*. Cambridge, MA: Harvard University Press, 1987.

————. *Political Writings*. Edited by Kenneth Sacks. Cambridge: Cambridge University Press, 2008.

Feyerabend, Paul. *Against Method: Outline of an Anarchistic Theory of Knowledge*. London: NLB, 1975.

Fifer, Elizabeth. "Is Flesh Advisable? The Interior Theater of Gertrude Stein." *Signs* 14.1 (1979): 472–483.

Franken, Claudia. *Gertrude Stein, Writer and Thinker*. Münster, Germany: LIT Verlag, 2000.

Freud, Sigmund. *Jokes and Their Relation to the Unconscious*. Translated by James Strachey. New York: W. W. Norton, 1960.

Goldsmith, Kenneth. *Uncreative Writing: Managing Language in the Digital Age*. New York: Columbia University Press, 2011.

Griffin, Farah, Magee, Michael, and Gallagher, Kristen, eds. "A Conversation with Harryette Mullen." *Electronic Poetry Centre.* 1997. wings.buffalo.edu/epc/authors/mullen/interview-new.html (accessed September 1, 2013).

Grosz, Elizabeth. *Volatile Bodies: Toward a Corporeal Feminism.* Bloomington: Indiana University Press, 1994.

Guattari, Félix. *The Guattari Reader.* Edited by Gary Genosko. Oxford: Blackwell, 1996.

Halewood, Michael. *A. N. Whitehead and Social Theory: Tracing a Culture of Thought.* London: Anthem, 2011.

———. "On Whitehead and Deleuze: The Process of Materiality." *Configurations* 13.1 (2005): 57–76.

Haraway, Donna. *Simians, Cyborgs and Women: The Reinvention of Nature.* New York: Routledge, 1990.

Heidegger, Martin. *Poetry, Language, Thought.* Translated by Albert Hofstadter. New York: HarperCollins, 1971.

Hejinian, Lyn. *The Language of Inquiry.* Berkeley: University of California Press, 2000.

Hoffman, Michael J., ed. *Critical Essays on Gertrude Stein.* Boston: G. K. Hall, 1986.

Holton, Gerald. *Thematic Origins of Scientific Thought.* Cambridge, MA: Harvard University Press, 1973.

James, William. *Essays in Radical Empiricism.* New York: Cosimo, 2008.

———. *Principles of Psychology.* Vol. 1. New York: Cosimo, 2007.

———. *The Will to Believe and Other Essays in Popular Philosophy.* New York: Cosimo, 2007.

———. *The Works of William James: Essays, Comments and Reviews.* Cambridge, MA: Harvard University Press, 1987.

Kant, Immanuel. *Critique of the Power of Judgment.* Translated by Paul Guyer. Cambridge: Cambridge University Press, 2000.

Katz, Leon. "Weininger and the Making of Americans." *Twentieth Century Literature* 24.1 (1978): 8–26.

Koestenbaum, Wayne. *Cleavage: Essays on Sex, Stars, and Aesthetics.* New York: Ballantine Books, 1999.

———. *Humiliation.* London: Picador, 2011.

Kucharzewski, Jan D. "'There is no "there" there': Gertrude Stein and Quantum Physics." *Amerikastudien / Amercian Studies* 49.4 (2004): 499–513.

Latour, Bruno. "An Attempt at a 'Compositionist Manifesto.'" *New Literary History* 41 (2012): 471–490.

———. "A Plea for Earthly Sciences." In *Bruno Latour.* 2007. www.bruno-latour.fr/sites/default/files/102-BSA-GB_0.pdf (accessed November 1, 2010).

———. *We Have Never Been Modern.* Translated by Catherine Porter. Cambridge, MA: Harvard University Press, 1993.

Leibniz, G. W. *Discourses on Metaphysics and the Monadology.* Translated by George R. Montgomery. Amherst: Prometheus Books, 1992.

———. *Philosophical Works.* Translated by George Martin Duncan. New Haven, CT: Tuttle, Morehouse & Taylor, 1908.

Levinson, Ronald B. "Gertrude Stein, William James, and Grammar." *Journal of American Psychology* 44. 1 (1941): 124–128.

Lin, Tan. *Selected Essays about a Bibliography.* Edited by Danny Snelson. New York: Edit, 2010.

———. *Seven Controlled Vocabularies.* Middletown, CT: Wesleyan University Press, 2010.

Love, Heather. *Feeling Backwards: Loss and the Politics of Feeling Backward.* Cambridge, MA: Harvard University Press, 2007.

Loy, Mina. *The Last Lunar Baedeker.* Highlands, NC: Jargon Society, 1982.

———. *The Lost Lunar Baedeker.* Edited by Roger L. Conover. New York: Noonday, 1996.

Lucretius. *On the Nature of the Universe.* Translated by R. E. Latham. London: Penguin, 2005.

Luhan, Mabel Dodge. *"Speculations, or Post-impressionism in Prose": A History of Having a Great Many Times Not Continued to Be Friends: The Correspondence between Mabel Dodge and Gertrude Stein, 1911–1934.* Edited by Patricia Everett. Albuquerque: University of New Mexico Press, 1996.

Luhmann, Niklas. "The Paradox of Observing Systems." *Cultural Critique* 31.2 (1995): 37–55.

Manguel, Alberto. *A History of Reading.* London: HarperCollins, 1996.

Massumi, Brian. *Parables for the Virtual: Movement, Affect, Sensation.* Durham, NC: Duke University Press, 2002.

McGann, Jerome. *The Scholar's Art: Literary Studies in a Managed World.* Chicago: University of Chicago Press, 2006.

Mellow, James R. *Charmed Circle: Gertrude Stein and Company.* New York: Henry Holt, 1974.

Meyer, Steven. "Creativity." *Configurations* 13.1 (2005): 1–33.

———. *Irresistible Dictation: Gertrude Stein and the Correlations of Writing and Science.* Stanford, CA: Stanford University Press, 2011.

Meyerowitz, Patricia. "Lesbian Never?" *New York Review of Books*, October 7, 1971.

Moretti, F. "Conjectures on World Literature." *New Left Review* 1 (2000): 54–68.

Muecke, Stephen. "Motorcycles, Snails, Latour: Criticism without Judgement." *Cultural Studies Review* 18.1 (2012): 40–58.

Ngai, Sianne. "The Cuteness of the Avant-Garde." *Critical Inquiry* 31 (2005): 811–847.

———. "Merely Interesting." *Critical Inquiry* 34.4 (2008): 777–817.

———. "Our Aesthetic Categories." *PLMA* 125.4 (2010): 948–958.

———. *Ugly Feelings.* Cambridge, MA: Harvard University Press, 2005.

Olson, Charles. *Collected Prose.* Edited by Donald Allen and Benjamin Friedlander. Berkeley: University of California Press, 1997.

Oxford English Dictionary online. S.v. "Gay. " Last updated February 2, 2011.

Peirce, C. S. *The Essential Peirce: Selected Philosophical Writings, Volume 1 (1867–1893).* Edited by Nathan Houser and Christian J. W. Kloesel. Bloomington: Indiana University Press, 1992.

———. *The Essential Peirce: Selected Philosophical Writings, Volume 2 (1893–1913).* Edited by Peirce Edition Project. Bloomington: Indiana University Press, 1998.

Perloff, Marjorie. "'Grammar in Use': Wittgenstein / Gertrude Stein / Marinetti." *South Central Review* 13.2/3 (1996): 32–62.

———. *Poetics of Indeterminacy.* Evanston, IL: Northwestern University Press, 1999.

Puar, Jasbir. " 'I would rather be a cyborg than a goddess': Intersectionality, Assemblage, and Affective Politics." *Transversal.* European Institute for Progressive Cultural Policies. 2011. eipcp.net/transversal/0811/puar/en (accessed May 1, 2013).

Quartermain, Peter. *Disjunctive Poetics: From Gertrude Stein and Louis Zukofsky to Susan Howe.* Cambridge: Cambridge University Press, 1992.

Reed, Brian. "Now Not Now: Gertrude Stein Speaks." *ESC* 33.4 (2007): 103–113.

Reid, B. L. *Art by Subtraction: A Dissenting Opinion of Gertrude Stein.* Norman: University of Oklahoma Press, 1958.

Riding, Laura. *Contemporaries and Snobs.* St. Clair Shores: Scholarly Press, 1971.

Retallack, Joan. Introduction to *Gertrude Stein Selections.* Edited by Joan Retallack, 3–81. Berkeley: University of California Press, 2008.

———. *Poethical Wager.* Berkeley: University of California Press, 2003.

Rich, Adrienne. "Compulsory Heterosexuality and Lesbian Experience." In *Blood, Bread, and Poetry.* New York: Norton, 1994.

Richardson, Joan. *A Natural History of Pragmatism: The Fact of Feeling from Jonathan Edwards to Gertrude Stein*. Cambridge: Cambridge University Press, 2006.

———. "Recombinant ANW: Appetites of Words." *Configurations* 13.1 (2005): 117–133.

Robertson, Lisa. "Time in the Codex." In *Nilling: Prose Essays on Noise, Pornography, the Codex, Melancholy, Lucretius, Folds, Cities and Related Aporias*. Toronto: Book Thug, 2012.

Ruddick, Lisa. *Reading Gertrude Stein: Body, Text, Gnosis*. Ithaca, NY: Cornell University Press, 1990.

Saunders, Katherine Elaine. "Tan Lin" (interview). *BOMB Magazine*. March 2010. bombmagazine.org/article/3467/.

Sedgwick, Eve. *Epistemology of the Closet*. Berkeley: University of California Press, 1990.

———. "A Poem Is Being Written." *Representations* 17 (1987): 110–143.

———. "Queer Performativity: Henry James's *The Art of the Novel*." *GLQ: A Journal of Lesbian and Gay Studies* 1 (1993): 1–16.

———. *Touching Feeling: Affect, Pedagogy, Performativity*. Durham, NC: Duke University Press, 2001.

Serres, Michel. *Atlas*. Paris: Editions Julliard, 1994.

———. *The Parasite*. Translated by Lawrence R. Schehr. Minneapolis: University of Minnesota Press, 2007.

Serres, Michel, and Bruno Latour. *Conversations on Science, Culture, and Time*. Translated by Roxanne Lapidus. Ann Arbor: University of Michigan Press, 1995.

Shaviro, Steven. *Without Criteria: Kant, Whitehead, Deleuze, and Aesthetics*. Cambridge, MA: MIT Press, 2009.

Silliman, Ron. *The New Sentence*. New York: Roof, 1987.

Simon, Linda. *Gertrude Stein Remembered*. Lincoln: University of Nebraska Press, 1993.

Skinner, B. F. "Has Gertrude Stein a Secret?" *Atlantic Monthly* 153 (1934): 50–57.

Spahr, Juliana. *Everybody's Autonomy: Collective Reading and Connective Identity*. Tuscaloosa: University of Alabama Press, 2001.

Stein, Gertrude. *The Autobiography of Alice B. Toklas*. London: Penguin, 2001.

———. *Everybody's Autobiography*. New York: Vintage Books, 1973.

———. *Geography and Plays*. Madison: University of Wisconsin Press, 1993.

———. *Gertrude Stein Selected*. Edited by Joan Retallack. Berkeley: University of California Press, 2008.

————. *How to Write*. Mineola, NY: Dover, 1975.

————. *How Writing Is Written*. Edited by Robert Bartlett Haas. Los Angeles: Black Sparrow, 1974.

————. *Ida: A Novel*. New York: Cooper Square, 1971.

————. *Last Operas and Plays*. Baltimore: Johns Hopkins University Press, 1995.

————. *Lectures in America*. Boston: Beacon, 1957.

————. *Lifting Belly*. Edited by Rebecca Mark. Tallahassee: The Naiad, 1989.

————. *The Making of Americans: Being a History of a Family's Progress*. Normal, IL: Dalkey Archive, 1997.

————. *Narration*. Chicago: University of Chicago Press, 2010.

————. *Portraits and Prayers*. New York: Random House, 1934.

————. *A Stein Reader*. Edited by Ulla E. Dydo. Evanston, IL: Northwestern University Press, 1993.

————. *Tender Buttons*. Mineola, NY: Dover, 1997.

————. *What Are Masterpieces*. New York: Pitman Publishing Corporation, 1970.

————. *Writings: 1932–1946*. New York: Library of America, 1998.

Stein, Gertrude, and Carl Van Vechten. *The Letters of Gertrude Stein and Carl Van Vechten*. Volume 2, *1913–1946*. Edited by Edward Burns. New York: Columbia University Press, 1986.

Stein, Gertrude and Thornton Wilder. *The Letters of Gertrude Stein and Thornton Wilder*. Edited by Edward M. Burns, Ulla E. Dydo, and M. R. William Rice. New Haven, CT: Yale University Press, 1996.

Stimpson, Catharine. "The Somagrams of Gertrude Stein." *Poetics Today*. 6.1/2 (1985): 67–80.

Stengers, Isabelle. "A Constructivist Reading of *Process and Reality*." *Theory, Culture and Society* 25.4 (2008): 91–110.

————. *Power and Invention: Situating Science*. Translated by Paul Bains. Minneapolis: University of Minnesota Press, 1997.

————. *Thinking with Whitehead: A Wild and Free Creation of Concepts*. Translated by Michael Chase. Cambridge, MA: Harvard University Press, 2001.

Tiffany, Daniel. *Infidel Poetics: Riddles, Nightlife, Substance*. Chicago: University of Chicago Press, 2009.

Turner, Kay, ed. *Baby Precious Always Shines: Selected Love Notes between Gertrude Stein and Alice B. Toklas*. New York: St. Martin's, 2000.

Wagers, Kelley. "Gertrude Stein's 'Historical' Living." *Journal of Modern Literature* 31.3 (2008): 23–42.

Watson, Dana Cairns. *Gertrude Stein and the Essence of What Happens*. Nashville: Vanderbilt University Press, 2005.

Weininger, Otto. *Sex and Character*. New York: Howard Fertig, 2003.

Whitehead, Alfred North. *The Concept of Nature*. Cambridge: Cambridge University Press, 1964.

———. *Essays in Science and Philosophy*. New York: Philosophical Library, 1947.

———. *The Function of Reason*. Boston: Beacon, 1929.

———. "Objects and Subjects." *Philosophical Review* 41.2 (1932): 130–146.

———. *Process and Reality*. Corrected version. Edited by David Ray Griffin and Donald W. Sherburne. New York: Free Press, 1978.

———. *Symbolism: Its Meaning and Effect*. New York: Macmillan, 1927.

Will, Barbara. *Gertrude Stein: Modernism and the Problem with Genius*. Edinburgh: Edinburgh University Press, 2000.

Wittgenstein, Ludwig. *Philosophical Grammar*. Translated by Anthony Kenny. Edited by Rush Rhees. Berkeley: University of California Press, 1974.

Wittgenstein, Ludwig. *Philosophical Investigations*. Translated by G. E. M. Anscombe, P. M. S. Hacker, and Joachim Schulte. Rev. 4th ed. Oxford: Blackwell, 2009.

———. *Philosophical Remarks*. Translated by Raymond Hargreaves and Roger White. Edited by Rush Rhees. Oxford: Basil Blackwell, 1975.

———. *Tractatus Logico-Philosophicus*. Translated by D. F. Pears and B. F. McGuinness. London: Routledge, 1974.

Winnicott, D. W. *Playing and Reality*. New York: Routledge, 1989.

Wolfe, Cary. Introduction to Michel Serres, *The Parasite*. Translated by Lawrence R. Schehr. Minneapolis: University of Minnesota Press, 2007.

Astrid Lorange is a poet and an associate lecturer at the College of Fine Arts, University of New South Wales.